FREEMASONRY

A
CELEBRATION
OF THE
CRAFT

FREEMASONRY

A
CELEBRATION
OF THE
CRAFT

FOREWORD BY
HRH THE DUKE OF KENT

General Editors
JOHN HAMILL   ROBERT GILBERT

JG
PRESS

GENERAL EDITORS

JOHN HAMILL

An internationally acknowledged authority on English Freemasonry, and author of *The Craft* which traces the development of English Freemasonry from its obscure beginnings to the present day. He was Master of the renowned Quatuor Coronati Lodge (of research) No 2076 during its centenary year 1985/86 and editor of Henry Sadlers's 'Masonic Facts and Fictions'. He is presently Librarian and Curator of the Grand Lodge and Museum in London

ROBERT GILBERT

Among his numerous books on Masonic subjects, he is the biographer of A. E. Waite, the Masonic scholar; he has also edited a collection of essays by Wynn Westcott and has contributed papers to the transactions of Quatuor Coronati Lodge (of research) No 2076, of which he is a member.

EDITORIAL RESEARCHER

ANDRÉE BUISINE

A French national who studied English at the Sorbonne, she was a member of the French underground movement during the Second World War. She has received French and American awards including the Legion d' Honneur. A Doctor of History and author of La Franc-Maçonnerie Anglo-Saxon. She is presently a long-time member of Feminine Freemasonry in France

CONTRIBUTORS

C. FRED KLEINKNECHT

FRANCIS G. PAUL

REV. NORMAN VINCENT PEALE

ROBERT C. SINGER

RICHARD E. FLETCHER

RICHARD H. CURTIS

SIDNEY R. BAXTER

PAUL D. FISHER

S. BRENT MORRIS

MARQUESS OF NORTHAMPTON

ROGER NATHAN-MURAT

DR. MAX TETAU

LIEUT. COMMANDER B. MILES

PUBLISHED IN THE USA 1998 BY J G PRESS.
DISTRIBUTED BY WORLD PUBLICATIONS, INC.
THE J G PRESS IMPRINT IS A TRADEMARK OF
J G PRESS, INC.
455 SOMERSET AVENUE
NORTH DIGHTON, MA 02764
ISBN 1-57215-267-2

Research, Editing, Compilation, Design
and Production Management
Terry Allen

Assistant Sub-Editors
Michael Cox and William Adams

Picture Research
Sylvie Basdevant

Additional Picture Research
John Ashby and Pierre Petit

Logo Calligraphy
Nicholas Skelton

Colour Origination
**PR Service Graphique,
Paris, France**

CONTENTS

FOREWORD

BY HRH THE DUKE OF KENT, KG, GCMG, GCVO, ADC, THE MW
THE GRAND MASTER OF THE UNITED GRAND LODGE OF ENGLAND

TWO hundred and seventy five years of continuous working is a major achievement for any human enterprise. In 1717 four London lodges came together to form a Grand Lodge, the beginnings of organised Freemasonry. In 1725 the Irish and in 1736 the Scots formed their own Grand Lodges. Between them the British Grand Lodges spread Freemasonry over the face of the globe. In time, independent Grand Lodges grew up in many parts of the world. Each developed in its own way with its own traditions and differences, but all subscribe to the same basic principles of Brotherly Love, Relief and Truth.

In such a long period many millions of men have enjoyed membership of Freemasonry. Amongst them have been some who were, and are, prominent in various areas of life and whose work and ideas have materially affected or greatly enriched the lives of not only their fellow members but mankind in general. Most of them however have been ordinary men who have attempted to live their lives by the practical lessons of morality, duty and service which they have learned in their lodges.

Their names may not be remembered today but in their times they were good citizens working for the common good and the betterment of society, not for their own self-interest.

This book celebrates two hundred and seventy five years of organised Freemasonry. It traces the complex history of the Craft's development world wide; considers the notable contributions of its members; but above all it demonstrates how Freemasonry has contributed in a practical way to improving the world and alleviating suffering and distress. The many contributors and the general editors are to be congratulated for producing such a concise and fascinating survey, enhanced by the splendid illustrations. I commend it to all who are interested in the subject, whether they be Freemasons or not.

GRAND MASTER

Left THEIR ROYAL HIGHNESSES THE DUKE AND DUCHESS OF KENT, SEEN HERE ARRIVING AT HAMPTON COURT PALACE, ENGLAND, TO CELEBRATE THE BICENTENARY OF 'THE TIMES' NEWSPAPER.

NORMAN VINCENT PEALE

A METHODIST MINISTER FOR SEVENTY YEARS, PEALE IS INTERNATIONALLY RECOGNIZED FOR HIS BEST-SELLING
BOOKS ON SELF-IMPROVEMENT – *A GUIDE TO CONFIDENT LIVING* AND *THE POWER OF POSITIVE THINKING* –
AND IS THE BEST KNOWN CHAMPION OF FREEMASONRY IN AMERICA TODAY,
UNIVERSALLY RESPECTED FOR HIS HONEST AND FORTHRIGHT VIEWS.

INTRODUCTION

FOR all those who are curious about Freemasonry, for those who are already Freemasons, and more especially, for those who are contemplating joining the Craft, this book answers the question, 'What is Freemasonry?' with the more meaningful question, 'What is a Freemason?' In the answer to *that* question lies the essence of the Craft.

Freemasonry is not, as most popular books portray it, little more than a series of strange ceremonies, involving curious symbols and odd regalia; nor is it a museum of Masonic mementoes. Rather it is a living structure, built up from the aspirations and achievements of every individual Freemason during the 275 years that the Craft as we know it has existed.

Above all, Freemasonry consists of *Men*: men who have joined the Craft because its eternal principles strike a chord within them. When Masons are asked what the Craft means to them, not one of their answers will be exactly the same as another, but the essence of that meaning will never vary and it is epitomised in these words of Dr. Norman Vincent Peale – perhaps, one of the most distinguished of living American Masons. For Dr. Peale, membership in the Craft brought its own rewards in all aspects of daily life.

> 'The values and ideas, the profound principles of religion, morality and honour for which Masonry stands, mean much to me as an American...
>
> There is, as I see it, nothing like Masonry. It is unique in its fellowship which spreads over much of the earth, in addition to our own country. Moreover, this in-depth fellowship spans the years, even the centuries, running back into antiquity. To me it means a personal relationship with great historical personalities and, taken by and large, also with about the finest body of men whom it is possible to assemble anywhere...
>
> Attending Lodge and participating in Masonic activities gave me confidence. I learned to work with people. I found that everyone, every single brother, had a special talent. All I had to do was bring it out. The Brother, then, saw quickly enough how to put his talent to use. And his success at Lodge work gave him confidence too! He passed it on to others, and they to still others. It wasn't necessary to repeat a self-help motto like 'I believe in me.' Just doing the work and seeing the results were enough.
>
> Confidence in self, in the Lodge, in Masonry, in the community and nation – it caught on, and I have seen it spread farther and farther as I continue my Masonic journey in life, meeting ever more Brothers and sharing with them the confidence Freemasonry can give...
>
> Ever since I became a Mason, the work has not only charmed me, but also impressed me. I can further add that, as a public speaker, it has also given me enhanced perception of the nobility of words and their inspirational power when used in skillful combination and for the expression of lofty thoughts.'

REV. NORMAN VINCENT PEALE

GOD AS THE GREAT ARCHITECT OF THE UNIVERSE circumscribing HEAVEN AND EARTH (13TH CENTURY).

CHAPTER I

ORIGINS

The Father to the Children shall make known Thy Truth

Isaiah 38:19

THE precise origins of Freemasonry are unknown, and may perhaps remain so. However, despite – or perhaps because of – this, there has never been any lack of theories put forward to explain the genesis and original purpose of Masonry. Examined objectively, some explanations are less fanciful than others; indeed, the balance of probability tips decidedly in favour of one theory in particular, and as more evidence is accumulated the likelihood is that investigations into Masonic origins will truly, as Bacon put it, 'end in certainties'.

The one fixed point in the early history of Freemasonry is 24 June (the Feast of St John the Baptist) 1717, when four previously-established London lodges met together to constitute the Grand Lodge of England – the premier Grand Lodge for Masons all over the world. Before this date there are only scattered references to Freemasonry in printed literature, supplemented by occasional entries in diaries and other private papers and by the records of a small number of lodges of working stonemasons in Scotland.

Beyond this are the earliest extant records of all: the documents known as the *Old Charges*. These manuscripts – some dating from the end of the fourteenth century, though the majority are dated after 1600 – set out a series of regulations, or Charges, for the social behaviour of Masons, both within their Craft and in society at large, together with a largely legendary history of geometry, architecture, and the craft of Masonry and a description of the Seven Liberal Arts and Sciences.

The 'Traditional' History

It is from the historical account enshrined in the *Old Charges* that the 'official' or 'traditional' history of Freemasonry, set out in the printed Constitutions of the eighteenth century, is derived. Romantic and wholly fictitious though it is, the traditional theory of Masonic origin long held sway. Like other more feasible theories it argued for a descent of modern Freemasonry from the working, or operative, stonemasons of the Middle Ages; but the traditional history goes back even further, to the biblical Patriarchs (notably Noah and Moses) and then (by way of Nineveh, Egypt and 'worthy Clarke Euclid') to King Solomon and the building of the Temple of Jerusalem, Nebuchadnezzar, and the classical civilizations of Greece and Rome.

Then comes what might be termed the 'Gothic leap' to the Dark Ages: to Charles Martel, St. Alban, King Athelstan and the mythical 'Great Assembly of Masons at York' under Prince Edwin in AD 930.

None of this has the slightest basis in truth; but to the eighteenth century Freemason, biblical history and chronology was literally true and an accurate knowledge

of ancient and medieval history was far from widespread. Under such conditions it was not self-evidently absurd that the Craft could lay claim to such a grandiose pedigree. By 1815 common sense had led to the traditional history being discreetly dropped from the Constitutions, although old ideas die hard and there has never been a shortage of enthusiastic romantics who seek for the fountainhead of the Craft in the mists of Antiquity.

Other masonic historians – such as John Yarker and J.S.M. Ward who leaned towards the mystic interpretation – have argued for a lineage every bit as ancient, and as grand, as that of the traditional history. Parallels have been evoked between Freemasonry and the building of the Egyptians pyramids, the construction of Stonehenge, and the Roman Collegia Fabrorum (Schools of Masons). Links have been sought with the so-called Comacines of the Middle Ages – masons from the region of Como in northern Italy who allegedly possessed secret knowledge of such importance that a (non-existent) Papal Bull was supposed to have been promulgated constituting them as a quasi-religious Order. From the Comacines, it is argued, came the medieval building guilds, and from them, in due course, Freemasonry as we now know it. The theory is an entertaining one, and although there is not a shred of evidence to support it, the *idea* of such an origin has been a significant factor in more than one offshoot of the Craft.

There is undoubtedly a connection between medieval operative masons and what we now call speculative Freemasonry: the very structure of the Craft makes this clear. But the exact nature of the connection remains uncertain and scholars continue to dispute the question, with some arguing for a direct descent from operative masonry, and others for a more complex, indirect link. We shall return to this debate in due course; for the moment two more claimed sources of the Craft must be mentioned – both improbable, but both of which still have adherents.

Right GRAND LODGE MS No. 1. OUR KNOWLEDGE OF THE REGULATIONS GOVERNING THE STONEMASONS IN THE MIDDLE AGES, AND OF THE 'TRADITIONAL' HISTORY THAT THEY ACCEPTED AS THE STORY OF THEIR CRAFT, IS DERIVED FROM THE DOCUMENTS KNOWN AS THE *OLD CHARGES*. THE OLDEST OF THESE DATE FROM THE 14TH CENTURY, BUT GRAND LODGE MS No. 1. WHICH IS DATED 1583, IS OF CRUCIAL IMPORTANCE BECAUSE IT IS THE EARLIEST OF THE POST-REFORMATION TEXTS.

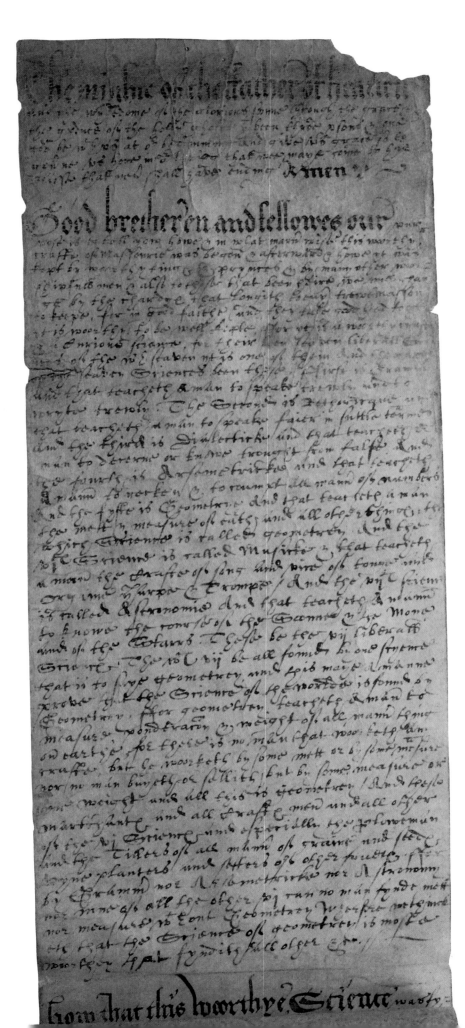

Septuaginta duo gigantes contra Deum
edificare volentes variis linguis ceperunt loqui
z ideo per universum mundum sunt disperfi

Haec turris vocata est Babel
quia ibi confusum est
labium universe terre

Left IN THIS 12TH CENTURY DRAWING
OF THE BUILDING OF THE TOWER OF
BABEL, MEDIEVAL MASONS CAN BE SEEN
WORKING WITH MANY OF THE
TRADITIONAL WORKING TOOLS – SQUARE,
CHISEL, HEAVY MAUL AND PLUMB-RULE.
THEY ARE ALL RETAINED IN THE
SYMBOLIC WORKINGS OF TODAY'S
SPECULATIVE CRAFT.

Below THE CONSTRUCTION OF THE
PRESENT, AND THIRD FREEMASONS
HALL, LONDON, ENGLAND, BUILT 1927-
1933, BY VOLUNTARY SUBSCRIPTION,
AS A MASONIC PEACE MEMORIAL TO
THOSE WHO GAVE THEIR LIVES IN
WORLD WAR ONE.

23.9.30
5985 B

THE CASTLE OF THE LOUVRE AT PARIS
(FROM THE 15TH CENTURY *TRES RICHES HEURES* OF JOHN, DUKE OF BERRY). WHEN
JACQUES DE MOLAY WAS BURNED AT THE STAKE IN 1314, THE KING OF FRANCE,
PHILIP THE FAIR, WATCHED FROM THE RIGHT-HAND TOWER ON THE OUTER WALLS.

JACQUES DE MOLAY, GRAND MASTER OF THE ORDER OF KNIGHTS TEMPLAR
As he bravely met his death, in March 1314, de Molay is said to have cried out to his persecutors
'I summon you, Philip the Fair and Pope Clement the Fifth, within a year before the tribunal of God.'
Within twelve months, both men were dead.

THE KNIGHTS TEMPLAR

IN 1737 the Chevalier Andrew Ramsay wrote an 'Oration', which, although never delivered, was widely circulated among French Freemasons in the 1740s. In it Ramsay wrote of a renewal of Freemasonry, described as 'an order founded in remote antiquity' among a certain group of Crusaders, and alluded to a resulting 'intimate union' between Freemasonry and the Knights of St John of Jerusalem, who brought the revived Order and its ancient ceremonies back to the British Isles. This account was widely misinterpreted as a claim that Freemasonry, as a symbolic system, had originated among the Knights Templar, and thus Ramsay's romantic dreams were transformed into an elaborate history that saw the Templars as the true founders of the Craft.

Though this theory has been much popularized in recent years it has no foundation in fact whatsoever, as the briefest glance at the actual history of the Templars' origins will reveal.

The Order of Poor Fellow-Soldiers of Christ and the Temple of Solomon, to give the Templars their full title, was founded in 1118 to protect pilgrims travelling to the Holy Places in Jerusalem. When the Crusaders were finally driven from Palestine, the order continued to flourish in Europe until 1307, when, for purely political reasons, it was violently suppressed and dissolved by the Pope in 1312. Its Grand Master, Jacques de Molay, was burned at the stake, in 1314 on trumped up charges of sorcery and blasphemy. One Masonic myth has it that those Templars who survived the purge are supposed to have fled to Scotland, where they avoided persecution by infiltrating court circles and perpetuated their Order in secret until it eventually resurfaced as Freemasonry. Thus, it is claimed, the 'secrets' of the Templars became the 'secrets' of Freemasonry. In fact the Papal Bull condemning the Templars was rejected in Scotland and the Templars were never subject to persecution there.

While there are certain superficial similarities between the two Orders (both have a hierarchical structure, both surround the admission of new members with secrecy, and both have a concern with King Solomon's Temple), their differences are far greater, and more striking. The outlines of the Templar admission ceremony are well known, despite the alleged secrecy, and they bear no resemblance to those of Freemasonry, which for one thing do not enjoin candidates to take up a monastic life of poverty and celibacy. Nor is there any connection between the 'secrets' of the two Orders. The 'secrets' of Freemasonry are nothing more than the modes of recognition used in the ceremonies, while – as far as objective history goes – the Templars had no 'secrets' at all.

Even the association with the Temple is misleading. Freemasons treat the construction of King Solomon's Temple as an allegory: the building of the morally upright and virtuous man. For the Templars, the Temple was simply their original headquarters and a place for quartering their horses.

The Templar theory of Masonic origin, then, is not supported by the historical record. James Anderson, in 1723, even suggested that the line of descent went in the other direction: 'Nay', he wrote, 'if it were expedient, it could be made to appear, that from this ancient Fraternity (i.e. Freemasonry) the Societies or Orders of the Warlike Knights, and of the Religious too, in process of time, did borrow many solemn usages.' And yet the supposed link with the Knights Templar had a prolonged effect on the popular Masonic mind, fostering associations between the Craft and the noble ideals of medieval chivalry. From this romantic notion sprang not only the purely Masonic Order of Knights Templar, but also a multitude of more exotic chivalric Orders that finally found their definitive expression in that most enduring and ubiquitous of the 'additional degrees': the Ancient and Accepted Scottish Rite of Freemasonry. The story of that Rite will be told in its proper place, but it may be noted here that within its ritual structure are several degrees whose traditional histories and ceremonies are based on the legendary story of the Knights Templar and which emphasize the righting of the wrongs done to the Order. The existence of these degrees has helped, though unwittingly, to perpetuate the Templar myth.

Right IN THIS IDEALIZED PORTRAYAL OF JACQUES DE MOLAY THE DETAILS OF THE DRESS OF THE KNIGHTS TEMPLAR CAN BE SEEN. AS BEFITTED THE MEMBERS OF A MONASTIC ORDER, THE KNIGHTS, THE 'MONKS OF WAR', WERE CELIBATE – SYMBOLIZED BY THE WHITE MANTLE WITH ITS RED CROSS, WORN IN THE MANNER OF A MONASTIC HABIT OVER THEIR CHAIN MAIL. THEY WERE FULLY ARMED IN ORDER TO CARRY OUT THEIR PRIMARY PURPOSE OF PROTECTING PILGRIMS IN THE HOLY LAND.

THE ROSICRUCIAN MYTH

THE last of the more imaginative theories of Masonic origin concerns the occult brotherhood known as the Rosicrucians. Like the Templar theory, this still finds popular support, although there is even less ground for believing in Rosicrucianism as the Craft's original source than in the Templars. At least the Templars existed: there is absolutely no historical evidence to establish the reality of the original Rosicrucian brotherhood.

And yet the myth took hold, and still survives. Elias Ashmole and Sir Robert Moray, both prominent figures in Masonic prehistory, were intrigued by the Rosicrucians, whilst the influential hermetic physician Robert Fludd – though his only connection with Freemasonry is the proximity of his London house to that of the Masons' Company – wrote fervently in their defence. Then in 1730 a satirical letter appeared in the English *Daily Journal* which stated that English Freemasons had based their ceremonies on those of the Rosicrucians, and towards the end of the eighteenth century various esoteric offshoots of Freemasonry sprang up proclaiming themselves to be true heirs of Christian Rosenkreutz, and declaring that Freemasonry and Rosicrucianism were intimately linked. This view found specious scholarly support in the work of J. G. Buhle, who stated in 1804 that 'The original Freemasons were a society that arose out of the Rosicrucian mania.' But, again, supporters of the Rosicrucian theory of origin have been consistently unable to bring forward any corroborative historical evidence for their belief.

Who, then, were the Rosicrucians? The earliest reference to the Fraternity of the Rosy Cross appeared in 1614 with the publication of the *Fama Fraternitatis*, the first of three pamphlets known collectively as the Rosi-crucian Manifestos (the others being the *Confessio* and the *Chymische Hochzeit*, or Chemical Wedding). All three were anonymous but are thought to have been the work of a German Lutheran theologian called Johann Valentin Andreae, who claimed to be the author of the third of the pamphlets.

As well as advocating a universal reformation of religion and manners, the Rosicrucian manifestos tell the story of Christian Rosenkreutz, the mythical founder of the Rosicrucian Order. The Rosenkreutz legend has clear parallels with the life of Christ and has obvious allegorical intent. The followers of Rosenkreutz are bound to a life of apostolic zeal and simplicity and are envisaged as a Protestant equivalent of a medieval mon-astic Order, with each member undertaking to heal the sick and to find a 'worthy person' to succeed him in the Order. The story also recounts the discovery of Rosen-kreutz's tomb, 120 years after his death, and describes the secret alchemical and kabbalistic symbolism it con-tained. Although a grave also figures in the ceremony of raising a Master Mason, both the structure and impli-cations of Rosicrucian rituals differ fundamentally from those of Freemasonry. Masonic ceremonies are intended to teach simple moral lessons; the emphasis of the Rosicrucian Manifestos is on spiritual attainment and on the acquisition of a hidden wisdom within Christianity. More significantly, there is no historical evidence of an established Rosicrucian Order until esoteric groups of the late seventeenth century – many years after the frag-mentary records of proto-Masonry began – assumed the name (or, like Johannes Kelpius in Pennsylvania, were described as Rosicrucians by others).

But if not Noah, or Nebuchadnezzar, or the Coma-cines, or the Templars, or the Rosicrucians, what or who can lay legitimate claim to have originated Freemasonry? The question leads us to consider the more rational theories of Masonic origins that are based upon actual historical records.

RIGHT REGALIA OF THE ROSE CROIX OF HEREDOM, 18° OF THE ANCIENT AND ACCEPTED RITE. THE ROSE-CROIX DEGREE IS ULTIMATELY DERIVED FROM THE ROSICRUCIAN MYTH, WHICH WAS AN ALLEGORY OF THE LIFE OF CHRIST. CHRISTIAN SYMBOLISM CAN BE SEEN ON THE JEWEL OF THE DEGREE (THE MEDAL THAT IS WORN SUSPENDED FROM THE COLLAR) WHICH DEPICTS, IN ADDITION TO THE CALVARY CROSS, THE ROSE OF SHARON AND THE PELICAN FEEDING HER YOUNG WITH HER OWN BLOOD – BOTH OF THEM SYMBOLS OF CHRIST.

Eighteenth Degree
Plate 1st

THE THREE-STAGE THEORY OF ORIGIN

UNTIL recently, most Masonic scholars accepted the idea of a direct line of descent from medieval Masonry to the modern Craft. According to this theory, there were three stages in the development of the Masonic lodge: operative, transitional and speculative. First came the lodges that regulated the trade of stonemasons employed in the building of the great cathedrals, abbeys, and castles of medieval England. By the early seventeenth century these operative lodges had begun to accept non-stonemasons – called Accepted Masons – as members. Gradually, Accepted Masons formed majorities transforming operative lodges into so-called speculative lodges, which were the forerunners of today's Masonic Lodges.

At first sight the existing evidence appears to support this theory. Medieval operative masons were certainly grouped in lodges, and in Scotland such operative lodges gradually became geographically defined units. This is clear from the *Schaw Statutes* of 1598-9, two documents drawn up by William Schaw, Master of Work and General Warden of the Masons under King James VI, which set out an elaborate code of organization and procedure for operative masons. Indeed, surviving minute books from Scottish operative lodges imply that some form of ritual work was carried on, in addition to the business of management and control of the trade. They also show the increasing admission of Accepted Masons, to the extent that by the early eighteenth century the operative content of some of the lodges had become completely eroded and they were, to all intents and purposes, speculative lodges. The process seems to have been similar in England. For example, the London Masons' Company admitted members who were neither operative craftsmen nor their employers, and there are also well-attested instances of non-operatives being initiated into other Masonic lodges.

The most famous of these is the case of the antiquarian Elias Ashmole. According to his diary, Ashmole was initiated into a lodge at Warrington, Lancashire, on 16 October 1646, during the English Civil War. (Five years earlier Alexander Hamilton and Sir Robert Moray, two generals of the Scots army then invading England, had been initiated at Newcastle-on-Tyne by members of an Edinburgh lodge, although this should be seen as a Scottish, rather than an English, event – an important distinction, as we shall see). Ashmole records only one other Masonic event at which he was present: the admission of six gentlemen, none of whom were operative

masons, to the 'Fellowship of Free Masons' at London in 1682. Six years later Randle Holme III, an heraldic painter, stated in print that he was a 'Member of that Society, called Free-Masons', while at the same period the antiquarian Robert Plot gave a brief comment on the Masonic admission ceremony emphasizing its 'secret signes'. Taken together, these pieces of evidence appear to support the three-stage theory; but several key questions remain unanswered and put the validity of the theory in doubt.

The first concerns the distinction between English and Scottish Freemasonry. A recent study has argued that Freemasonry before 1717 developed entirely in Scotland, citing not only the evidence quoted above, but also the fact that ritual elements in the working of Scottish Masonic lodges (for example, the use of the Mason Word from 1638 onwards) can be shown to have crept into English lodge working. But the same study does not distinguish clearly between operative and speculative Masonry when discussing 'masonry' in general; more importantly, it does not take into account the great differences – social, cultural, political, religious and legal – that existed between England and Scotland in the sixteenth and seventeenth centuries. The two nations had separate rulers until 1603, and they remained politically distinct for a further century until the Act of Union in 1707. It is thus dangerous to draw conclusions about Masonic activities in one country from apparent parallels in the other.

Further, there is as yet no evidence of operative lodges in England after 1500, just as there is none for the existence of similar lodges in Scotland before the end of the sixteenth century. And if the *Old Charges* are the essential evidence for the development of speculative out of operative Masonry, why do the Scottish versions – few in number – all date from the late seventeenth century and demonstrate a clear derivation from earlier English versions ?

It must be agreed that non-operatives were admitted to Scottish lodges; but we do not know what form their admission ceremonies took, nor how they differed – if at all – from those used for operatives. Indeed, we know little about *any* Masonic ritual prior to the publication of Samuel Prichard's *Masonry Dissected* (1730). Nor can it be shown that these Scottish non-operatives were anything other than purely honorary members admitted simply because they were burgh dignitaries and who took no active part in the workings of their wholly operative lodges. At the same time in England, where operative lodges had been unknown for more than a century, gentlemen Masons were being admitted to Masonic lodges for purposes quite unconnected with the stonemason's trade.

From all this arises the most important question of all: why were Elias Ashmole and others admitted into Masonic lodges (of whatever kind) and why did they seek such admission? In short, why did Freemasonry appear when it did and in the way that it did? The theory of a direct descent from the medieval builders cannot supply an answer to these questions; but there is one theory that can.

THE SCHAW STATUTES (AS PRESERVED IN THE FIRST MINUTE BOOK OF THE LODGE OF EDINBURGH, MARY'S CHAPEL). IN 1598 AN ELABORATE CODE OF RULES GOVERNING THE ACTIVITIES OF OPERATIVE MASONS WAS DRAWN UP IN SCOTLAND – WHERE PERMANENT LODGES IN FIXED LOCATIONS HAD BEGUN TO APPEAR BY THE END OF THE 16TH CENTURY – BY WILLIAM SCHAW. A SECOND SET OF STATUTES, ISSUED IN 1599, WAS CONCERNED WITH QUESTIONS OF LOCAL ORGANIZATION, AND THE RULES IN GENERAL CAN BE SEEN AS A KIND OF PROTOTYPE OF THE REGULATIONS GOVERNING THE PROVINCIAL STRUCTURE OF MODERN FREEMASONRY.

FAC-SIMILE OF A PORTION OF THE SCHAW STATUTES, 1598.

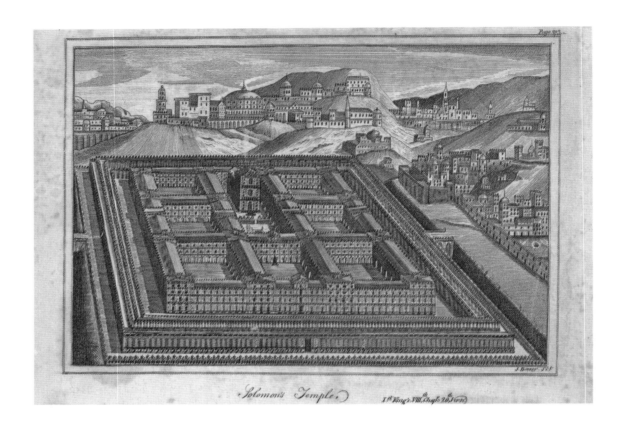

KING SOLOMON'S TEMPLE
'I HAVE BUILT THE HOUSE FOR THE NAME OF THE LORD, THE GOD OF ISRAEL.' THIS EARLY 19TH CENTURY RECONSTRUCTION OF
KING SOLOMON'S TEMPLE AT JERUSALEM IS BASED ON THE BIBLICAL DESCRIPTION OF ITS BUILDING.

'BROTHERLY LOVE, RELIEF AND TRUTH'

A systematic examination of the *Old Charges* manuscript reveals a clear distinction between the two oldest Charges, dating from the late fourteenth and early fifteenth century, and those of a later date, many of which were written, or copied, after the founding of the Grand Lodge of England in 1717. The third oldest version, known as the *Grand Lodge MS No. 1*, is dated 1583, but internal evidence now leads scholars to place it well after 1600. The oldest manuscripts have a purely operative content and were plainly devised by and for working stonemasons. The later versions, however, contain much that is irrelevant to operative Masonry while being very pertinent to Freemasonry as we now know it. From a consideration of these differences, one Masonic scholar, the late Colin Dyer, developed a new and startling theory.

The context of Dyer's arguments is the religious and political turmoil of the seventeenth century. The period was one of growing intolerance in both politics and religion. No forum existed in which men of differing views could meet in harmony. Opinions became polarized and divisions over matters of belief were so acute that families, friendships, and eventually society itself were torn apart by the English Civil War in 1642. Despite this, there were still men who believed passionately in tolerance and the free exchange of views. They saw the need for an organization in which men of widely differing opinions and beliefs could meet together in harmony and work to promote the ideal of tolerance in a troubled and fragmented world. And so they founded a fraternal order that eschewed sectarianism in both religion and politics whilst continuing to root itself firmly in a belief in God and in an unwavering loyalty to the three great principles of Brotherly Love, Relief and Truth.

During the seventeenth century, as in earlier ages, it was common for philosophical and moral ideas to be taught through allegory and symbolism. Since the essential aim of this brotherhood was to promote the building of a better man in a better world, no more appropriate allegory could have been found than the building of King Solomon's Temple. The working tools of the stonemason also became symbols of the brotherhood's moral aspirations. And so the outward forms of the old operative Masonic lodges became adapted to a new purpose. Not only did this provide a means of propagating the ideals of Freemasons, it also gave the founders of the new Order a cloak for their activities. Being suspected of 'subversion' could have dire consequences in those dangerous times, and even those dedicated to promoting tolerance in an intolerant world had to go about their work with the utmost discretion – even secrecy.

So runs the theory of the indirect descent of Freemasonry from the old operative lodges. But what historical evidence is there to support it?

The initiation of Elias Ashmole took place at the height of the English Civil War. Ashmole, a royalist, was a prisoner of the Parliamentarians. Also on the side of Parliament was his father-in-law, Colonel Henry Mainwaring, who was initiated at the same time as Ashmole. None of the seven other Freemasons who were present at their induction – all of whom must have been 'made' Masons at an earlier date – was an operative Mason. Thus we have a gathering of non-operative Masons from both sides of the political and religious divide – a striking instance of tolerance in action.

Further support for the indirect theory comes from a consideration of the period in which early Freemasonry grew up and consolidated its organization. After the Civil War, Oliver Cromwell showed himself to be an even greater tyrant than the executed Charles I, and the restoration of Charles's son in 1660 did little for the cause of tolerance. England in the late seventeenth century was effectively an absolute monarchy that came to an end only with the expulsion of James II after the 'Glorious Revolution' of 1688. The constitutional monarchy brought in by the accession of William and Mary gradually brought about a greater degree of religious toleration, but the process was a slow one and England remained unsettled until the end of the century.

As long as the threat of religious persecution remained real, Freemasonry needed to disguise its activities. Exiled Jacobites continued to plot against the new constitutional settlement, and the effects of persecution were only too visible in the form of Huguenot refugees from France. These French Protestants had been driven from their homes as a result of the Revocation of the Edict of Nantes. In 1598 the Edict had granted them liberty of conscience and the right·to worship in public. In 1685 these freedoms were stripped from them by Louis XIV, a supreme absolutist monarch. It cannot be shown conclusively that Huguenots entered Masonic lodges before 1717; but the obvious appeal of an organization devoted to tolerance and their prominence in the early years of the Grand Lodge of England lends strong support to the possibility.

The date of the foundation of the Grand Lodge is also significant. In 1715 the Jacobite rebellion against George I, the new German king, failed in its attempt to replace parliamentary government with an autocratic monarchy. By its failure, open political debate and freedom of conscience were assured. There was no longer any need for Freemasonry to hide itself or its purpose. And so in 1716 the lodges in London determined to create a governing body, and within a year organized Freemasonry had come into being.

Despite the plausibility of Dyer's theory the possibility cannot be ruled out that Freemasonry was still basically a trade-orientated society even at the time the premier Grand Lodge was founded. It has been argued that the original medieval lodge system, which had withered away by the time of the Reformation, was revived at the beginning of the seventeenth century by artisans who adapted to new working conditions by forming a self-help organization for their craft. If the lodge is thus seen primarily as a means of providing 'help to a brother', the practice of 'accepting' Masons from areas outside the immediate locality becomes more explicable. Lodges could have offered assistance – in the form of money collected as dues from the members, or perhaps by providing work – to itinerant Masons. The use of secret signs of recognition would have helped to ensure that the system was not abused and that the charity, or 'Relief', that was the lodge's principal function was properly disbursed. If this view is accepted, seventeenth-century Freemasonry can be seen as a trade club – the 'Society of Freemasons' described by Robert Plot – into which speculative Masons, who were not of the artisan class and who had never been working Masons, were gradually, and increasingly, admitted.

In fact, there is no conflict between the idea of Freemasonry as a charitable, trade-based body and the notion of it as a vehicle for the promotion of religious and political tolerance. For different reasons, secrecy, allegory, and symbolism were appropriate to both functions, making this the most reasonable – even, perhaps, the most probable – theory of Masonic origin. And yet it remains a hypothesis. How, when, and why Freemasonry arose are still questions to which we have no final answers.

ANTHONY SAYER (1672-1742),
THE FIRST GRAND MASTER OF THE PREMIER GRAND LODGE.

CHAPTER II

HISTORY OF THE CRAFT

'HISTORY IS PHILOSOPHY TEACHING BY EXAMPLES'

HENRY ST. JOHN, VISCOUNT BOLINGBROKE

WITH the founding of the premier Grand Lodge on 24 June 1717, organized Freemasonry was born. The four 'Old Lodges' that met at the Goose and Gridiron ale house in St Paul's Churchyard elected one of their number, Anthony Sayer, as 'oldest Master Mason and then Master of a Lodge', as Grand Master and agreed to hold a Grand Feast once a year. Sayer also appointed Grand Wardens and 'commanded the Master and Wardens of Lodges to meet the Grand Officers every Quarter in Communication', although there is no evidence that these meetings ever took place. For the first three years of its existence Grand Lodge simply provided an opportunity of an annual social gathering of the London lodges. There was no attempt, nor apparently any intention, to exercise control over provincial lodges. But this casual state of affairs was soon to change.

The Grand Masters who succeeded Sayer – George Payne and the Revd. Dr. Theophilus Desaguliers – were men of a different stamp who, with the help of the astute and inventive Revd. Dr. James Anderson, remodelled and revitalized the Craft. Following the codification of Grand Lodge regulations by Payne in 1720, and the election of a Grand Secretary in 1723 (with the consequent establishment of official Minutes), Anderson compiled and published the first official *Constitutions of the Free-Masons* (1723), which set out those regulations, together with a history of the craft derived partly from the *Old Charges* but expanded and embellished by Anderson's fertile imagination. Fanciful though this history was, the effects of Anderson's *Constitutions* was to establish the idea of Freemasonry firmly in the public eye – to such an extent that contemporary writers seized upon it as a worthy object of satire.

This did not mean that the Craft was inimical to the intelligentsia of the time – far from it – and for this much of the credit must go to Dr. Desaguliers, among whose many achievements was his invention of the planetarium. Associate and friend of Isaac Newton, Desaguliers was the archetypal speculative Mason. As the child of Huguenot refugees he was deeply committed to the ideal of tolerance, while as a natural philosopher (or what we should now call a physicist) he was an eager student of the 'Hidden Mysteries of Nature and Science'. There seems little doubt that the many Fellows of the Royal Society who became Freemasons were influenced by Desaguliers's example, and it is surely no accident that no less than twelve Grand Masters were also Fellows of the Royal Society during the twenty years following Desaguliers. Many others – among them Martin Folkes, who was President for twelve years, and John Arbuthnot, who introduced both Alexander Pope and Jonathan Swift to the Craft – served as Grand Officers.

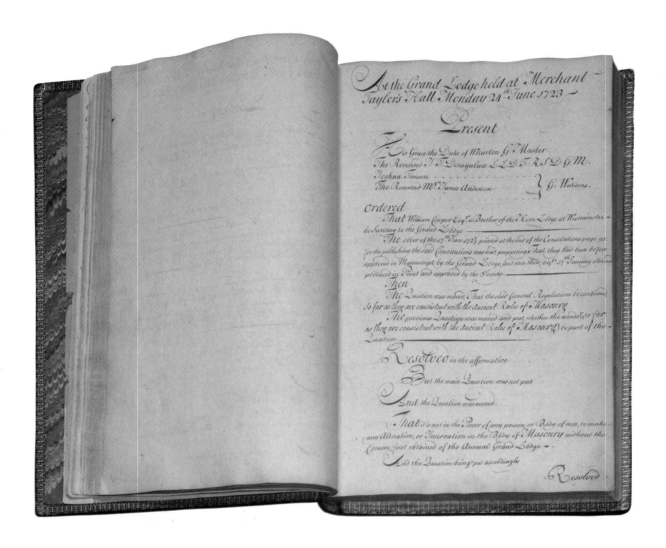

THE FIRST MINUTE BOOK OF THE GRAND LODGE OF ENGLAND, CONTAINING THE FIRST OFFICIAL RECORD OF SPECULATIVE FREEMASONRY. THE ENTRY DATED MONDAY 24 JUNE 1723 APPOINTED WILLIAM COWPER OF THE HORN LODGE TO BE 'SECRETARY TO THE GRAND LODGE', AND APPROVED THE PRINTING OF THE CONSTITUTIONS.

It is also significant that, after 1720, every Grand Master was of either noble or royal rank. By this time a subtle shift had taken place. The old operative element – such at is was – lost control of the Craft, whilst Grand Lodge, the governing body, became increasingly associated with the upper echelons of society. This was to have a profound effect on the development of English Freemasonry. But the history of the Craft is not simply the history of Freemasonry in London. By the mid-1720s many provincial lodges began to accept the jurisdiction of Grand Lodge; others, however, denied its authority – notably at York, where an independent Grand Lodge sprang up.

There are few surviving records of the earliest provincial lodges, but it is clear that support for the Craft grew throughout the eighteenth century. The Industrial Revolution brought out significant shifts in the pattern of population. As new industries expanded and brought wealth to particular towns and districts, so Freemasonry flourished. Conversely, population decline in other areas led to the disappearance of local Lodges. But what exactly did the Grand Lodge govern?

Masonically, the term 'Lodge' has been applied to the building or room in which Freemasons work; to the specific body or group of people using that room; or to the meeting of such a group. During the early days of the Craft there were no permanent Masonic Halls or Temples and Lodges were usually held in taverns or coffee-houses. We can build up a picture of those early days from the surviving Minute Books of some of the oldest lodges, and the manner of their working is known from early eighteenth century manuscript catechisms and from the unofficial printed rituals, the 'Exposures', that appeared from 1730 onwards.

Above THE EARLIEST ENGLISH LODGES MET IN TAVERNS AND COFFEE HOUSES. THIS TAVERN ON THE RIVER THAMES,
AT PELICAN STAIRS, OLD WAPPING, LONDON, ENGLAND WAS THE HOME OF OLD DUNDEE LODGE NO. 18 FROM 1739 TO 1820.

Following page JAMES ANDERSON'S *THE CONSTITUTIONS OF THE FREE-MASONS* OF 1723: THE FIRST OFFICIAL,
PRINTED MASONIC DOCUMENT, WHICH TOOK THE PLACE OF THE MANUSCRIPT *OLD CHARGES*.

THE CRAFT DEGREES

THE lodge room would have an oblong table in its centre, with the properties required laid upon it (when not in use these were kept in the lodge box). Around it sat the Master and brethren. An oblong enclosing the emblems and symbols appropriate to the ceremony to be worked was drawn on the floor in chalk ('drawing the lodge'), to be erased by the candidate with mop and pail after his initiation had taken place. The feasting and drinking that followed the ceremony took place in the same room. The same procedure was more or less standard for the Craft degrees throughout the eighteenth century, although it is not known precisely when they were introduced. About the structure of the ceremonies themselves, however, we can be more certain.

From the latter part of the seventeenth century the following pattern was followed. First, the candidate took an Obligation on the Bible to preserve the mysteries of the Craft. The Mason Word and Sign were then communicated and the Charges – telling the new Mason of his duty to God, his Master, and his fellow-men – and the legendary history were read. By 1700 a two-degree system, of Entered Apprentice and Fellow Craft, was in place, and in the 1720s a third degree, that of Master Mason, made its appearance.

Gradually, the ceremonies became more elaborate. The Obligation, accompanied now by a physical penalty, was followed by the communication of the Sign and Word of the degree in question, while in the second part of the ceremony there was a short catechism, using a simple symbolism based on the stonemason's tools, in which the ceremony and the purpose of the degree were explained. From the 1770s these explanations began to be expanded, incorporating additional working tools as symbols of particular virtues and symbolical explanations of the

CONSTI
TU
TIONS

Engrav'd by John Pine in Aldersgate Street London

THE
CONSTITUTIONS
OF THE
FREE-MASONS.

CONTAINING THE

History, Charges, Regulations, &c.
of that moſt Ancient and Right
Worſhipful *FRATERNITY.*

For the Uſe of the LODGES.

L O N D O N:

Printed by WILLIAM HUNTER, for JOHN SENEX at the *Globe,*
and JOHN HOOKE at the *Flower-de-luce* over-againſt *St. Dunſtan's
Church,* in *Fleet-ſtreet.*

In the Year of Maſonry —— 5723
Anno Domini —— —— 1723

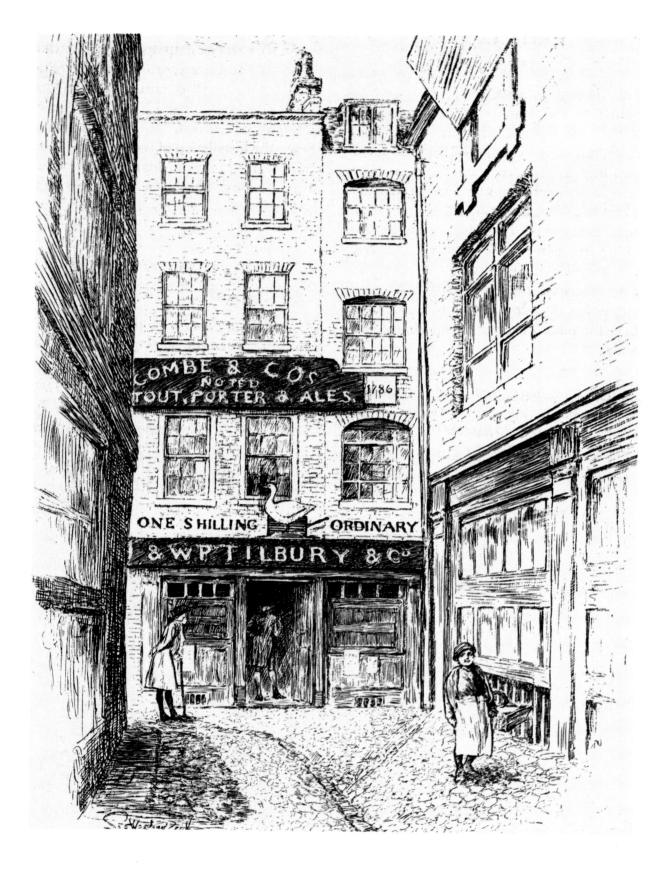

THE FIRST MEETING OF THE PREMIER GRAND LODGE WAS HELD ON 24 JUNE 1717
AT THE GOOSE AND GRIDIRON ALEHOUSE IN ST. PAUL'S CHURCHYARD,
THE HOME OF THE FIRST OF THE FOUR OLD LODGES THAT ESTABLISHED THE GRAND LODGE.

candidate's preparation for each degree, as well as of the lodge furniture and members regalia. Today there is a wide variety of degree ceremonies, or workings, practised within the Craft in England; but the basic framework is effectively the same as it has been since a standard form of ritual was introduced in 1816.

The government of the Craft also follows a standard pattern. Since Freemasonry is a hierarchical system, the descent of authority from the Grand Master downwards in the Grand Lodge is mirrored in the structure of individual lodges. The Master, the lodge's principal officer, conducts the ceremonies and administers the lodge with the assistance of two Wardens. Below them come the two Deacons, who act as messengers between Master and Wardens, as well as guiding and conducting candidates during the ceremonies. There are also two guardians of the Lodge, one inside and one outside. The Outer Guard, the Tyler, keeps out all intruders and prepares the candidate for the ceremonies. It was also his duty, before painted cloths and, later, Tracing Boards were used to display the emblems and symbols of each degree, to 'draw the lodge' in chalk. Inside, the door is guarded and candidates admitted, when properly prepared, by the Inner Guard, although this office did not exist in the eighteenth century and these duties were carried out by the Junior Warden, or by one of the Stewards.

The office of Steward, who originally attended the Wardens and was responsible for the refreshments, is a living reminder that, in the early days of Freemasonry, conviviality was an important part of the lodge's social functions. Today the duties of the British Stewards are largely confined to serving wine at the Festive Board (the meal that usually follows the completion of the lodge's work). The ritual and ceremonial is overseen by a Director (formerly Master) of Ceremonies, while the day- to-day administration is now, as in the past, carried out by the Secretary and Treasurer.

Communications in the eighteenth century were much slower than today, and as the number of lodges under the jurisdiction of Grand Lodge, but at a distance from London, increased it became more difficult to administer them directly. Consequently, Provincial Grand Lodges were established governing provinces that were more or less coincidental with the old county boundaries, although they had no clearly defined official status until 1813. Indeed, the main function of a Provincial Grand Master was not to administrate but, rather, to constitute new lodges in his province. The founding of new lodges overseas – in British possessions or in places where English merchants had settled – remained a matter for the Grand Lodge, but outside England proper, wholly independent Grand Lodges arose.

EARLY FREEMASONRY IN SCOTLAND

GIVEN the existence of active operative lodges in Scotland, it is surprising that a Grand Lodge did not arise there until 1736. When it did, it was – as in England – the result of four old lodges combining. Their initial gathering led to a meeting of thirty-three lodges on 30 November 1736 at which William St. Clair was elected Grand Master Mason of Scotland. However, a considerable operative element remained in Scottish Masonry; new lodges did not proliferate to the same extent as in England, and to dissension between operatives and non-operatives was added argument over historical precedence. In 1743 the latter controversy led to the Canongate Kilwinning Lodge resuming its independence, which lasted for almost seventy years and during which it chartered lodges both in Scotland and in North America. It was also involved in the even greater disruption of Scottish Masonry caused by Jacobite Rebellion of 1745.

True to the principles of Freemasonry, the majority of Scottish Masons avoided sectarian politics; but in many lodges there were supporters both of the Crown and of Charles Edward Stuart, the young Pretender (c1745). The members of Kilwinning were more partisan: the majority were Jacobites, although it is not clear if they gave active support to the Pretender's cause, and as the rebellion began to fail harmony was restored in the lodges.

Among the many distinguished Scottish Masons was Robert Burns, always a great favourite at the lodges he visited – particularly at Kilwinning (although the story of his being the lodge's Poet Laureate seems to be a romantic fiction). Burns's prominence and popularity illustrates an important fact of Masonry: the ability of members to cross social, political and religious divides. Burns came from a poor family and was a political radical with Deistic views; yet he was welcomed by all the Masonic brethren whatever their beliefs or social standing.

EARLY IRISH FREEMASONRY

THERE is no certain evidence that operative lodges existed in Ireland, and there is only a single literary allusion to a Speculative Lodge at Dublin in 1688. The first certain date is 26 June 1725, when a meeting of the Grand Lodge at Dublin elected the Earl of Rosse as its 'New Grand Master'. The Dublin Grand Lodge, however, was not the only one in Ireland. Just as in England, provincial lodges were wary of submitting to a central authority. Many of them paid little attention to directives from Dublin, while in Cork an independent Grand Lodge of Munster survived for seven years until 1733. For the rest of the eighteenth century the Grand Lodge of Ireland had no rivals and, except for the brief emergence of a Grand Lodge in Ulster in the early nineteenth century, it has continued to act as the sole Masonic authority in Ireland.

In Masonic terms, Ireland was also a model of religious tolerance. Protestants and Catholics came together in the Craft, and for many years the statesman and patriot Daniel O'Connell played an active part in Irish Freemasonry, resigning from the Craft only when a misguided belief that Freemasons were to blame for the excesses of the French Revolution led the Roman Catholic hierarchy to enforce the anti-Masonic Bulls of 1738 and 1751. This foolish action led to a great exodus of Catholics from the Craft, for which a terrible price in sectarian violence has subsequently been paid.

But despite such setbacks, Irish Masonry flourished. Lodges under the Irish Constitution were founded overseas and from 1732 it was the Grand Lodge of Ireland that issued the first travelling warrants to regiments of the British Army. While this had little impact on English Freemasonry, a later influence in English Masonry was to create an upheaval in the Craft that would have dramatic and far-reaching consequences.

Above right FRONTISPIECE TO *AHIMAN REZON* (1764), SECOND EDITION. THE 'ANTIENTS' GRAND LODGE THAT WAS SET UP IN 1751 BY LAURENCE DERMOTT HAD ITS OWN BOOK OF CONSTITUTIONS, KNOWN AS *AHIMAN REZON*, THAT REGULATED THE CONDUCT OF ITS MEMBERS.

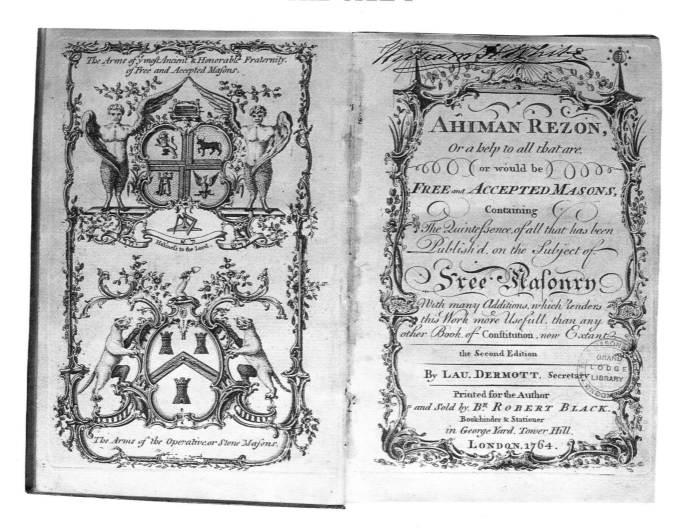

ANTIENTS AND MODERNS

LITTLE more than ten years after the founding of the premier Grand Lodge of England, changes in both custom and ritual began appearing which some members of the Craft viewed with alarm. Becoming increasingly concerned with what they saw as unwarranted interference with the 'landmarks' of the Order, they eventually threw in their lot with a group of Irish Masons who had been denied entry to London lodges – primarily because they were artisans, and because their ritual did not conform to English usage. In 1751 these disaffected Masons formed themselves into six lodges and set up a Grand Committee that within two years had transformed itself into a vigorous and wholly independent Grand Lodge. Through the efforts of one remarkable man this 'Antients' Grand Lodge – so called because it claimed to have restored ancient usages – went from strength to strength until it became a formidable rival of the earlier, and now paradoxically nicknamed, 'Moderns' Grand Lodge.

Laurence Dermott, was an Irish journeyman painter (later he would prosper as a wine merchant) who came to London in 1748. Dermott supported the 'Antients' and for twenty years acted as their Grand Secretary. In this role he wrote, and published in 1756, the curiously titled *Ahiman Rezon; or, A Help to a Brother*, in which the Constitutions of the 'Antients' were set out. Successive editions soon followed that were increasingly hostile to the Moderns and, by virtue of Dermott's polemical but engaging style, highly influential within the Craft. Within twenty years of its foundation the 'Antients' Grand Lodge had founded some two hundred lodges in London, the provinces, and overseas (almost half the number of lodges under the authority of the much older premier Grand Lodge). Even more galling to the 'Moderns' was the fact that the 'Antients' were also recognized as the legitimate Masonic authority in England by the Grand Lodges of both Ireland and Scotland.

ENGLISH FREEMASONRY IN THE AGE OF REVOLUTION

IN spite of its quarrel with the 'Antients' and its problems with more recent rival Grand Lodges, the 'Moderns' Grand Lodge also flourished – due mainly to the work of William Preston whose *Illustrations of Masonry* remained in print for almost a century after its first appearance in 1772. Preston's book undoubtedly helped to reassure ordinary Masons that the principles of the Craft were more important than the petty squabbles in which their hierarchy indulged. But for all their feuding, the two Grand Lodges still offered notable examples of tolerance and harmony. In an overwhelmingly Protestant country that still proscribed Catholicism, it was a salutary example, both to the Craft and to the nation as a whole, to see Freemasonry ruled by Roman Catholic Grand Masters – Thomas Mathew for the 'Antients' in 1767 and, five years later, Lord Petre for the 'Moderns'.

As the 1800s drew to its close Freemasonry was increasingly seen as an institution dedicated to the benevolence and the moral good of mankind: the image of the carousing Freemason established in the 1740s by the satirical engravings of William Hogarth (himself a Mason and Grand Steward) had become a thing of the past. The Craft was avowedly non-political, and the political repercussions of the American Revolution had very little effect on the institution as a whole. The effects of the French Revolution, however, were to be very different.

Initially, the events of 1789 were greeted in England with a degree of sympathy. Many saw the removal of an absolutist tyranny and its replacement by a constitutional monarchy and elected government as a desirable political end. But with the coming of the 'Terror' sympathy was replaced by revulsion and hostility towards those who professed 'Liberty, Equality and Fraternity'. The superficial similarity between the revolutionary slogan and the basic principles of Freemasonry was seized upon by detractors who hysterically blamed the Craft for unleashing the violence of the Revolution. Luckily, common sense prevailed and it was generally recognized that English Freemasonry – which, from 1782 onwards, could point to a succession of royal Grand Masters – was in no way a subversive organization; in fact when the Unlawful Societies Act (for the suppression of seditious organizations) was passed in 1799, Freemasonry was specifically exempted.

The trauma of the French Revolution and its aftermath led to a general desire to heal national and social divisions, and within the Craft a new generation of Freemasons sought to close up the rift in their own ranks. The first move came from the 'Moderns' in 1798, and slowly, in 1813, the 21 Articles of Union were drawn up and agreed upon, and the United Grand Lodge of England was born.

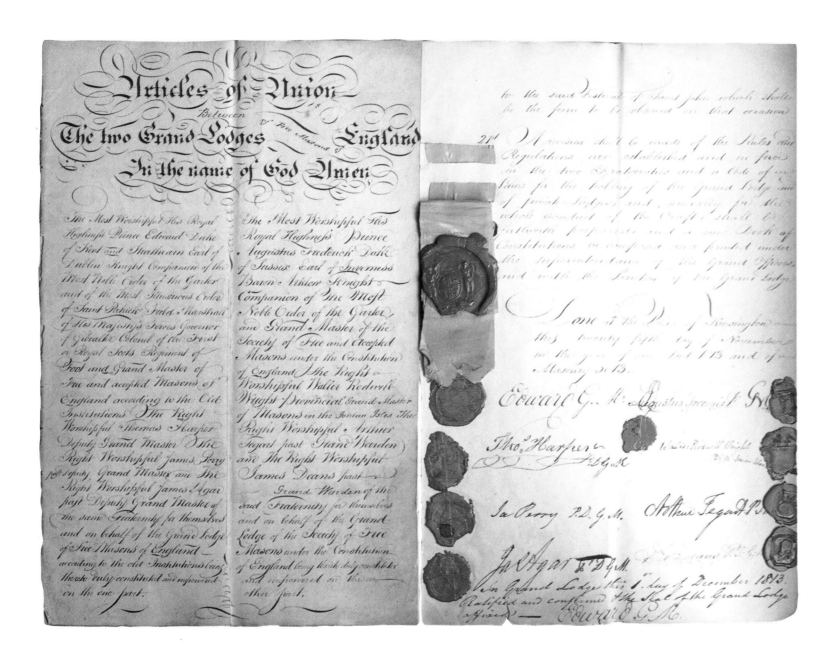

THE ARTICLES OF UNION. AFTER SIXTY YEARS OF DIVISION, HARMONY WAS RESTORED TO ENGLISH FREEMASONRY IN 1813 WITH THE UNION OF THE TWO RIVAL GRAND LODGES OF THE 'ANTIENTS' AND 'MODERNS' UNDER THE DUKE OF SUSSEX, WHO HAD BEEN GRAND MASTER OF THE 'MODERNS'. WITH FEW EXCEPTIONS THE GRAND MASTERS OF THE UNITED GRAND LODGE OF ENGLAND HAVE BEEN OF ROYAL RANK, DOWN TO THE CURRENT GRAND MASTER, EDWARD, DUKE OF KENT.

ENGLISH FREEMASONRY IN THE NINETEENTH CENTURY

THE year 1813 was a watershed in English Free-masonry. On 27 December the rival 'Modern' and 'Antient' Grand Lodges came together to form the United Grand Lodge of England under the Grand Mastership of Augustus Frederick, Duke of Sussex, a son of King George III. The Duke was a student of theology and Hebrew, and to scholarship he united unusual religious and political tolerance. In an age when religious bigotry was still rife in public affairs, the Duke of Sussex was an outspoken supporter of Catholic emancipation and went out of his way to associate himself with a number of Jewish causes.

In reorganizing the Craft after the Union, the Duke was determined to make the Antient Charge 'Of God and Religion' the centrepiece of the reconciled fellowship: 'Let a man's religion or mode of worship be what it may, he is not excluded from the Order, provided he believe in the glorious architect of heaven and practise the sacred duties of morality'. It was intended that the Craft and the Royal Arch should become truly universal and open to men of all faiths. And so when the Craft ritual was being revised in 1814-16, and the Royal Arch in 1834-35, the process of de-Christianization that had been steadily occurring since the late eighteenth century was accelerated, resulting in the removal of all overt Christian references from both sets of rituals.

As a result non-Christians could now participate in Freemasonry without compromising their principles, while Freemasonry itself could demonstrate that, although it supported religion in general, it was not attempting to replace or challenge any particular denomination. In short, the revisions made clear that while Freemasonry had an archaic religious basis, it was not in any sense a religion in itself. Instead, again in the words of the 'Antient' Grand Lodge, it sought to be 'the centre of union between good men and true, and the happy means of conciliating friendship among those who must otherwise have remained at a perpetual distance'.

The revisions of the English Craft rituals also had a profound effect on the nature of English Freemasonry itself. In the eighteenth century the rituals, while attempting to instil in members a simple moral code, had been basically a means of gaining admission into what was essentially a social society. The new rituals, which exemplified the three great Masonic principles of Brotherly Love, Relief and Truth, and emphasized the centrality of God in human existence, became the whole basis of Freemasonry, not simply entrance ceremonies for a club whose main purpose was social. Those societies that grew up in emulation of Freemasonry, but which emphasized the convivial, beneficial, or charitable sides and neglected the moral code that lay at the heart of the new rituals, either faded away or survived only as benefit clubs or insurance societies. Freemasonry, by contrast, firmly rooted in morality and religion, has expanded on a scale that would have been unimaginable to those who revised the Craft rituals in the early nineteenth century.

The Grand Lodges of Ireland and Scotland had carefully observed the negotiations that led to the formation of the United Grand Lodge of England. The three British Grand Lodges, whilst retaining their individual sovereignty and developing differences in practice, maintained a close rapport that has continued to the present day. In all three jurisdictions, Freemasonry was becoming part of the fabric of social life. As Britain was rapidly transformed into a major industrial power, Freemasonry grew on an unprecedented scale. With this social upheaval went an explosion of new ideas, especially in the field of science. What had been regarded as fundamental, inviolate truths now began to be questioned. In the midst of such social and intellectual ferment Freemasonry appeared to many to offer a haven of calm and certainty with its core of unchanging principles, and within the Masonic lodge men from all sections of society, who might be separated by class and political ideology in their daily lives, came together as equals.

Left AUGUSTUS FREDERICK DUKE OF SUSSEX (1773-1843), GRAND MASTER OF THE UNITED GRAND LODGE OF ENGLAND FOR THIRTY YEARS, WAS A PILLAR OF POLITICAL AND RELIGIOUS TOLERANCE IN AN ERA WHEN SUCH OPEN-MINDEDNESS WAS RARE.

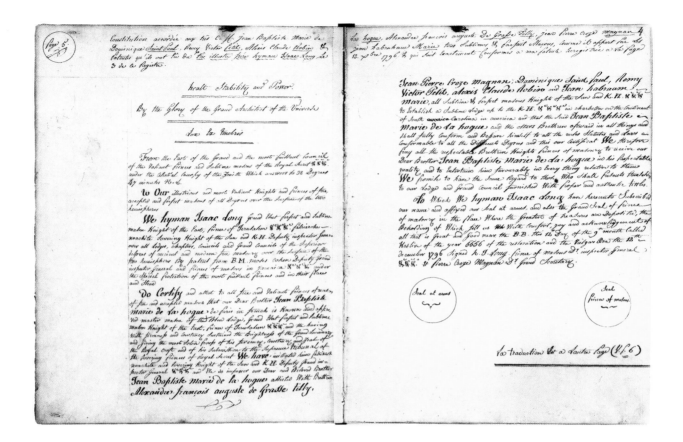

FREEMASONRY IN FRANCE

THE history of Freemasonry in France is immensely complex. For 150 years it displayed a tangled web of Grand Lodges, Chapters, Rites and Orders, Councils that united, divided, vanished, revived and interlocked. But underlying the complexity was one major factor that would eventually bring about a dramatic change in the way Freemasonry was viewed – from both within and without.

In its basic form, 'pure Ancient Masonry' consists of three degrees, and no more: 'the Entered Apprentice, the Fellow Craft, and the Master Mason (including the Supreme Order of the Holy Royal Arch)'. But while the three Craft degrees have remained essential and inviolate since the early eighteenth century, other Masonic degrees have proliferated, and most of these can trace their origins, directly or indirectly, to France. Exactly why so many more degrees – 34 quasi-Masonic Orders, and 26 Orders admitting both men and women, containing between them a total of more than 1,400 degrees – should rise up in France is not fully understood. But rise up they did, and those that survived the test of time have played an important part in the growth of Masonry.

The Ecossais Degrees

For all their apparent diversity, the majority of additional degrees – especially those created during the Age of Enlightenment – are based on the virtues of chivalry and on legends such as that linking Freemasonry to the Knights Templar. Perhaps the simplicity of the Craft did not satisfy the tastes of the French aristocracy; perhaps novel and extravagant rituals struck a chord in those used to Catholic ceremonial; or perhaps high-sounding titles appealed to the elitism characteristic of French Masonry.

Whatever the reason for this proliferation, a common thread united those degrees and grades known as 'Ecossais' (i.e. Scottish). They have, of course, no true connection with Scotland but owe their name to the popularity of Ramsay's Oration (see p. 15), which made the impossible claim that Freemasonry began as a chivalric Order and then travelled from France to Scotland some four hundred years before its re-emergence in 1717. Precisely when the Ecossais degrees first arose is unknown. While at first many of them were independent of each other, by 1760 they had been brought together into the semblance of an organized Masonic rite under the nominal control of the Grand Lodge of France.

The following year, 1761, a patent was granted to one Stephen Morin, appointing him 'Grand Inspector in all parts of the New World' and empowering him to found lodges in order to 'multiply the Royal Order of Masonry in all the Perfect and Sublime Degrees'. And so what was to become the Ancient and Accepted Scottish Rite first made its way to North America.

The same tendency towards esoteric speculation was apparent among German Freemasons, who developed numerous Masonic rites based on alchemy, hermeticism, and the Templar myth. As in France, these, too, embodied the ideals of chivalry – most spectacularly in the Rite of the Strict Observance, created in 1755 by Baron Von Hund. It was perhaps inevitable that some of those exotic rituals attracted not only speculative philosopher such as Martines de Pasqually and Louis Claude de Saint-Mart, but also occult adventurers typified by Giuseppe Balsam, who called himself Count Cagliostro. (see p 84) Others gave birth to quasi-Masonic secret societies with avowedly political ends, notably the Order of the Illuminati in Bavaria, the creation of a certain Adam Weishaupt, which was dedicated to fighting secular and religious tyranny. Weishaupt's order was tiny and was snuffed out after eight years of life in 1785; but because of its revolutionary nature it bred suspicion and hostility to the Craft in general.

When the Revolution broke out in France, Freemasonry was well established. But, by the time of the 'Terror' in 1793-4 the Craft had virtually ceased to exist. It is a perpetual irony for Freemasonry that the great symbol of the 'Terror', the guillotine, was named after Dr. Joseph Guillotin, an active Mason, associate of Benjamin Franklin, and a humanitarian whose desire had been to ensure that death by capital punishment should be as swift and painless as possible.

After the Revolution came the rise of Napoleon and twenty years of war in Europe. This was a period of mixed fortunes for Freemasonry. It was banned in Austria and Russia but experienced a renaissance throughout much of the continent. The revolutionary promise of 'Liberty, Equality and Fraternity' had proved an empty one; but men of goodwill still struggled to bring about social transformation based on Brotherly Love, Relief and Truth, and as long as such men existed Freemasonry's place was unequivocally assured in the new Europe.

In 1877 the Grand Orient, reflecting the prevailing anti-clerical and anti-religious climate that followed the defeat of Napoleon III and the savage repression of the Commune, abolished the necessity for Masonic candidates to profess a belief in a Supreme Being. It also erased all references to God from its *Constitutions* and rituals, removed the Bible from its lodges, and no longer required candidates to take their obligations on the sacred books of their religion. Henceforth the Grand Orient admitted unbelievers, atheists and free-thinkers into its lodges. Having rejected the religious basis of Freemasonry the Grand Orient went on to involve itself as a body directly in politics and social policy, thus discarding another of Freemasonry's fundamental principles. The Masonic world was appalled. At a stroke the Grand Orient had altered the whole nature of the Craft.

The reaction of the other Grand Lodges was immediate and the Grand Orient was given an ultimatum: either it reverted to its former constitution or it – and all of its members – would be rejected as an irregular body by every regular Masonic jurisdiction in the world. But the Grand Orient refused to recant, and so was cast out of the Masonic fold.

The shock to regular Freemasonry was severe. Bodies had grown up in the past (for example, so-called Grand Orients in Spain and Portugal) that had been known for what they were – political groups masquerading as Freemasons – and had been duly rejected. But they were of little or no consequence: to all intents and purposes the Grand Orient *was* Freemasonry in France.

There had been, since 1804, a Supreme Council 33° for Scottish Rite Masonry in France and in 1880 this body, unhappy with the Grand Orient's actions, set up a Grand Lodge of France. However, because of its origins and because it has not insisted that every lodge should contain the Volume of the Sacred Law, this Order was, as it remains unrecognised, and the light of regular Freemasonry was extinguished in France until the National Grand Lodge of France was constituted in 1913.

Above left THE EARLIEST AUTHENTIC DOCUMENT MENTIONING DE GRASSE-TILLY PRIOR TO THE FOUNDATION OF THE SUPREME COUNCIL AT CHARLESTON IN 1801

Next page A COPPER ENGRAVING, (1823) OF THE DECLARATION OF INDEPENDENCE OF THE 13 UNITED STATES OF AMERICA.

THE CRAFT IN THE NEW WORLD

CERTAIN knowledge of the Craft in America begins in 1730 with the appointment of Daniel Coxe as Provincial Grand Master for New York, New Jersey, and Pennsylvania. Three years later Henry Price took up a similar post for New England and founded lodges at Boston and elsewhere – although the oldest known lodge is St. John's at Philadelphia, which was active by 1731 when Benjamin Franklin is recorded as being a member. By 1734 the Craft had progressed sufficiently for Franklin to print an American edition of Anderson's 1723 *Constitutions*, while within another twenty years the first Masonic hall was built at Philadelphia.

In that same year, 1755, Henry Price noted that forty lodges had sprung from his first lodge in Boston alone. Lodges, indeed, proliferated all down the eastern seaboard – all of them, until after the outbreak of the War of Independence in 1775, under the direction of Provincial Grand Masters appointed in England.

During the American Revolution the Craft was divided and there were prominent Masons on both sides. Support for, or opposition to, the struggle for independence was a matter solely for an individual's conscience, with which Freemasonry never interferes. Of the 55 signatories of the Declaration of Independence, only nine were unquestionably Masons, and out of the 55 delegates who signed the Constitution of the United States in 1787 only 13 were, or were to become, Freemasons. On the other hand, many of the most prominent heroes of the Revolution were members of the Craft – among them George Washington, Benjamin Franklin, Paul Revere, John Paul Jones, John Hancock, and the Marquis de Lafayette.

In 1781 the War of Independence came to an end and the new nation turned to the task of political consolidation. Vast tracts of largely unexplored territory began to be opened up, and Freemasonry travelled with pioneers who mapped out and settled the newly claimed lands. In the early years of independence there was an attempt to establish a National Grand Lodge, but this came to nothing and, as now, each State of the Union was governed Masonically by its own State Grand Lodge.

Hostility and Dissension

During the early part of the nineteenth century, Freemasonry in America came under fierce attack from various quarters. Organised anti-Masonry came to full flower in 1826 in the person of William Morgan, an unsavoury character who, although a Mason, turned against the Craft and announced his intention of publishing an exposure of Masonic ceremonies. Local Freemasons were alarmed; but instead of simply calling Morgan's bluff they took fright and allegedly kidnapped him. Morgan was never seen again and it was widely believed the he had been murdered by his fellow Masons. Although this was never proven, Morgan's kidnappers were brought to trial and punished.

The alleged murder of Morgan led to an outcry against Masonry in general which spread rapidly throughout New York State, New England, and even further afield. Within a year anti-Masonic conventions were being held and anti-Masonic political candidates were successfully fielded in State elections. In 1832 William Wirt, a Mason and the anti-Masonic party candidate, failed to capture the presidency and the whole hysterical movement began to wither away. Its pernicious work, however, had already been done, and Freemasonry in the North-eastern States fell into a catastrophic decline from which it took many decades to recover.

Hostility towards Freemasonry also came from the Mormons, who attempted to gain control in a few Lodges in Illinois. The resulting animosity between the two groups has unfortunately persisted to the present day. And then there was the abiding problem of Prince Hall Masonry – the Lodges of Black Freemasons deriving from Prince Hall's own African Lodge, warranted at Boston in 1784 by England. This Lodge was perfectly regular, until 1813 when erased by England for not submitting reports or payments. But Prince Hall took it upon himself to constitute, without authority, a further lodge at Providence, Rhode Island. After his death in 1808 African Lodge continued without regularity and in 1827 declared itself to be the independent African Grand Lodge No. I – a wholly irregular step. Further Lodges were chartered, and within twenty years Prince Hall State Grand Lodges began to appear. They remain unrecognized by most regular U.S. Grand Lodges but there is no question concerning the sincerity of their members and their intentions, or of their acceptance of the basic principles of Freemasonry.

The harmony of American Freemasonry was further shattered in 1861 by the outbreak of the American Civil War, during which division among Masons was as acute as it had been in the War of Independence. But when the war ended the Craft played its full part in bringing the divided nation together.

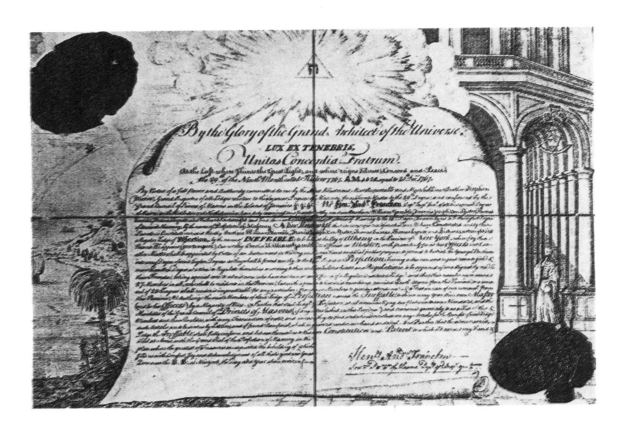

THE FRANCKEN PATENT TO THE LODGE OF PERFECTION, ALBANY, N.Y., 1767.

THE ANCIENT AND ACCEPTED SCOTTISH RITE

AS the century wore on, one branch of the Craft, the Ancient and Accepted Scottish Rite, was undergoing turmoil but would eventually provide vigorous reinforcement for the fraternity. The Scottish Rite had been brought to America by Stephen Morin in 1761.

By 1763 Morin had organized his own 'Rite of Perfection' of 25 degrees in the British West Indies, and by 1767 this was taken to North America by his close associate Henry Francken, who established a Lodge of Perfection at Albany in New York and continued to propagate the Rite after Morin's death in 1771. Francken in turn was succeeded by the Comte de Grasse-Tilly, who was ultimately responsible for adding the eight degrees that gave the Rite its present structure of 33 degrees. De Grasse-Tilly, as well as establishing the first Scottish Rite Supreme Council at Charleston, South Carolina, was also unquestionably involved in creating the *Grand Constitutions of 1786*, supposedly drawn up at Berlin under the direction of Frederick the Great of Prussia (at whose court Voltaire had found refuge in 1750) but almost certainly produced some ten years after 1786 by

De Grasse-Tilly and his colleague J.B.M. Delahogue. Whenever it was compiled, the *Grand Constitutions of 1786* formed the basis of the 'Mother Supreme Council 33°, Ancient and Accepted Scottish Rite' that was formed on 31 May 1801 by Col. John Mitchell and the Revd. Dr. Frederick Dalcho with the probable help of De Grasse-Tilly and Delahogue.

For almost seventy years the Scottish Rite in America followed a complex and convoluted course. In the northern States the story was one of virtual chaos, with divisions, rivalries, schisms, and even spurious Supreme Councils. In the South the Rite was dominated by one man, Albert Pike – poet, lawyer, Civil War general, mystic, and a Masonic ritualist of genius. His work, *Morals and Dogma of the Ancient and Accepted Scottish Rite of Freemasonry*, was extremely popular and widely printed for more than a century.

Albert Pike entered the Scottish Rite in 1853, taking it up with enthusiasm in spite of a deep dissatisfaction with its ceremonies. With typical energy Albert Pike set out rewriting degrees. He constructed liturgies and in-

ALBERT PIKE (1809-1891) A PAINTING BY CHARLES LORING ELLIOTT,
OF PIKE WHEN HE WAS 34 YEARS OF AGE).

structional lectures and effectively remoulded the Rite's very structure. It was said of Albert Pike that 'He found the Scottish Rite in a cabin and left it in a Temple'. He 'revised the Rituals from the Fourth to the Thirty-second Degree, and had printed his work for the benefit of The Supreme Council at a cost to himself of twelve hundred dollars' when he was elected in 1859 Sovereign Grand Commander of the Supreme Council (Southern Jurisdiction) which office he held for a total thirty-two years until his death in 1891. Nationally, the scale of achievement was shown by the phenomenal growth of the Rite.

The Scottish Rite offers a spiritual and philosophical approach to Freemasonry that is very different from the simple moral precepts that underpin the Craft degrees, and while there are many Masons who enter the Rite purely for social reasons there are as many who do so because of the rich symbolism of the ceremonies and their meaning.

THE ANCIENT AND ACCEPTED SCOTTISH RITE AS WE KNOW IT TODAY
WAS EFFECTIVELY BORN ON 31 MAY 1801 AT CHARLESTON, SOUTH CAROLINA, WHEN
THE FIRST SUPREME COUNCIL WAS FORMED THERE BY COL. JOHN MITCHELL,
THE REVD. DR. FREDERICK DALCHO AND THEIR COLLEAGUES. (IN THIS PAINTING BY ALLYN COX
THE HOUSE IN WHICH THEY MET IS SHOWN AS IT APPEARED AT THE TIME.)

Above PRESENT OFFICES OF THE SUPREME COUNCIL, ANCIENT ACCEPTED SCOTTISH RITE,
NORTHERN MASONIC JURISDICTION, U.S.A.

Below HOUSE OF THE TEMPLE OF THE SUPREME COUNCIL, ANCIENT ACCEPTED SCOTTISH RITE,
SOUTHERN MASONIC JURISDICTION, U.S.A.

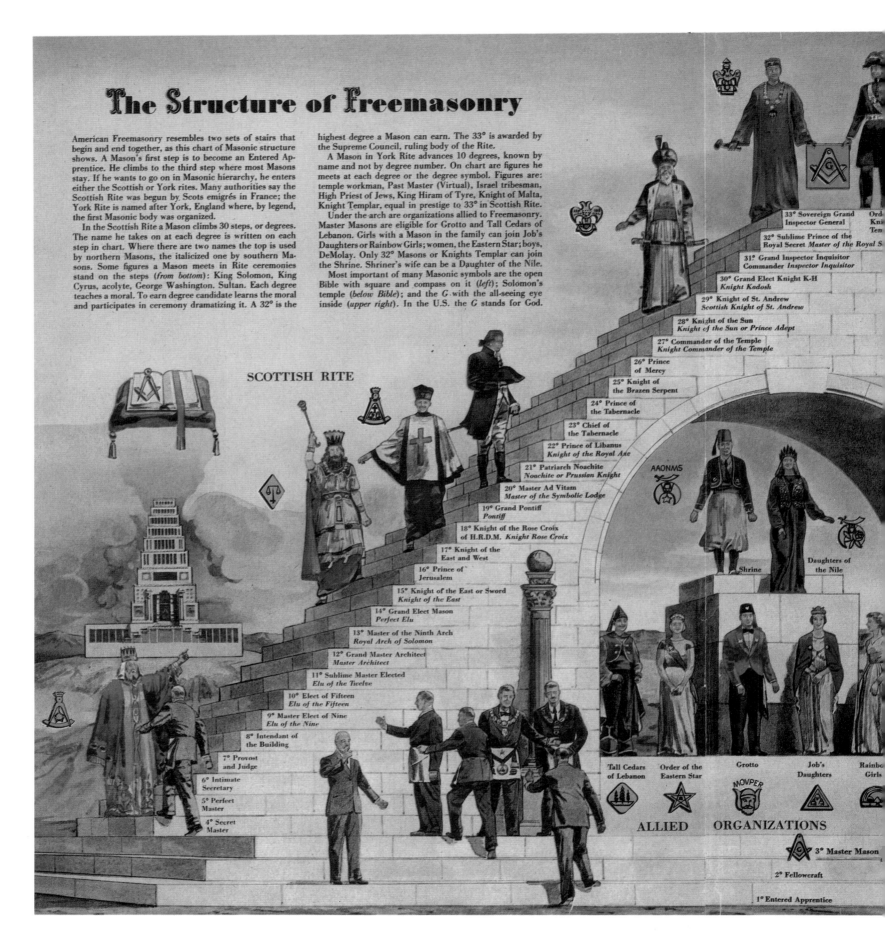

The Structure of Freemasonry

American Freemasonry resembles two sets of stairs that begin and end together, as this chart of Masonic structure shows. A Mason's first step is to become an Entered Apprentice. He climbs to the third step where most Masons stay. If he wants to go on in Masonic hierarchy, he enters either the Scottish or York rites. Many authorities say the Scottish Rite was begun by Scots emigrés in France; the York Rite is named after York, England where, by legend, the first Masonic body was organized.

In the Scottish Rite a Mason climbs 30 steps, or degrees. The name he takes on at each degree is written on each step in chart. Where there are two names the top is used by northern Masons, the italicized one by southern Masons. Some figures a Mason meets in Rite ceremonies stand on the steps (*from bottom*): King Solomon, King Cyrus, acolyte, George Washington, Sultan. Each degree teaches a moral. To earn degree candidate learns the moral and participates in ceremony dramatizing it. A 32° is the

highest degree a Mason can earn. The 33° is awarded by the Supreme Council, ruling body of the Rite.

A Mason in York Rite advances 10 degrees, known by name and not by degree number. On chart are figures he meets at each degree or the degree symbol. Figures are: temple workman, Past Master (Virtual), Israel tribesman, High Priest of Jews, King Hiram of Tyre, Knight of Malta, Knight Templar, equal in prestige to 33° in Scottish Rite.

Under the arch are organizations allied to Freemasonry. Master Masons are eligible for Grotto and Tall Cedars of Lebanon. Girls with a Mason in the family can join Job's Daughters or Rainbow Girls; women, the Eastern Star; boys, DeMolay. Only 32° Masons or Knights Templar can join the Shrine. Shriner's wife can be a Daughter of the Nile.

Most important of many Masonic symbols are the open Bible with square and compass on it (*left*); Solomon's temple (*below Bible*); and the *G* with the all-seeing eye inside (*upper right*). In the U.S. the *G* stands for God.

SCOTTISH RITE

33° Sovereign Grand Inspector General
32° Sublime Prince of the Royal Secret *Master of the Royal S*
31° Grand Inspector Inquisitor Commander *Inspector Inquisitor*
30° Grand Elect Knight K-H *Knight Kadosh*
29° Knight of St. Andrew *Scottish Knight of St. Andrew*
28° Knight of the Sun *Knight of the Sun or Prince Adept*
27° Commander of the Temple *Knight Commander of the Temple*
26° Prince of Mercy
25° Knight of the Brazen Serpent
24° Prince of the Tabernacle
23° Chief of the Tabernacle
22° Prince of Libanus *Knight of the Royal Axe*
21° Patriarch Noachite *Noachite or Prussian Knight*
20° Master Ad Vitam *Master of the Symbolic Lodge*
19° Grand Pontiff *Pontiff*
18° Knight of the Rose Croix of H.R.D.M. *Knight Rose Croix*
17° Knight of the East and West
16° Prince of Jerusalem
15° Knight of the East or Sword *Knight of the East*
14° Grand Elect Mason *Perfect Elu*
13° Master of the Ninth Arch *Royal Arch of Solomon*
12° Grand Master Architect *Master Architect*
11° Sublime Master Elected *Elu of the Twelve*
10° Elect of Fifteen *Elu of the Fifteen*
9° Master Elect of Nine *Elu of the Nine*
8° Intendant of the Building
7° Provost and Judge
6° Intimate Secretary
5° Perfect Master
4° Secret Master

AAONMS

Shrine

Daughters of the Nile

Tall Cedars of Lebanon

Order of the Eastern Star

Grotto

MOVPER

Job's Daughters

Rainbow Girls

ALLIED ORGANIZATIONS

3° Master Mason

2° Fellowcraft

1° Entered Apprentice

THE DIVERSITY OF THE MANY ADDITIONAL MASONIC DEGREES
WORKED IN AMERICA IS SHOWN BY THIS ILLUSTRATION FROM AN
ISSUE OF *LIFE MAGAZINE* (8 OCTOBER 1956).

THE GROWTH OF FREEMASONRY IN EUROPE

EARLY Freemasonry in Europe had no connection at all with operative masonry. Almost all the earliest European lodges were founded by English speculative Masons working under the authority of the premier Grand Lodge, which set up Provincial Grand Lodges throughout Europe in order to constitute new local Lodges and to direct the spread of the Craft in each host country. Some individual lodges, especially in France and Prussia, constituted new lodges quite unofficially – themselves – and took on the role of 'Mother' lodges to their offspring. The creation of yet another stratum of lodges was brought by the military lodges that moved through Europe with their regiments as the shifts of war and political alliances dictated.

Gradually, the European lodges, already independent to a large degree from English control, sought and obtained Masonic self-government. By 1736 a Grand Lodge of France had been established in Paris, but it controlled only a limited number of lodges (the English lodge at Bordeaux, founded in 1732, maintained its independence for many years afterwards). Elsewhere lodges sprang up in many European states from the 1720s onwards. In Madrid, Hamburg, The Hague, Florence, Rome, Lisbon, Vienna, and in many other towns and cities, Freemasonry began to flourish, although in many cases its flowering was all too brief.

On the continent of Europe the Craft has displayed a remarkable resilience during three centuries of mixed fortunes. In general terms its growth, decline and recovery in Europe has depended on the complex shifts of political allegiance and national boundaries, which have in turn been the consequences of dynastic changes, war, and social upheaval.

Thus there could be no independent Masonic jurisdiction in Belgium, for example, until that land became a nation state in 1830. After independence, King Leopold I – who was himself a Mason – became Protector of the new Grand Orient of Belgium. In a similar fashion Norway had no Grand Lodge until shortly before the country's separation from Sweden, whose own Grand Lodge had been constituted in 1759.

The Scandinavian countries also strikingly illustrate the great variety in Masonic working around the world. During the 1750s a number of chivalric 'higher degrees' were brought to Stockholm and became very popular among Swedish Masons; in 1780 the system which was developed from them – the Swedish Rite – was established by the future King Charles XIII, and it is this Rite that has been worked ever since throughout Scandinavia.

It consists of eleven degrees, of which the first three correspond to the Craft degrees; beyond these are three Scots degrees (Scottish Apprentice; Fellow of St. Andrew; and Scottish Master of St. Andrew) and four Chapter degrees (Stewart Brother; Confidant of Solomon; Confidant of St. John; and Confidant of St. Andrew) The eleventh and highest degree, Knight Commander of the Red Cross, is a chivalric Order conferred by the King.

The fountain-head of additional degree systems, as we have seen, was France, and the profusion of Rites and degrees – with all the confusion that their internecine rivalry brought – continued throughout the nineteenth century. But Craft Masonry in France was effectively controlled by the Grand Orient, which had been founded in 1773, and it was the Grand Orient of France who brought about the greatest crisis in Masonic history.

In England, government was vested in a constitutional monarchy and an elected parliament drawn not only from the aristocracy but also from the landed gentry and from the merchant and professional classes. Social mobility, while difficult, was not impossible, and – perhaps most important of all – the Church held little political power.

By contrast, most of the nations of Europe were ruled by absolute monarchs; society was rigidly stratified and the Church of Rome was strong in temporal influence. To such rulers Freemasonry represented liberty of conscience and political freedom – concepts that were anathema to them – and they kept a wary eye on the growth of the Craft.

But the Church of Rome saw things in a different light. Masonic privacy was wrongly interpreted as anti-clerical secrecy and a cloak for clandestine activities directed against the temporal authority of the Catholic Church. In 1738 Pope Clement XII issued *In Eminenti*, the first Bull to condemn the Craft. His successor, Benedict XIV, confirmed it in 1751 with the Bull *Providas*; but neither had a major effect upon Freemasonry.

Even in the most fervently Catholic countries the papal action was recognized as being largely political in purpose and Freemasonry, which was seen as a supporter of religion, was not only tolerated but often actively encouraged. This is best exemplified by Austria, where Francis, Duke of Lorraine, was both joint ruler with his wife, Maria Theresa, and also, from 1745, Emperor of Germany. Francis had been initiated into Freemasonry at The Hague in 1731 and throughout his rule he protected the Craft, which counted Catholic bishops amongst its members, from the hostility of the Empress. Until 1790 Freemasonry prospered throughout the Empire – enriched alike by the philosophy of the Enlightenment and by the music of Mozart and Haydn, both of whom were active in the Craft. But, as in so many countries, the French Revolution had a blighting effect on Masonry.

Initially, opposition to Freemasonry was political, stemming from fears that its activities would disturb public order. But where proscription of the Craft was actually enacted (in Holland, France and Sweden, in the 1730s and in the Swiss Cantons in the 1740s) it was invariably short lived, for it was soon realized that Masonic principles forbade subversion and enjoined obedience to lawful authority.

Because of political activities by Masons, or the belief – usually quite unjustified – that the Craft was involved in politics, undemocratic and totalitarian regimes have sought to suppress Freemasonry. In Russia the Craft was banned in 1822 and this ban continued under the Communist dictatorship that followed the Revolution and Civil War – although there was a brief flowering of Masonry during the few months of 1917 when Alexander Kerensky, who was himself a Mason, led the only democratic government that Russia had ever known. A fledgling Grand Lodge of the Ukraine, which developed at this time, was suppressed when the Ukraine was absorbed into the U.S.S.R.

Dictatorships of the Right behaved in the same manner: in Italy under Mussolini; in Spain and Portugal while they were fascist dictatorships; and in Nazi Germany, Freemasonry was rigidly suppressed. But it was in Germany that the Craft suffered most.

Although Germany had been politically unified in 1870 there had been no real attempt to establish a unifying Grand Lodge and those Grand Lodges that had evolved during the eighteenth and nineteenth centuries continued to operate. After World War One the anti-Masonic and anti-semitic sentiments engendered by Ludendorff's rabid publications, based on the notorious forgery known as *The Protocols of the Learned Elders of Zion*, which allegedly revealed a Judeo-Masonic plot for world domination, foreshadowed the anti-masonic measures of the years after 1933 when Hitler came to power. The German Grand Lodges were closed down, Freemasons were removed from the army and the civil service – many being transported to concentration camps – and Masonic records, regalia, and artefacts were seized.

As the Nazis overran Europe the same policy was pursued in each occupied country. It says much for the fortitude of German Masons, and of Freemasons in lands under Nazi occupation, that despite terrible persecution Freemasonry survived, and within a few months of Hitler's death plans were already being laid for its revival in Germany, and for the reorganization of the old Grand Lodge.

After World War One the break-up of the Austro-Hungarian Empire led to the spread of Freemasonry in Central Europe and in the newly liberated countries of the Balkans. There had been a Grand Lodge in Greece for many years, and in Hungary since 1870, but Grand Lodges were now established, or re-established, in Austria, where the Craft had been banned since 1794, Romania, Czechoslovakia, and Yugoslavia.

Most of them were destined, however, to be short-lived, for after suppression by the Nazis, the revival that Freemasonry enjoyed in eastern Europe immediately after World War Two was all too brief: with the rise of Communism the Craft was again proscribed. (To a French Mason, asking him if there were any Masonic lodges in the U.S.S.R., Stalin replied: 'Would you enjoy having fleas in your shirt?')

But, yet again, the resilience of Freemasonry has been demonstrated by its rapid reappearance in the new democracies of Eastern Europe. Both Hungary and Czechoslovakia have Grand Lodges again, while there are signs of renewed Masonic activity in Romania and Yugoslavia. A similar revival has taken place in both Spain and Portugal since their totalitarian regimes have been replaced by democracy.

THE GROWTH ON OTHER CONTINENTS

AFRICA

DURING the nineteenth century Britain, France and other European nations grew as imperial powers, and Freemasonry expanded abroad as new territories were opened up and colonized. In many parts of the world Freemasonry already had a hold – albeit often a tenuous one – and to some extent the ground was well prepared for establishing the Craft.

The first inroad into Africa had been the granting of a patent in 1726 to one Richard Hull as Provincial Grand Master for the Gambia, but he never made use of it (the first known lodge in West Africa was not founded until 1792) Dutch Masons had established lodges at Capetown before 1800, to be followed by the English in 1811; while at the other end of the continent a National Grand Lodge of Egypt had been created in 1864 from Italian Greek and French Lodges, the earliest of which had been active since 1786. Egypt was not under the control of any European power but it was a part of the Ottoman Empire, and the only truly independent nation in Africa at the time of European expansion was Liberia, although its Grand Lodge was not founded until 1867.

Inevitably the pattern of Masonic growth in African countries followed that set by their European colonists and this tradition has, for the most part, persisted after independence, the principal exception being those North African coutries where Islamic fundamentalism has led to the prohibition of all Masonic activity. (although irregular Lodges are said to work) Lodges in many former British colonies work under the Grand Lodges of England, Ireland and Scotland, while in countries that had been French dependencies Masonry is largely controlled by either the Grand Orient or the Grand Lodge of France, although the National Grand Lodge of France is currently expanding its involvement in Benin, Senegal, and in the French West African countries.

West Africa, perhaps more than other parts of the continent, has been fertile ground for Masonic growth. Nigeria and Ghana have many Lodges of the English, Irish, and Scottish constitutions; there are independent Grand Lodges in Gabon, the Ivory Coast and Liberia; and Togo – through its complex colonial history – has German Lodges as well as those under the three British Grand Lodges. In all of these countries, as in the rest of the continent, Masons of all races can meet in perfect harmony – although it was not always so. Until the recent repeal of the apartheid laws in the Republic of South Africa, members of different races were prevented from meeting together, but from 1977 the two Prince Hall Lodges in South Africa were admitted to membership of the Grand Lodge of South Africa, and, through the efforts of that Grand Lodge, their members were exempted from the racial law in question. In this way true brotherhood was displayed and an affront to humanity was overcome.

THE FIRST MASONIC LODGE OF MOROCCO WAS FOUNDED IN 1867 BY THE SUPREME COUNCIL OF FRANCE.
THIS WAS FOLLOWED IN 1882 BY LODGE, AL MOGHREB AL AKSA (WHOSE MEMBERS ARE SEEN HERE),
FOUNDED AT TANGIERS BY THE GRAND LODGE OF MANITOBA, CANADA.

AMERICA

WHILE Masonry was putting down its roots in North American soil it was also being firmly established in the West Indies. By the end of the eighteenth century there were Lodges in English, French, Dutch and Danish islands, and in most of these Freemasonry has flourished ever since, as it does in the American territory of Puerto Rico. There are also Lodges in the Guianas, perhaps the most remarkable being at Kourou, the space centre in French Guyana, where engineers, physicists, and scientists from many coutries meet in Masonic harmony. Even in Cuba, where the first Masonic lodge was founded in 1804 Masonry has survived through all the tribulations of the island's history – not excepting the present Communist government, which has permitted regular Masonry to work freely, and has celebrated the Craft by issuing a postage stamp showing the Grand Lodge building.

The story of the Craft in South and Central America is more complex. Freemasonry was virtually unknown before the yoke of Spanish and Portuguese rule was thrown off, but since that time it has been continuously active and has enjoyed popular support in every part of the continent – due, perhaps, to the fact that Simon Bolivar, the liberator of South America, was himself a Mason. Indeed, Masons have played an important role in directing the affairs of their countries, and there have been many Masonic presidents – of Costa Rica, Columbia, El Salvador, Peru, Uruguay, and Venezuela, for example – and the first ruler of independent Brazil, the Emperor Pedro I, was also a Mason. It is worthy of note that many of these men were practising Catholics whose faith was no bar to their Masonic membership.

However, the history of Freemasonry in the region is very intricate and extraordinarily difficult to disentangle because of the complexity of the political history of the coutries concerned. Perhaps most complex of all is the story of Masonry in Mexico, where the Craft first appeared in the early years of the nineteenth century. From its beginnings Masonry was closely associated with the struggle for freedom from foreign rule: General Vicente Guerrero,

who brought that freedom and also abolished slavery; and Benito Juarez, who in 1866 threw off the yoke of the Emperor Maximilian,were all Masons. But the complex course of Mexican history, with its many interwoven social and political rivalries, has resulted in a proliferation of Grand Lodges: over twenty at the present time.

Today, despite the existence of many irregular bodies, regular Freemasonry thrives throughout the region and is, for the most part, in amity with regular Masonry world-wide.

In Masonic terms North America is sometimes treated as if it is synonymous with the United States. But such an approach unjustly ignores the significant presence of Free-masonry in Canada, where the Craft has worked contin-uously since 1749, when a lodge was founded at Annapolis Royal in Nova Scotia. During the Seven Years' War (1757-1763) military lodges worked in Quebec and their activi-ties led to the setting up of a Provincial Grand Lodge in 1767. Not all Canadian Lodges were English in origin: both the Scottish and Irish Grand Lodges founded military and stationary Lodges, and at least one Lodge was founded by the Grand Lodge of New York. But after the Revolution American influence ceased when the Loyalists left the newly independent United States and settled in Canada. The Masons among them played an active and important part in founding the Provincial Grand Lodges of Upper and Lower Canada, while in 1858 their descendants created the first Grand Lodge of Canada.

In the same year gold was discovered in British Col-umbia, drawing many settlers from the East and leading to the founding of both English and Scottish Lodges in the far West of Canada.

After the formation of the Dominion of Canada in 1867 – which followed the highly important Report on the state of the country, by John George Lambton, First Earl of Durham and an active Freemason, and the passing of the subsequent Canada Act – Grand Lodges were con-stituted (between 1866 and 1906) for each of the nine Canadian provinces. (Newfoundland did not join the Dominion until 1949 and is still linked Masonically with Britain, having eighteen Lodges of the English Con-stitution, and nine of the Scottish.) The Royal Arch and the additional Degrees also thrive in Canada: there are Grand Chapters for most of the Provinces (except for Prince Edward Island and Newfoundland which are under the jurisdiction of Nova Scotia), a Great Priory of Knights Templar, and a sovereign Supreme Council 33° which was chartered in 1874, Most of the other Masonic Degrees have independent controlling bodies, but some are governed from the United States.

Many prominent Canadians have been active Masons, – no fewer than six of the Dominion's Prime Ministers, from the first, Sir John Macdonald, to John Diefenbaker, one of the greatest of Canada's statesmen in this century.

ASIA

MASONRY has maintained a continuous presence in India since 1730, when the first lodge was founded at Calcutta. Ten years later it was followed by Star in the East lodge (which is still working), and within twenty years lodges had also been founded at Madras and Bombay. In the early years of the Craft in India native Indians were rarely admitted, principally for religious reasons as it was believed that Hindus did not believe in a single God; but in the 1830's it was decided – under the sensible guidance of the Duke of Sussex – that the gods of the Hindu pantheon were really personifications of aspects of the one Supreme Being and Hindus could quite properly be made Masons. As the Duke made clear, a Mason's religion was his own concern: 'It is necessary to ascertain what religion (the candidate) professes in order to obligate him in the most formal and solemn manner, (but) when once admitted into the Fraternity, all questions of religion cease.'

Soon after this,in 1844, Dr. George Burnes, the Pro-vincial Grand Master for Western India, under the Grand Lodge of Scotland, founded a lodge at Bombay for the general admission of Indians, and from then on Free-masonry became increasingly popular among Hindus, Muslims, Parsis and Sikhs, as a true symbol of brotherly love in a land that has suffered terribly from religious strife.

Among the British in India, Freemasonry was es-pecially popular with servicemen – an association im-mortalized by Kipling – but after independence in 1947, most Britons left the country and in 1961 the Grand Lodge of India was inaugurated. Today the Craft flou-rishes throughout India, but sadly this is not true of Pakistan where, for political and sectarian reasons, Masonry has been suppressed.

Elsewhere in Asia the Craft also has both a long history and a bright future. A military Lodge met in Sri

Lanka (then Ceylon) in 1761, and there are now thirteen English, Scottish, and Irish Lodges. Malaysia, whose Lodges are also under the three British jurisdictions, is Masonically younger (the first Lodge was founded at Penang in 1809) but much stronger, its greatest strength being in Singapore. Masonry also thrives in other former British possessions; in the Philippines, where a Grand Lodge was formed with American help in 1917; and, from 1957,in Japan.

Before 1949 Masonry had been avtive for many years in the cities of mainland China, but since that time many of the Chinese Lodges have worked in Hong Kong under the English, Scottish, and Irish jurisdictions, while Freemasonry on the island of Taiwan is governed by an independent Grand Lodge of China. In the Middle East the rise of Islamic fundamentalism has not helped Freemasonry: the Grand Lodges of Egypt and of Iran have both been closed down (although the Grand Lodge of Iran in exile is permitted to meet in Boston Massachusetts.) and Masonic activity is forbidden in Iraq. There is no Masonry permitted in the Gulf states, where the earliest Lodge in the region – a Scottish Lodge at Aden – was founded in 1850; no regular Masonic activity survives in Lebanon, and only a few Lodges meet in Jordan. There is a strong Masonic presence in Israel that crosses the religious boundaries; the Grand Lodge of Israel was founded in 1953 and one of its first Grand Masters was a Christian Arab. The only Islamic country in the region where there is significant Masonic activity is Turkey, where the Grand Lodge (originally founded in 1909 and derived from the old National Grand Lodge of Egypt) was revived in 1970.

AUSTRALASIA

FREEMASONRY in Australia had an inauspicious start: after one of the earliest meetings, in 1803, many of the brethren were arrested, but later freed, because the Governor had believed such meetings to be illegal. When Masonry was permitted, Irish Military lodges played an important part in its early spread, particularly in New South Wales. As the Australian colonies gained statehood, so Masonic activity increased – helped by the influx of men drawn to Australia by the various gold rushes. In Western Australia, for example, twenty-six Lodges were founded as a consequence of the gold rush of the 1890s.

By 1900 Grand Lodges had been established in every state except Queensland, where squabbles over jurisdiction delayed the formation of an all-embracing Grand Lodge until 1921. (New South Wales in 1888; South Australia in 1884; Tasmania in 1890; Victoria in 1889; Western Australia in 1899) Today, happily, Masonic harmony prevails throughout Australia and the Craft continues its healthy growth. In a similar manner the other Masonic Rites and Degrees also flourish, although many of their governing bodies did not become fully independent from British jurisdiction until the 1980s, when a sovereign Supreme Council 33º was constituted for the whole of Australia, and Great Priories for Knights Templar were formed in most of the states.

Nor do Australian Masons neglect charity. Masonic hospitals and retirement homes have been established throughout the coutry and are generously supported. But financial support is not all: in many rural communities Masonry is an intagral part of social life and the brethren give freely of their time for community projects and play an active role in relieving the distress caused by drought, fire and other natural disasters.

Freemasonry is also found on the many islands – both large and small – scattered across the Pacific Ocean. In Masonic terms Hawaii, which is an American State, is the most significant: the Craft has been active since 1842 when a French Lodge was founded, and since 1989 there has been a Grand Lodge of Hawaii. On other islands there is also Masonry, demonstrating that Freemasonry is truly a worldwide fraternity.

Small though the country is in terms of population, Freemasonry in New Zealand has not only flourished but also retained a remarkable diversity. The first Lodge was founded in 1842 and although a Grand Lodge of New Zealand was established in 1890, many lodges remain under District or provincial Grand Lodges of England Scotland and Ireland – but without any lack of harmony. New Zealand Masons are also noted for their interest in the study of Masonic history and philosophy. The extent of their enthusiasm – far greater than might be expected from their numbers – is shown in their active support for ten Lodges of Research and one Chapter of Research.

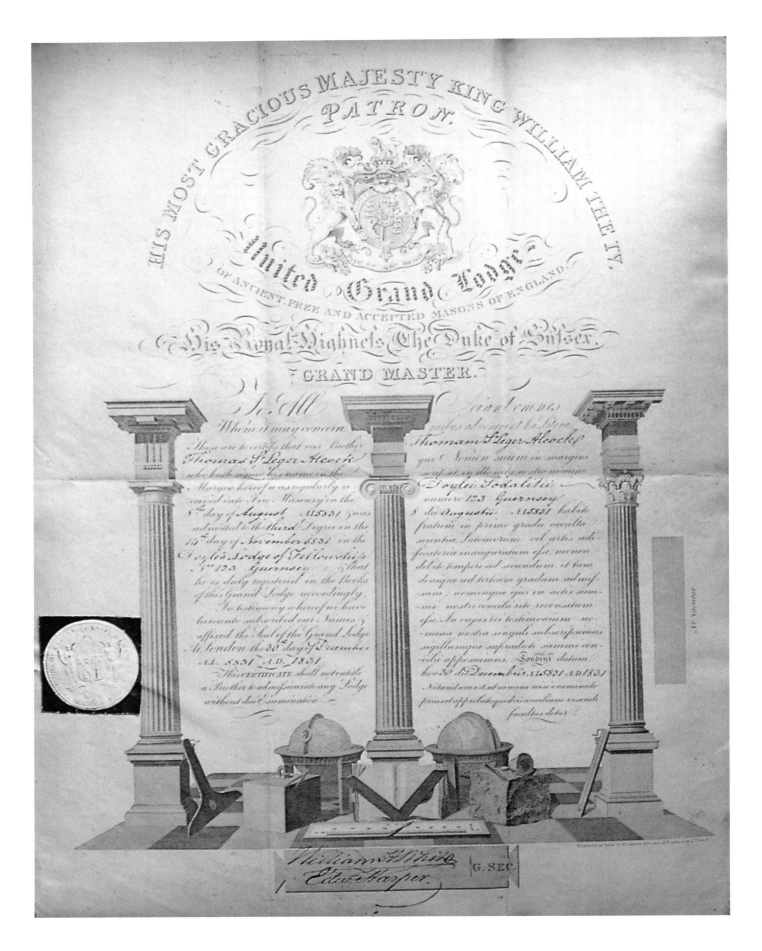

CHAPTER III

MASONIC IDEALS

'BE SO TRUE TO THYSELF AS THOU BE NOT FALSE TO OTHERS.'

FRANCIS BACON: ESSAY ON WISDOM

ALL the rich symbolism of Freemasonry that is visible in the decoration and furnishing of the Masonic lodge and displayed in the course of the ceremonies, serves to remind the Freemason of the Ideals of the Craft. From the very beginning of his Masonic career, the Freemason is exhorted to live by the principles of Brotherly Love, Relief (i.e. Charity or philanthropy), and Truth; to practice the four cardinal virtues of Temperance, Fortitude, Prudence and Justice; and to have as his distinguishing characteristics, the qualities of Virtue, Honour and Mercy.

As he proceeds through the ceremonies of the three Craft degrees, the Mason is first impressed with the need to maintain his faith in God and his hope in salvation, and to epitomise charity in his dealings with his fellow men. He is next taught the importance of understanding God's creation by unlocking the 'hidden mysteries of Nature and Science' through study of the seven liberal arts and sciences: Grammar, Rhetoric, Logic, Arithmetic, Geometry, Music and Astronomy. Finally he is enjoined to maintain his honour at all times and to display stoic fortitude in the face of death, placing his faith in the certainty of immortality.

All these principles, qualities and ideals are presented to him in symbolic form in the visible ornamentation of the Lodge, in the pictorial diagrams for each degree on the Tracing Boards and in the working tools of operative Masonry that are symbolically utilised in the ceremonies. But perhaps the most powerful symbols are the three pillars of Wisdom, Strength and Beauty, representing divine omniscience and omnipotence, and the symmetry and order of God's creation. They are displayed within the Lodge both in material form as Ionic, Doric and Corinthian columns respectively, and figuratively in the persons of the Worshipful Master, and his Senior and Junior Wardens. As such, they are always present on every occasion that the Lodge is open.

When the Mason returns to the everyday world he is inspired by the principles inculcated and reinforced by the teachings of the Craft. Whatever his walk of life may be, he brings to it an awareness that he embodies in himself all the ideals of the Craft. It is the putting into practice of these essential principles that has resulted – as it continues to do – in so many men of note giving so much of themselves to all mankind in the labour of their daily lives.

Left GRAND LODGE CERTIFICATE OF THE UNITED GRAND LODGE OF ENGLAND, THE BASIC DESIGN, SHOWING THE THREE PILLARS OF WISDOM, STRENGTH, AND BEAUTY (REPRESENTED BY IONIC, DORIC, AND CORINTHIAN COLUMNS).

Francis G. Paul
Sovereign Grand Commander Ancient Accepted Scottish Rite,
Northern Masonic Jurisdiction,
United States of America.

WISDOM

POINTED IN THE RIGHT DIRECTION THE WISDOM OF OUR FRATERNITY

I HAVE found it interesting that age is held in the highest regard in most countries other than the United States. Throughout the world, age and wisdom are interrelated. Across the globe and down through the ages, there is the belief that the young can learn invaluable lessons from their elders.

Unnecessary mistakes can be avoided, the most beneficial path can be followed, and the sacred continuity of one generation to another is unbroken. In other words, with age comes wisdom.

Only now in the United States are we beginning to recognize that the future is more secure if we look backward as well as forward, if we listen to voices other than our own.

Although a few have had their mentors in politics, business, the arts and education, we are now coming to appreciate and even celebrate the value of learning from those who walk before us.

All this, of course, is nothing new to Freemasons around the world.

It has long seemed to me that the wisdom of our Fraternity is one of its most significant gifts to our members, one that may not be fully appreciated by today's Masons.

There is an utter simplicity to Masonic wisdom. Perhaps this is the definition of wisdom: seeing life simply and clearly. Wisdom is the pane of glass that's so clean we do not even see it.

My idea of Masonic wisdom rests in our Fraternity's unique ability to help a man stay pointed in the right direction. Since we all make mistakes, there are those who urge us to learn from these errors. This is only partially true. We all know those who make one mistake after another and never seem to learn from what they're doing. They repeat – time after time – the same mistake. They never move forward.

There are others who are able to view what they have done against a standard of performance. They make the necessary adjustments and move forward. Have they learned from their mistake? Not really. They have actually learned to compare what they had done against a better standard.

The unique contribution of Masonic wisdom of a man's life is simply keeping him pointed in the right direction. He has a standard by which to measure his actions. He gets more out of life because he remains on the right path more than others.

Our Masonic symbol of the Square and Compasses is no accident. It serves a unique purpose. No matter how many times a Mason sees these tools, he cannot escape being reminded of how he is expected to live! This is the wisdom of our Fraternity.

FRANCIS G. PAUL
SOVEREIGN GRAND COMMANDER
ANCIENT ACCEPTED SCOTTISH RITE, N.M.J.,U.S.A.

VISIONS OF LIBERTY

NO better example of the practical application of Masonic ideals can be found than in the life's work of Benjamin Franklin (1706-1790). Through his writing, his creation of the American Philosophical Society, his help in founding of the first subscription library in the American Colonies, he can lay claim to be called the greatest educator of colonial America. At the same time he carefully prepared the ideological ground for the American Revolution – thus epitomizing the Masonic fusion of wisdom and freedom.

The Masonic vision of liberty was first enshrined in the Constitution of the United States, described by the greatest British prime minister of the nineteenth century, William Ewart Gladstone, as 'The most wonderful work ever struck off at a given time by the brain and purpose of man.' The Constitution has become the touchstone for every other written political constitution ever since. It also includes the ten amendments of the 1791 Bill of Rights that guaranteed – among other essential liberties – freedom of speech, worship, and the press. No other document more clearly encapsulates the fundamental social principles of Freemasonry.

The influence of the American Constitution, and thus of Masonic ideals, was soon felt: it inspired the liberation movements led by Simon Bolivar, Jose de San Martin and Bernardo O'Higgins in South America, Vicente Guerrero, and, later, Benito Juarez in Mexico, Jose Marti in Cuba, and Jose Rizal in the Philippines. But it is, perhaps, best epitomized by the struggle for independence in Texas.

The first Americans in Texas, who had settled along the Brazos River with Stephen Austin in 1823, had been content to live as Mexican subjects, but discontent with Mexican rule led to a desire for secession, and in1835 the American colonists revolted, resulting in the beginnings of The Republic of Texas. In the following year, Santa Anna attempted to crush the new republic – he was defeated by the heroism of the defenders of the Alamo: they gave their own lives to enable Houston's forces to prepare for the decisive battle of San Jacinto at which the Mexicans were routed and Santa Anna captured.

Texan freedom was now secure, until it joined the Union in 1845, Texas was an independent republic. It was also, in many ways, virtually a Masonic republic, for almost all of its principal founders, liberators and leaders were Freemasons: Stephen Austin, Sam Houston, many of the defenders of the Alamo – Captain Travis, and Mirabeau Lamar, who broke the Mexican line at San Jacinto with the rallying cry 'Remember the Alamo!'. During the years of independence that followed, the Presidents of The Republic of Texas – David Burnet, Sam Houston, Mirabeau Lamar – were all Masons, as were every one of its Vice-Presidents, most of the principal government officers, much of the judiciary, and many other Texan patriots who preserved their territory's hard-won freedom.

All these patriots – of so many lands, and so different in their origins and lives – were united by their passionate love of liberty and by their membership of the Craft, which gave a form and structure to their political ideals. In Europe the same process was at work. British Freemasons such as Henry Brougham (1778-1868) worked hard to extend the benefits of education as a means of political emancipation. Lord Brougham's enthusiastic application of Masonic principles helped the founding of London University – the first in England to remove religious barriers to entry – and to the passing of the Reform Bill of 1832 that swept away political abuses and ushered in true parliamentary democracy.

Left BENJAMIN FRANKLIN (1706-1790) FROM A MINIATURE BY THOURON, 1782.
FRANKLIN PUT MASONIC IDEALS INTO PRACTICE IN HIS WORK AS A STATESMAN, POLITICAL PHILOSOPHER, AND SCIENTIST. HE WAS THE ONLY FREEMASON TO SIGN BOTH THE DECLARATION OF INDEPENDENCE AND THE CONSTITUTION OF THE UNITED STATES.

SAMUEL HOUSTON (1793-1863), ONE OF THE LEADERS IN TEXAS' FIGHT FOR INDEPENDENCE FROM MEXICO.
HE SERVED AS PRESIDENT OF THE REPUBLIC OF TEXAS AND LATER AS UNITED STATES SENATOR AND GOVERNOR OF THE STATE.
THE CITY OF HOUSTON WAS NAMED IN HIS HONOUR.

THE HEROISM DISPLAYED BY THE DEFENDERS OF THE ALAMO – MANY OF WHOM WERE MASONS –
INSPIRED THEIR COMPATRIOTS AND ENSURED THE FREEDOM OF TEXAS. THE STORY OF THE SIEGE
WAS IMMORTALIZED IN THE FILM, *THE ALAMO*, STARRING JOHN WAYNE, WHO WAS HIMSELF A MASON.

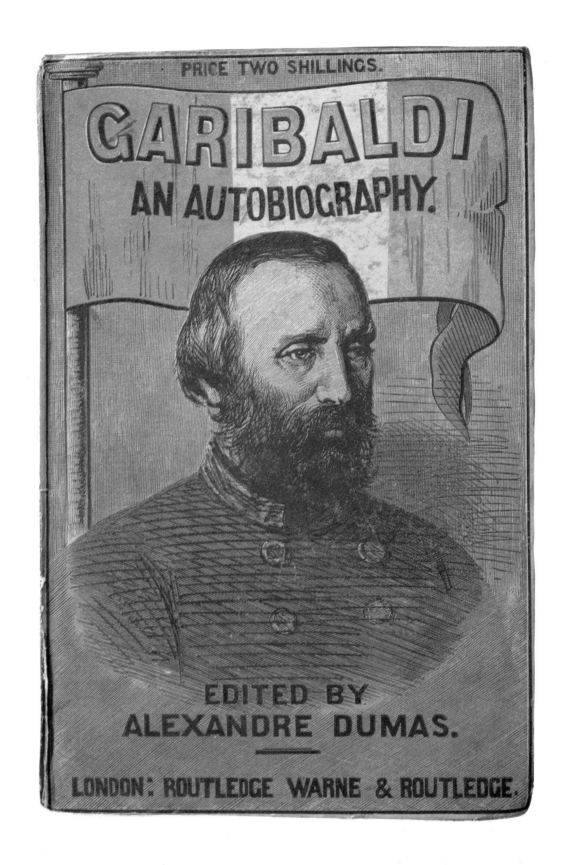

GARIBALDI'S *AUTOBIOGRAPHY* (1860) WAS EDITED BY ALEXANDRE DUMAS, WHO WAS SUBSEQUENTLY
MADE A MASON AT NAPLES IN 1862. GEORGE ROUTLEDGE, WHO PUBLISHED
THE ENGLISH TRANSLATION OF GARIBALDI'S BOOK, WAS ALSO A MEMBER OF THE CRAFT.

Elsewhere in Europe, Freemasons were at the forefront of political change. Giuseppe Mazzini and Giuseppe Garibaldi freed Italy from foreign despotism and forged a new sense of national unity. Garibaldi himself made an explicit link between the Craft and his political vision: 'Whenever there is a human cause, we are certain to find Freemasonry, for it is the fundamental basis of all true liberal associations. For ever I will pride myself upon my Masonic connection.'

The liberation of Italy came in the wake of a long struggle for freedom in France. In the early days of that struggle the works of two seminal figures – Baron de Montesquieu's *De l'Esprit des Lois* (The Spirit of Law) and Voltaire's writings against religious intolerance – were infused with Masonic principles. Both men died before the full horrors of the revolutionary period were unleashed in the 1790s. But during the course of the next century, as despotism and democracy alternated, Freemasons continued to play a leading role in securing the final triumph of freedom.

VOLTAIRE DID NOT BECOME A MASON UNTIL APRIL 1778 – TWO MONTHS BEFORE HIS DEATH – BUT HE PROPAGATED THE MASONIC PRINCIPLES OF TOLERANCE AND TRUTH THROUGHOUT HIS LIFE.

GEORGE WASHINGTON

WASHINGTON was a Freemason for the whole of his adult life, having been initiated into Freemasonry at Fredericksburg, Virginia, on 4 November 1752, when only twenty years of age. When the Revolution came in 1775 Washington was made Commander-in-Chief of the Continental Army, and, more than any other Revolutionary patriot, it was his leadership and courage that brought the country through the long years of war, just as his direction of affairs as the country's first President brought it to true nationhood. And throughout all, Washington remained a dedicated Mason. In 1798, near the end of his life, he wrote of the principles of Freemasonry, that 'I conceive them to be founded in benevolence, and to be exercised only for the good of mankind.' He could have written nothing else, or they were the principles on which his whole life had been based.

A PAINTING OF WASHINGTON LAYING THE CORNERSTONE OF THE UNITED STATES CAPITOL, SEPTEMBER, 18, 1793. PAINTED BY JOHN MELIUS, AND COMMISSIONED BY THE SUPREME COUNCIL, 33° SOUTHERN JURISDICTION USA.

George Washington Laying the Cornerstone of the United States Capitol, Sept. 18, 1793

GEORGE WASHINGTON (1732-1799) 'FATHER OF HIS COUNTRY', MILITARY LEADER OF THE
AMERICAN REVOLUTION, FIRST PRESIDENT OF THE UNITED STATES OF AMERICA.

THE POST-WAR WORLD

EUROPE'S final liberation – from the tyranny of the Nazis in 1944 – was spearheaded by two great political leaders of the twentieth century, Franklin Delano Roosevelt and Winston Churchill, both of whom were Freemasons. Masonic principles were an inspiration for both men, providing a continuing source of moral strength at a time of intense national stress. The leadership and oratory of Winston Churchill galvanized the British spirit in the face of the Nazi threat, whilst the political genius of Roosevelt brought America out of the Depression.

Below CHURCHILL AND ROOSEVELT WERE THE TWIN ARCHITECTS OF VICTORY OVER NAZI TYRANNY IN EUROPE, BUILDING THE POLITICAL WILL OF THE PEOPLE AND INSPIRING THE ARMED FORCES IN THE MILITARY STRUGGLE. *Right* THE LIBERATION OF EUROPE BEGAN WITH THE NORMANDY LANDINGS IN JUNE 1944; CHURCHILL INSPECTED THE LANDING BEACHES IN MARCH 1945.

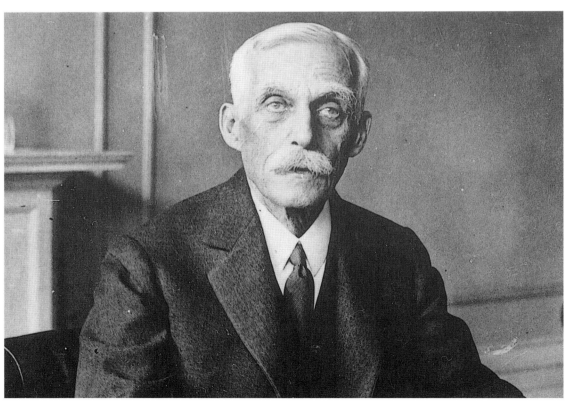

IDEALS IN PRACTICE

MASONIC idealism continued to play a key role in the making of the post-war world. The fragile democracies of liberated Europe needed aid on an unprecedented scale if they were to survive, and this was supplied through the efforts of an American president and an American general who were both proud to acknowledge their allegiance to the Craft. The Marshall Plan, devised by President Harry S. Truman and General George C. Marshall, was vital in bringing about political and industrial recovery in Europe, and thus helping to ensure a continuing state of peace. It also enabled nations shattered by war to begin rebuilding their educational and cultural infrastructures. In recognition of General Marshall's humanitarian services he was awarded the Nobel Peace Prize in 1953.

The practical application of wisdom and other Masonic principles can be seen in many ways in the great humanitarian and cultural enterprises of our time. For instance, there is the work of the industrialist and Freemason Andrew W. Mellon (1855-1937), who founded the educational and charitable trust that bears his name in 1930 and that was largely responsible for funding the American National Gallery of Art, to which Mellon bequeathed his extensive private art collection. Another example can be found in Belgium, where pioneering schools for the developement of intelligence and independence of children were established by Ovide Decroly – he was a disciple and co-worker of the great educationalist Maria Montessori.

If such public benefactors demonstrate the Masonic concept of 'Wisdom', then the establishment of the International Red Cross can be seen as epitomizing the principle of Brotherly Love. After organizing emergency medical aid for the wounded of both sides during the Battle of Solferino in Northern Italy in 1859, the Swiss humanitarian Henri Dunant (1828-1910) worked to bring about the conference that resulted in the Geneva Convention of 1864, which established internationally agreed upon rules for the treatment of those wounded in war and created the voluntary relief organization we know as the Red Cross.

Dunant's work was carried to America in 1881 by Clara Barton, who had experienced the full horror of war when working as a nurse during the Civil War. Later she was initiated into the Order of the Eastern Star by its founder, Rob Morris. After the end of World War One, the work of the Red Cross was complemented by the Belgian Mason Ernest Nys (1851-1920), who helped establish the international code for the humane treatment of prisoners of war.

Above left GENERAL GEORGE C. MARSHALL (1880-1925) *(CENTRE)* CHIEF OF STAFF, IS SHOWN WITH MEMBERS OF HIS GENERAL STAFF AT THE WAR DEPARTMENT, WASHINGTON.

Below left ANDREW W. MELLON (1855-1937), FORMER SECRETARY OF THE UNITED STATES TREASURY AND FORMER UNITED STATES AMBASSADOR TO BRITAIN.

Above ROOSEVELT DIED SUDDENLY IN 1945 AND HIS PLACE WAS TAKEN BY HARRY S. TRUMAN, THE MOST ACTIVE AND ENTHUSIASTIC OF MASONIC PRESIDENTS. IN THE PRESIDENTIAL ELECTION OF 1948 – HIS OPPONENT, DEWEY, WAS ALSO A MASON – TRUMAN WON A LANDSLIDE VICTORY AGAINST ALL PREDICTIONS: A REFLECTION OF PUBLIC APPRECIATION FOR HIS PERSONAL QUALITIES, WHICH WERE EPITOMIZED BY THE SIGN ON HIS DESK THAT READ, 'THE BUCK STOPS HERE'.

Right FOR THE PEOPLE OF EUROPE LIBERATION WAS SYMBOLIZED BY THE LIFTING OF THE OPPRESSIVE WEIGHT OF TYRANNY FROM THEIR LANDS. FREEMASONRY, TOO, WAS LIBERATED AND ONCE AGAIN THE CRAFT BEGAN TO FLOURISH ACROSS THE CONTINENT.

LIBERTIES OF THE MIND

IF Masons have played a prominent part in political emancipation, they have also been active in promoting the less tangible, but no less important, freedom of speech and belief. The fundamental principles on which the Craft is based encourage constant exercise of the creative and intellectual faculties, always with the intention of improving and enriching the quality of human life.

Of the many authors who have been Freemasons some, such, as the Rev. J. G. Wood, the greatest populariser of natural history in the nineteenth century, have written to disseminate knowledge, while others have sought to express the essence of the Masonic ideal in their works. The most influential of these have often been 'popular' writers in the best sense of the term – story-tellers for whom fiction has been a medium for conveying eternal truths through entertainment. For instance, the historical novels of Sir Walter Scott (1771-1832) and Lew Wallace (1827-1905) and the romances of Sir Henry Rider Haggard, creator of *King Solomon's Mines* and *She*, all convey the virtues of chivalry, loyalty and honour through tales of high adventure.

Masonic themes in literature are not confined to the work of initiated Masons. In Thomas Hardy's last novel, *Jude the Obscure* (1895), for example, the unfolding tragedy is interwoven with episodes of the hero's life as a stonemason, as in the passage where Jude reflects on the significance of his craft and what it symbolizes:

> The yard was a little centre of regeneration. Here, with keen edges and smooth curves, were forms in the exact likeness of those he had seen abraded and time-eaten on the walls... For a moment there fell on Jude a true illumination; that here in the stone yard was a centre of effort as worthy as that dignified by the name of scholarly study within the noblest of colleges.

Perhaps the most perfect artistic presentation of Masonic themes is to be found in the work of Rudyard Kipling, whose pride in the Craft can be seen not only in his overtly Masonic poetry and prose, but also in more subtle fashion in those stories in which the leading qualities of the characters are consonant with the ideals of Freemasonry. Kim's touching faith in the help and support that will come to him when his father's Craft certificate is recognized are well known. In the story *Thrown Away*, the quality of brotherly love is expressed in an especially forceful way. A young subaltern, 'The Boy', commits suicide in despair but to spare his family unnecessary suffering they go to extraordinary lengths to hide the true cause of his death. Truth, in this instance, lies in being true to the memory of a friend.

The roll-call of Masonic authors is a long and distinguished one and ranges from James Boswell to Anthony Trollope, and Oscar Wilde to Mark Twain and Sir Conan Doyle. Even longer is the list of writers who have incorporated Masonic themes, settings, images, and phrases from masonic ritual ('on the level', 'squared off', etc.) in their work. Examples include the deliberate use of Masonic allusion in James Joyce's *Ulysses* and the reference to the research work of Quatuor Coronati Lodge in H.G. Wells's story of *The Inexperienced Ghost*. It extends to the comic world of P. G. Wodehouse (in *Blandings Castle*, Lord Emsworth's prize sow is described as being 'to the pig world what the Masonic grip is to the human') and to the world of science fiction in the stories of Robert Heinlein, Avram Davidson, and others, such as Charles De Vet, whose colonists in the story *Return Journey* establish Masonry on an alien planet within a few years of their arrival: 'A stray mongrel dog followed them up the street past the Masonic Lodge as they started out.'

SIR WALTER SCOTT WAS THE MOST SUCCESSFUL BRITISH NOVELIST OF HIS DAY.
IN TWO OF HIS NOVELS (*IVANHOE* AND *THE TALISMAN*) THE TEMPLARS ARE FEATURED, AND IN 1823
HE WAS OFFERED THE GRAND MASTERSHIP OF THE MASONIC KNIGHTS TEMPLAR IN SCOTLAND,
BUT ILL-HEALTH LED HIM TO DECLINE.

THE MOTHER-LODGE
(The Seven Seas, 1896)

THERE was Rundle, Station Master,
    An' Beazely of the Rail,
An' Ackman, Commissariat,
    An' Blake, Conductor/Sergeant,
    Our Master twice was 'e,
With Jim that kept the Europe-shop,
    Old Framjee Eduljee.
Outside – Sergeant! Sir! Salute! Salaam!
Inside – Brother, an' it doesn't do no 'arm.
We met upon the Level an' we parted on the Square,
An' was Junior Deacon in my Mother-Lodge out there!

We'd Bola Nath, Accountant,
    An' Saul the Aden Jew,
An' Din Mohammed, draughtsman
    Of the Survey Office, too;
There was Babu Chuckerbutty,
    An' Amir Singh the Sikh,
An' Castro from the fittin'-sheds,
    The Roman Catholick!

We 'adn't good regalia,
    An' our Lodge was old an' bare,
But we knew the Ancient Landmarks,
    An' we kep' 'em to a hair;
An' lookin' on it backwards
    It often strikes me thus,
There ain't such things as infidels,
    Excep', per'aps, it's us.

For monthly, after Labour,
    We'd all sit down and smoke
(We dursn't give no banquits,
    Lest a Brother's caste were broke),
An' man on man got talkin'
    Religion an' the rest
An' every man comparin'
    Of the God 'e knew the best.

Full oft on Guv'ment service
    This rovin' foot 'ath pressed,
An' bore fraternal greetin's
    To the Lodges east an' west,
Accordin' as commanded
    From Kohat to Singapore,
But I wish that I might see them
    In my Mother-Lodge once more! ...

                              RUDYARD KIPLING

RUDYARD KIPLING'S EARLY POETRY REFLECTS THE ETHOS OF THE RAJ,
BUT IT EXPRESSES ALSO THE RACIAL AND RELIGIOUS TOLERANCE
THAT EPITOMIZES THE CRAFT – AND NOWHERE MORE CLEARLY THAN
IN HIS POEM, *THE MOTHER-LODGE*.

JOHANN WOLFGANG VON GOETHE, GERMANY'S GREATEST LITERARY FIGURE,
WHOSE WORK EXEMPLIFIED BOTH THE ENQUIRING SPIRIT OF THE ENLIGHTENMENT
AND THE IMAGINATION OF THE ROMANTIC MOVEMENT.

TRANSFORMATION

GREAT works of the imagination – like *Faust*, whose author, J. W. von Goethe (1749-1832) was a Freemason – can transform our view of the world and humanity's place in it. Goethe laid the foundations of modern German literature with his succession of masterly poems and plays, and seems to have been responsible for bringing his great contemporary, Schiller, into the Craft. But though *Faust* is unquestionably Goethe's greatest work, it does not contain the Masonic allusions that abound in *Wilhem Meister*; and although Faust is finally redeemed, the spirit of enquiry that he represents contrasts markedly with the Freemason's quest for self-knowledge that is governed by caution and self-discipline.

Literature is not the only path by which the Craft appeals to the human spirit. Masonic initiation, too, is a transforming event. It is a true rite of passage, which produces that 'decisive alteration' in the spiritual and social status of the person concerned referred to by Mircea Eliade in his classic definition of initiation. Eliade went on to say that, 'In philosophical terms, initiation is equivalent to a basic change in existential condition: the novice emerges from the ordeal endowed with a totally different being from that which he possessed before his initiation; he has become another.'

WISDOM

GOETHE AT THE COURT OF FREDERICK, MARGRAVE OF BADEN. WHILE HE WAS AT STRASBOURG
GOETHE BEGAN HIS LIFE-LONG FRIENDSHIP WITH HIS FELLOW MASON, THE ROMANTIC POET
HERDER, AND LAID THE FOUNDATIONS OF HIS LITERARY CAREER.

Eliade's words precisely describe the effect of initiation on a candidate who is truly committed to the principles of Freemasonry. The three stages of a rite of passage are all present: the preliminary state of separation, in which the initiate is taken out of his previous state (when he is prepared for the ceremony); the transitional stage, which involves ritual trials and disorientation that take place during the first part of the initiation ceremony; and the final stage, when the initiate is integrated into a wholly new condition – symbolized by his receiving the Sign, Word, and Token of the degree, and the regalia that identifies him with his new brothers. He is now a Freemason who has taken his first regular step.

In some respects the ritual dramas that constitute the three ceremonies of Craft Masonry are stages of a single initiation; only when he has completed all three degrees is the initiate a full-fledged Master Mason. Even so, throughout the ceremonies it is made clear to the initiate that, while they have a spiritual purpose, the overt content of the rituals is moral rather than religious, for Freemasonry is not a religion (though it has a religious basis) but a fraternity dedicated to teaching moral precepts and inculcating the three great practical ideals of Brotherly Love, Relief, and Truth.

The exhortations made through the ceremonies are all to moral rectitude, and it cannot be stressed too strongly that the symbolically presented myth is one of death in the cause of honour – not of death and resurrection. Even so, the rich symbolism of the ceremonies has inspired the spiritual quests of many.

79

THE SPIRITUAL QUEST

THE inspiration of Masonic symbolism has been taken over by many seekers after truth for their own ends – as with such picturesque characters as Joseph Balsamo (Count Cagliostro), Court de Gebelin (The Tarot theoretician), and many other occult adventurers who are the ultimate source of today's esoteric and 'New Age' movements.

Ancient Egypt offered a particularly fertile field of speculation for Masons with esoteric interests. In the legendary history of the *Old Charges* it was claimed that Abraham taught the Egyptians the seven sciences and that among his pupils was Euclid, who became so proficient that he trained the sons of the Egyptian nobility in 'the science of Geometry in practice, for to work in stones all manner of worthy works that belonged to building of temples and churches, castles, manors, towers and all there manner of buildings.'

But the real stimulus to armchair Egyptology among Freemasons of the Enlightenment was provided by a novel and a play. *Sethos*, the work of the Abbé Jean Terrasson, appeared in 1731; was rapidly translated from French into English, German, and Italian; and was widely assumed to be based on historical fact. It tells the story of an Egyptian prince who is initiated into the Mysteries of Isis, the ideals and precepts of which – brotherhood, truth, justice, and the importance of knowledge and education – has much in common with those of the Enlightenment, and especially with those of Freemasonry.

Sethos may have had few literary merits, but it provided inspiration for Mozart's *Die Zauberflöte* ('The Magic Flute'). Mozart's interest in Ancient Egypt was also displayed in 1773 when he set to music *Thamos, King of Egypt* by his fellow Mason, the Freiherr von Gebler.

Right MOZART'S *DIE ZAUBERFLÖTE* ('THE MAGIC FLUTE') AT GLYNDEBOURNE, 1978. DAVID HOCKNEY'S DESIGNS WERE ONE OF THE STRONGEST FEATURES OF JOHN COX'S PRODUCTION.

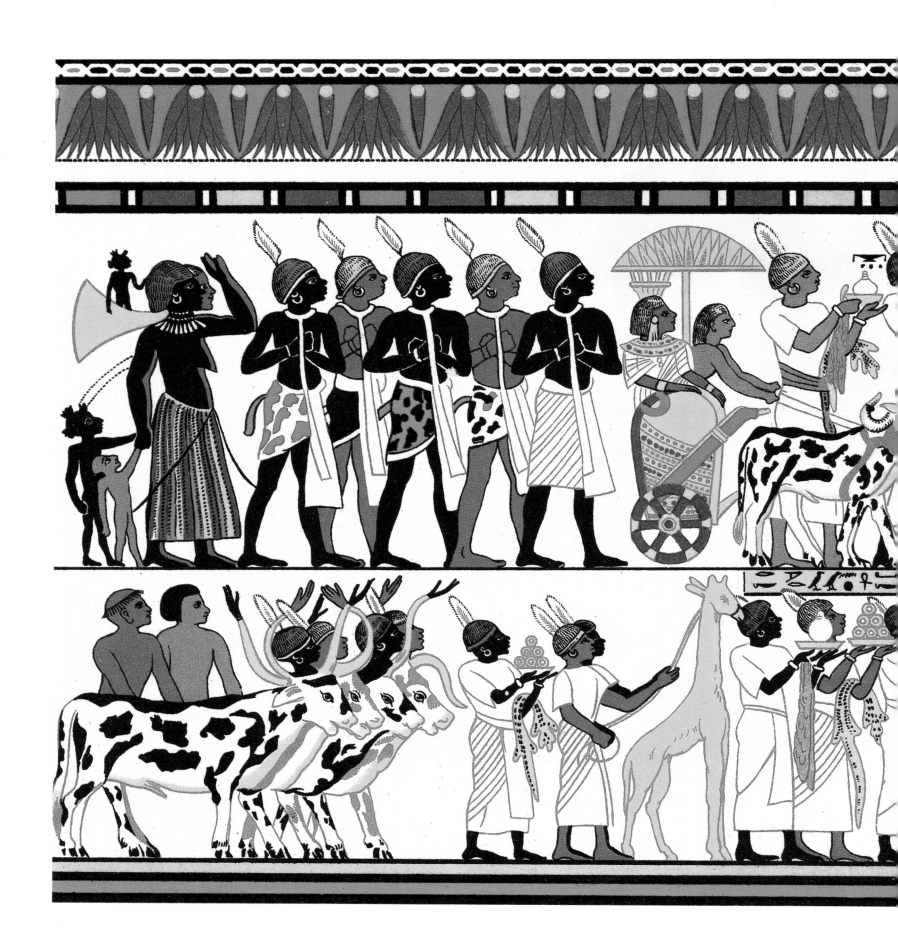

EGYPTIAN WALL-PAINTING FROM AN
18TH DYNASTY TOMB AT THEBES.
BECAUSE OF REFERENCES IN THE *OLD
CHARGES* – AND IMAGINED SIMILARITIES
BETWEEN EGYPTIAN COSTUME AND
MASONIC REGALIA – MANY MASONS
HAVE BEEN BOTH FASCINATED AND
INSPIRED BY EGYPTIAN SYMBOLISM.

A deep interest in Egypt also led two German Masons to create a quasi-Masonic Rite of Seven Degrees known as the Krata Repoa, or Initiations of Egyptian Priests. It was a curious Rite that probably progressed no further than the paper on which the rituals were printed; but it had a significant influence on Giuseppe Balsamo (1743-1795) who styled himself Count Cagliostro. In this guise he is best remembered for his part in the murky affair of Marie Antoinette's necklace and for his imprisonment at Rome by the Inquisition. Before his downfall, however, Cagliostro displayed his dramatic genius to the full in the quasi-Masonic 'Egyptian Rite of Freemasonry', devised in 1777. This sumptuous Rite involved both splendid pageantry and flowery language. It was also designed to accommodate women as well as men, and it enjoyed great – if fleeting – popularity as the author took it with him on his journeys around Europe. It had no effect on the development of genuine Masonic ritual, and when Cagliostro ceased to be a novelty his Rite withered away. But the fascination with Egypt remained.

Public interest was further stimulated by Napoleon's expedition to Egypt in 1798. While this ended in disaster, it resulted indirectly in the decipherment of Egyptian hieroglyphs from the Rosetta Stone, which was brought back to Paris. This seemingly intractable problem of translation was eventually solved through the labours of a French Freemason, Jean François Champollion (1790-1832), aided by the inscriptions discovered by an Italian fellow Mason, Giovanni Belzoni (1778-1823).

Left CAGLIOSTRO (JOSEPH BALSAMO) PORTRAYED AS A PHILOSOPHER AND MYSTIC.
THE TRUTH ABOUT CAGLIOSTRO WAS VERY DIFFERENT FROM THE PUBLIC PERCEPTION.
Above THE IMAGE OF CAGLIOSTRO AS MAGICIAN, MYSTIC, AND GRAND COPHT OF EGYPTIAN FREEMASONRY
HAS PERSISTED FOR TWO HUNDRED YEARS, AND ENTERED POPULAR CULTURE THROUGH
THE *CAGLIOSTRO* WALTZ OF JOHANN STRAUSS THE YOUNGER.

RELIGION

WHAT such curious leaps of imagination like Cagliostro's have done is to illustrate clearly the wisdom of those who created Freemasonry as we now know it, when they eschewed religious debate. Instead they emphasized that the Craft is neither a religion nor a substitute for it. They laid down that the only religious criterion for membership was a belief in God. This is the essential, unchangeable landmark of Freemasonry, acknowledged even by hostile critics of the Craft like the Jesuit Herbert Thurston, who in 1939 wrote,

> It is, however, only fair to note that the United Grand Lodge of England has lately reaffirmed that 'the first condition of admission and membership of the Order is a belief in the Supreme Being'.

All religious polemic and speculation was – and is – forbidden within the lodge. Sectarian division has thus been avoided, leaving the Craft open to all men of goodwill, whatever their personal religious beliefs. In this way, Freemasonry has overcome sectarian division and has crossed the boundaries between the faiths of the world.

The practical result of this has been a steady growth in religious tolerance. From its earliest days the Craft has brought together Protestant and Catholic Christian, Arab and Jew, Hindu and Moslem. Religious leaders such as Sir Israel Brodie (former Chief Rabbi of the United Kingdom), Geoffrey Fisher (Archbishop of Canterbury), the third Aga Khan (the father of the United Nations High Commissioner for Refugees), Stephen Wise (the American Zionist), and the Swami Vivekananda (who was, in his day, the leading interpreter of Yoga and Hinduism in the West) were all proud to be Freemasons and illustrate, in a powerful way, the Craft's essential spirit of tolerance and conciliation.

It is no coincidence that when countries with an overwhelming bias towards a single faith have been ruled by leaders who were also Masons there has been a notable increase in political and religious tolerance. For instance, until recently Egypt never enjoyed such an open society as it had done under the Khedive Ismail Pasha (1830-95), or Afghanistan the tolerance and freedom seen during the reign of the Amir Habibullah Khan (d. 1919). Today there is a growing acceptance of the Craft throughout the world, and, in societies that are still divided by racial and religious hatred, the continuing growth of Freemasonry offers real hope for the future.

Wisdom, then, means the constant striving after the good. The acquisition of Wisdom involves moving outwards into the world to bring about change and to lead others towards a full appreciation of what is noble and true – whether it be through political changes that shake continents, by acts of individual generosity and compassion that produce a new sense of moral purpose, through the works of the creative imagination, or though tolerance and understanding of the views of others.

Taken as a whole, the Craft and its underlying principles offer a means of transcending social, political, and religious divisions and lead to stability – the essential foundation of civilization that is represented symbolically by the second of the three Masonic pillars: Strength.

Right ISMAIL PASHA, KHEDIVE (VICEROY) OF EGYPT FROM 1863 TO 1879, WAS GRAND MASTER OF THE GRAND LODGE OF EGYPT. UNDER HIS ENLIGHTENED RULE THE SUEZ CANAL WAS CONSTRUCTED AND OPENED TO SHIPPING IN 1869. THE NEW YORK OBELISK WAS HIS GIFT TO THE UNITED STATES.

GEOFFREY FISHER (1887-1972), LORD FISHER OF LAMBETH, WAS
ARCHBISHOP OF CANTERBURY FROM 1945 TO 1961, AND A GREAT CHAMPION OF THE CRAFT.

Right SULTAN SIR MAHOMED SHAH, THE THIRD AGA KHAN (1877-1957), WAS THE SPIRITUAL LEADER OF THE WORLD'S ISMAILI MUSLIMS.

Left SIR ISRAEL BRODIE (1895-1979) WAS CHIEF RABBI OF THE UNITED CONGREGATIONS OF THE BRITISH COMMONWEALTH.

'TO SAY LITTLE AND TO HEAR AND THINK MUCH; TO LEARN THAT WE MAY BE ABLE TO DO; AND THEN TO DO, EARNESTLY AND VIGOROUSLY, THAT IS REQUIRED BY DUTY, BY THE INTERESTS OF OUR FELLOW, OUR COUNTRY, AND MANKIND.'

ALBERT PIKE

C. FRED KLEINKNECHT
SOVEREIGHN GRAND COMMANDER
ANCIENT AND ACCEPTED SCOTTISH RITE, SOUTHERN JURISDICTION,
UNITED STATES OF AMERICA

STRENGTH

AS the following pages of this chapter entitled 'Strength' prove, Freemasons are rightly proud of the many, many Brothers in the Craft who have contributed so much to the welfare of humankind in so many ways. You will find described herein, though of necessity all too briefly, famous Masons who have excelled in architecture, invention, diplomacy, medicine, education, industry, exploration, the military, and numerous other areas of significant endeavour.

This biographical approach is gratifying to modern Masons. Each can see himself as the contemporary personal representative and continuation of a great Masonic tradition. But life stories are surfaces. They show the public achievement, not the private motivation behind it. Many questions still remain. What caused this outstanding accomplishment? What is the spiritual foundation supporting such success?

One conclusion becomes evident from the massed biographies of this book. There must be something in Freemasonry itself, something interior and intimate, something at the core of a person's being, which provides an enduring strength of character as a foundation on which all else is built.

This is what Masons call the 'inner temple'. And it is from this inward temple that all other outward temples, our many Masonic achievements, originate. I first glimpsed the outlines of this inner temple in my own father, C. F. Kleinknecht, 33°. Now, a son's respect for his father comes naturally. In my case, however, I early on began to note my dad was somehow different than the fathers of my friends. Gradually, I realized he worked day and night, year after year, for something beyond supporting his family and benefiting his community. His special concern for others, his obsession with truth and principle, his tireless energy and determination – these seemed well beyond the concerns and interests of most other men and made him a better man than most.

There were some men, however, that seemed to share Dad's special intensity. They met together at regular intervals on what our mother dubbed 'Lodge night'. Dad never missed these meetings, nor did his closest friends. He seemed to draw a strength from each meeting, an energy that carried over to our family's rich involvement in church activities, civic groups, service clubs and, school organizations. Dad was always busy, always cheerful, always someone you could count on to complete the job and make any occasion a success.

Finally, at age 21, I discovered the source of his strength. I petitioned admission to Dad's Lodge, was accepted and initiated. First in the Blue Lodge and then in the Scottish Rite and Shrine, I found what made my father special. Freemasonry made him what he was. It strengthened his faith in a Supreme Being. It cemented his bonds of brotherly love with all humankind. It gave him the courage and dynamic spirit to meet – and over-come – all challenges. Freemasonry gave him a view of life and of himself which never failed him and has never failed me.

Here is the fundamental strength of our Craft. Rising above sectarian differences, Freemasonry affirms our individual faith. Transcending all differences between men – whether geographical, cultural, or economic – our gentle Craft teaches every person to live according to the principles of brotherhood, relief, and truth. On this foundation, my father built his life. On this foundation, all men everywhere can draw the strength to make the world a happier, wiser, and better place for all humankind.

C. FRED KLEINKNECHT
SOVEREIGN GRAND COMMANDER
ANCIENT ACCEPTED SCOTTISH RITE, S.M.J., U.S.A.

SPIRITUAL STRUCTURES

THAT the unknown men who founded the Craft should have taken the story of the building of King Solomon's Temple as the central theme of their allegorical ritual drama is not surprising. The richness of its symbolism, the opportunities it provides for imaginative embellishment and development, and its familiarity to all educated men of the time made it peculiarly fitting as a means of representing both the moral regeneration of the individual and the moral aims of the Craft itself. It would, indeed, be impossible to find a better universal symbol of the building of the spiritual temple within. The tools of the stonemason, too, symbolized the qualities essential to the perfection of that inner temple - tools that were used in the building of the Temple at Jerusalem, by the masons who built the great Gothic cathedrals, and by the builders of the new St. Paul's Cathedral and the elegant churches that rose from the ashes of the Great Fire of London of 1666.

The perfect proportions of the Gothic cathedrals, their delicate tracery, the symmetry and harmony of the pinnacles and soaring vaulting that carry the eye of the worshipper upwards, are balanced by the strength of their massive walls and immense columns – all of which can be taken as representing the inner qualities that characterize Freemasonry. For the stonemasons who built them, these symbols in stone were a source of justifiable pride, reflected in their eagerness to leave their personal marks on the stones of the abbeys, cathedrals, and churches they were erecting with such care and commitment. The techniques of their craft were carefully maintained within the building yards – the original lodges that adjoined the cathedrals – and kept from the eyes of the world This was done partly to guard their skilled techniques from the risk of poor imitation by

untrained workmen, but also to ensure that the structures to which they were dedicating their working lives truly mirrored their spiritual purpose.

The same dedication doubtless also inspired the craftsmen who built Solomon's Temple, as we certainly know it inspired both the Speculative Masons of the eighteenth century who were their spiritual heirs, and such men of genius as Isaac Newton and Sir Christopher Wren who preceded them in the decades before the founding of the first Grand Lodge. Their remarkable visions of the vanished Temple were based solidly on the biblical accounts of its building, but their plans and elevations were more than an architectural exercise: the Temple was seen as a cosmic symbol, and it was its spiritual significance that such drawings and descriptions sought to convey. Perhaps the most successful of such attempts was by William Stukeley, the Masonic antiquarian whose search for the origins of the Craft led him to analyse all the religious structures of the ancient world, from Stonehenge to the Roman Collegia.

When Masonic Temples began to be especially built their architects consciously looked back to the past, though not always to classical or Hebrew models. Many lodge rooms have been designed and decorated in Egyptian fashion – notably at Philadelphia, Dublin, Edinburgh, and Sydney – and at least one entire Masonic Hall, at Boston in Lincolnshire, was built as a miniature Egyptian temple.

There was also strong Masonic involvement in the transportation and re-erection of ancient Egyptian obelisks in Paris, London, and New York. The French obelisk was raised with Masonic ceremony in 1836. Forty years later 'Cleopatra's Needle' was transported to London and set up on the Victoria Embankment, the whole project initiated and financed by Freemasons. In America, erection of an obelisk was an even more spectacular affair. The foundation stone of its base was laid in October 1880 by the Grand Master of New York, Jesse Anthony, watched by over nine thousand Masons who had earlier marched through the city. The obelisk itself was put up four months later.

Grundriß

Far left 'OF EXQUISITE DESIGN AND WORKMANSHIP'. THE WEST FRONT OF REIMS CATHEDRAL, FRANCE THE CORONATION CHURCH OF THE FRENCH KINGS, BUILT IN THE 13TH CENTURY BY BERNARD DE SOISSONS.

Left CHARTRES CATHEDRAL, FRANCE IS A MASTER-PIECE OF GOTHIC ARCHITECTURE. BUILT IN THE 13TH CENTURY BUT ITS ARCHITECT IS UNKNOWN.

Below WILLIAM STUKELEY'S EMBLEM AND *bottom* 'PERSPECTIVE VIEW OF THE INFIDO OF THE HOLY PLACE: THE SANCTUM' DATED 6TH MARCH 1785

THE OBELISK DE LUXOR, IN THE PLACE DE LA CONCORDE, PARIS, WAS CARVED IN THE 13TH CENTURY BC AND BROUGHT FROM EGYPT IN 1836 AS A GIFT TO KING LOUIS PHILIPPE.

ST. PAUL'S CATHEDRAL, LONDON: THE NORTH TRANSEPT.
WREN BEGAN HIS PERFECTLY PROPORTIONED MASTERPIECE IN 1675 AND WORKED ON IT
FOR MORE THAN THIRTY YEARS, LAYING THE TOP STONE IN 1710.

VISIONS OF THE CITY

THE ancient world is not the only inspiration for Masonic building. Gothic architecture has been the model for many of the proud Scottish Rite cathedrals of America, while every Masonic Temple around the world, however mighty or humble, has sought to emulate the ideal of King Solomon's Temple. And this concept of the ideal temple can also be seen as the very basis of whole cities.

Many great city architects have been Freemasons, including Wren and Nicholas Hawksmoor, who were responsible for building most of the City churches lost in the Great Fire of London, Sir John Soane, who built the Bank of England, and Sir Robert Smirke, whose lasting memorial is the British Museum.

In America the same line of influence can be seen in the Catholic Cathedral in Baltimore, the magnum opus of Benjamin Latrobe, a Freemason and 'the father of American architecture'. Latrobe was also responsible for rebuilding the Capitol in Washington after the war of 1812, although the flanking wings and the great dome were the creation of a younger architect and Mason, Thomas Ustick Walter.

Even more significant is the work of Daniel Burnham, the Chicago architect who pioneered the construction of the skyscraper and who exerted a seminal influence on modern town planning with his great 'Plan of Chicago' of 1909 – a massive blueprint for the ideal city. This stemmed from his building of the White City of the Chicago World's Fair of 1893 – itself an archetype of municipal government. Burnham's aim with both was to create the Spiritual Temple on earth (it was with unwitting justice that his White City had earlier been described as the 'New Jerusalem'). The plan of 1909 was the first regional plan for a modern metropolis, and although it never came to fruition as Burnham envisaged it, the city still follows his plan and in its provision of a cultural centre at Grant Park (devoted in Burnham's plan to literature, science, and art – or, in other words, to wisdom, strength, and beauty) it presents a fine application of both Masonic principles and Masonic symbolism.

A more modest, but even more striking example of Masonic symbolism in city planning can be found in Sandusky, Ohio, where the diagonal streets are deliberately designed to intersect in the form of the Square and Compasses. But for Masonic associations, few cities in the world can compare with Paris.

Preceding pages THE EGYPTIAN HALL IN THE MASONIC TEMPLE, PHILADELPHIA, UNITED STATES OF AMERICA.

Right THE BRITISH MUSEUM, ONE OF LONDON'S MOST FAMOUS LANDMARKS, WAS BUILT BETWEEN 1823 AND 1847 BY SIR ROBERT SMIRKE.

Below TWO PAGES FROM SIR BANISTER FLETCHER'S BOOK, *A HISTORY OF ARCHITECTURE ON THE COMPARATIVE METHOD*, ILLUSTRATRATING ST. PAUL'S CATHEDRAL DESIGNED BY WREN WHO WAS ALSO A MASON.

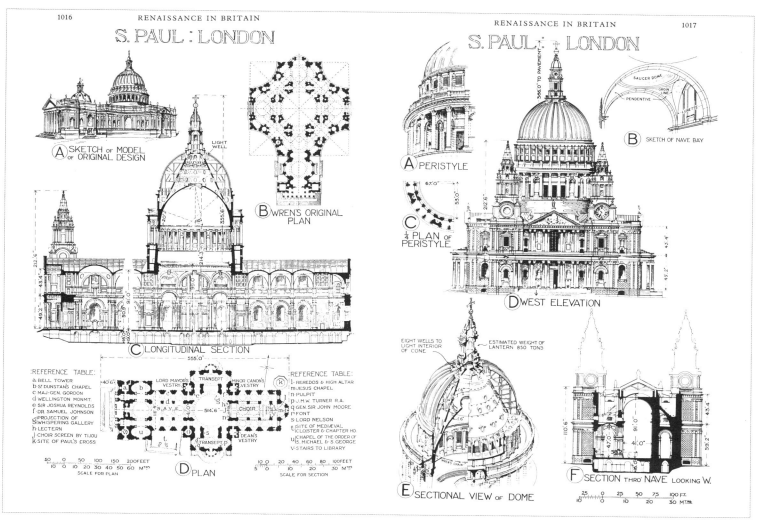

THE OFFICIAL RESIDENCE OF THE PRESIDENTS OF THE UNITED
STATES, THE WHITE HOUSE, AT WASHINGTON, D.C., WAS
DESIGNED AND BUILT BY JAMES HOBAN, WHO LAID THE
CORNERSTONE OF THE FIRST WHITE HOUSE IN 1792. AFTER
THE DESTRUCTION OF WASHINGTON'S PUBLIC BUILDINGS DURING
THE WAR OF 1812, HE ALSO DESIGNED THE PRESENT BUILDING.

ONE OF THE WORLD'S BEST-KNOWN
BUILDINGS, THE UNITED STATES
CAPITOL, AT WASHINGTON, D.C., WAS
THE CREATION OF A SUCCESSION OF
ARCHITECTS WHO WERE ALMOST ALL
FREEMASONS. ORIGINALLY DESIGNED
BY WILLIAM THORNTON (1759-1828),
THE WORK WAS COMPLETED BY
BENJAMIN LATROBE (A PUPIL OF THE
ENGLISH ARCHITECT SAMUEL PEPYS
COCKERELL, 1754-1827) WHO ALSO
REDESIGNED IT AFTER THE WAR OF
1812. THE FLANKING WINGS AND THE
GREAT DOME WERE ADDED LATER BY
THOMAS USTICK WALTER.

IN ADDITION TO HIS INNOVATIVE PLAN OF CHIGAGO OF 1909, DANIEL BURNHAM WAS THE ARCHITECT FOR THE FLATIRON BUILDING, NEW YORK CITY, 1903, (*RIGHT*) AND (*BELOW*) THE MASONIC TEMPLE AT CHICAGO OF 1892.

THE REALISED CITY

AS the city of Paris grew out of the original 'Ile de la Cité' it became surrounded by four successive rings of fortified walls, which were pulled down and replaced by broad avenues. Finally a new ring of fortifications was built around the city during the 1840s, and in 1864 the military road inside the ring was given over to civil use, broadened and planted with trees. The boulevards were laid out during the reign of Napoleon III, the nephew of Napoleon Bonaparte, who tried to bolster his own position, against both the republicans and royalists who opposed him, by appealing to the glories of his uncle's reign. Thus he named the boulevards after Bonaparte's marshalls (and one admiral), many of whom had also been Freemasons. His naming of the Parisian boulevards was clearly an act of homage to Freemasonry, and the perpetuation of their names under the republican government that followed Napoleon's downfall is a striking testimony of the esteem in which the Masonic Order was held, as well as French military glory.

It is not known for certain whether Napoleon Bonaparte was a Mason, although current French opinion inclines to accept him as such. However, the Empress Josephine was the widow of a Mason and an active member of Adoptive Masonry, while Napoleon himself elevated a number of active Masons to high government office. His nephew never joined the Craft, but he maintained an intense interest in it – even going so far as to impose a Grand Master of his own choosing, Marshal Magnan, on the Grand Orient of France. One of the most enduring symbols of Paris is also linked to the Craft. The Arc de Triomphe is the work of the eighteenth-century architect and Freemason, Jean-François Chalgrin.

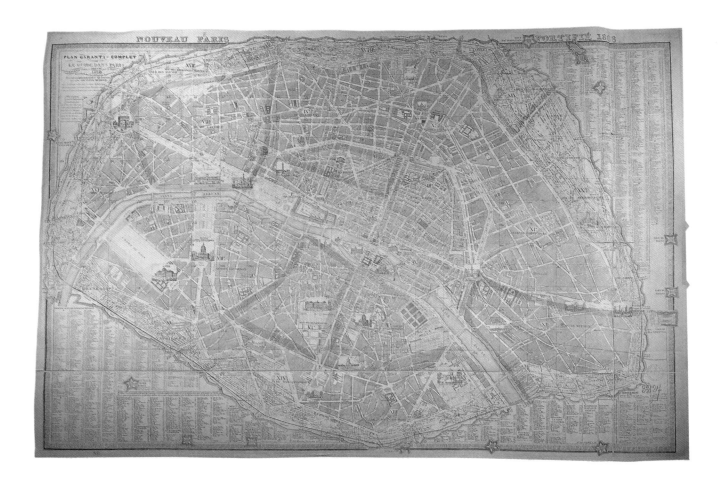

A MAP OF PARIS (1868) SHOWING THE ORIGINAL FORTRESS BOUNDARIES.

THE BOULEVARDS AROUND PARIS

ALTHOUGH he was often described as an 'illustrious Brother' by contemporary French Freemasons, it has never been proved that Napoleon was a Mason. But what is certain is that the Craft in France recovered from the disastrous effects of the Revolution and firmly re-established itself under his regime. Equally certain is the Masonic membership of the majority of his marshals.

At least three of Napoleon's marshals were members of military Lodges; five became Grand Officers of the Grand Orient; and seven were active in the Ancient and Accepted Scottish Rite. And while Napoleon III named the Parisian boulevards after his uncle's marshals in an attempt to profit by their reflected glory, it was their honourable careers in Masonry that ensured the survival of their names after 1870.

The twenty were: Michel Ney (1769-1815); Jacques MacDonald (1765-1845); Philibert Sérurier (1742-1819); Edouard Mortier (1768-1835); Nicolas Davout (1770-1823); Jean-de-Dieu Soult (1769-1851); Joseph Poniatowski (1763-1813); André Masséna (1756-1817); François C. Kellermann (1735-1820); Jean-Baptiste Jourdan (1762-1833); Guillaume Brune (1763-1815); Jean-François Lefebvre (1755-1820); Claude-Victor Perrin (1766-1814); Remy Exelmans (1775-1852); Louis Gabriel Suchet (1776-1826); Jean Lannes (1769-1809); Eustache Bruix (1759-1805); Laurent Gouvion (1764-1830); Louis Berthier (1753-1815); Jean-Baptiste Bessières (1768-1813).

108

THE ARCHETYPAL SYMBOL OF PARIS, THE ARC DE TRIOMPHE DE L'ETOILE,
WAS DESIGNED IN 1808 BY JEAN FRANÇOIS CHALGRIN (1739-1811) AS A TRIUMPHAL
CELEBRATION OF NAPOLEON'S VICTORIES. UNDER THE MASSIVE 162-FOOT ARCH AN ETERNAL
FLAME MARKS THE RESTING PLACE OF FRANCE'S UNKNOWN SOLDIER.

RAFFLES AND SINGAPORE

SIR Thomas Stamford Raffles (1781-1826) joined the Honourable East India Company as a boy, and in 1805 was sent to Penang as assistant secretary to the first Governor. From 1811 to 1815 (when it was returned to the Dutch) he was lieutenant-governor of Java, where he introduced a new system of land tenure to improve trade, and used his time to acquire an encyclopaedic knowledge of the East Indies, which he embodied in his *History of Java* (1817). In 1819 he acquired the island of Singapore for the East India Company and founded 'my city of Singapore', laying the foundations of the great international trading centre that it is now: 'I have declared that the port of Singapore is a free port and the trade thereof open to ships and vessels of every nation.' He was initiated into Freemasonry in Java, two months after the British conquest of the island in 1811; the Master of the Lodge being a former Dutch governor of Java, who, although he was naturally hostile to the British in public life, welcomed Raffles into the Craft.

Above right AN ENGRAVING OF SINGAPORE RIVER, c1870.
Below right THE PORT OF SINGAPORE, AND ITS MAGNIFICENT SKYLINE TODAY.

STRENGTH

FRÉDÉRIC AUGUSTE BARTHOLDI (1834-1904).

SYMBOL OF LIBERTY

THE best known of all Masonically-inspired monuments, and unquestionably the most ubiquitous icon of freedom, is the Statue of Liberty. Designed to celebrate the centenary of the American Revolution, although not completed until 1886, the statue was the work of Frédéric Auguste Bartholdi (1834-1904), who conceived its design while on a visit to America. As his ship sailed into New York, Bartholdi had a vision of a woman standing on a pedestal, holding a torch and welcoming immigrants to a new life in a free land. Initially it was a 'revolutionary' image, but in 1874 Bartholdi was initiated into Freemasonry and the values he found in the Craft greatly influenced his work. Now, Liberty became a serene but mighty matriarch, offering succour to the weak, hope to the despairing, and freedom to the oppressed.

Funding for the statue came largely through the efforts of Freemasons in France and America – including the future President, Theodore Roosevelt – while the task of supplying the steel inner structure of the colossal statue was given to Gustave Eiffel. When the cornerstone of the pedestal was laid in 1884, the Grand Master of New York asked rhetorically why Freemasons should become involved in such an enterprise and gave the answer: 'No other organization has ever done more to promote Liberty and to liberate men from their chains of ignorance and tyranny than Freemasonry'.

THE IDEA OF A STATUE SYMBOLIZING LIBERTY WAS CONCEIVED IN THE AFTERMATH OF THE CIVIL WAR AND WAS SOON LINKED WITH THE FRENCH PROJECT TO PRESENT A STATUE TO THE AMERICAN PEOPLE AS A TOKEN OF MUTUAL FRIENDSHIP. THE HONOUR OF CREATING THE STATUE WAS AWARDED TO THE FRENCH SCULPTOR FRÉDÉRIC BARTHOLDI, WHO IS SEEN IN THE CENTRE OF THIS SOMEWHAT ROMANTIC IMAGE HOLDING THE DESIGNS; IN FRONT OF HIM STANDS WILLIAM EVART, THE EDITOR OF THE POPULAR NEWSPAPER, *THE WORLD*, WHO CHAIRED THE COMMITTEE APPOINTED TO OVERSEE THE PROJECT.

Above and right THE CONSTRUCTION OF LIBERTY'S HAND AND HEAD. BARTHOLDI FIRST MADE A ONE METRE HIGH CLAY MODEL OF THE STATUE, THEN PROGRESSED TO A THREE METRE PLASTER VERSION AND GRADUALLY ENLARGED IT SECTION BY SECTION, UNTIL THE FULL SCALE WAS ACHIEVED. THE FINISHED STATUE OF *LIBERTY ENLIGHTENING THE WORLD* WAS PRESENTED TO THE AMERICAN AMBASSADOR IN PARIS, LEVI MORTON, ON 4 JULY 1884.

Above LIBERTY'S SERENE BUT STRONG-FEATURED FACE WAS MODELLED ON THAT OF THE DESIGNER'S MOTHER, CHARLOTTE BYSSER BARTHOLDI. LIKE THE HAND, IT WAS EXHIBITED SEPARATELY BEFORE THE STATUE WAS COMPLETED.

Right IN 1876 THE HAND OF THE STATUE, HOLDING ALOFT THE TORCH OF FREEDOM, WAS SHOWN TO THE PUBLIC AT THE PHILADELPHIA CENTENNIAL EXPOSITION.

Above LIBERTY'S MASONIC CORNERSTONE CEREMONY IN AUGUST 1884.

Below THE 1984 LIBERTY PLAQUE SIGNIFYING THE DEDICATION TO KEEP THE
TORCH OF LIBERTY LIGHTED FOR ALL MANKIND.

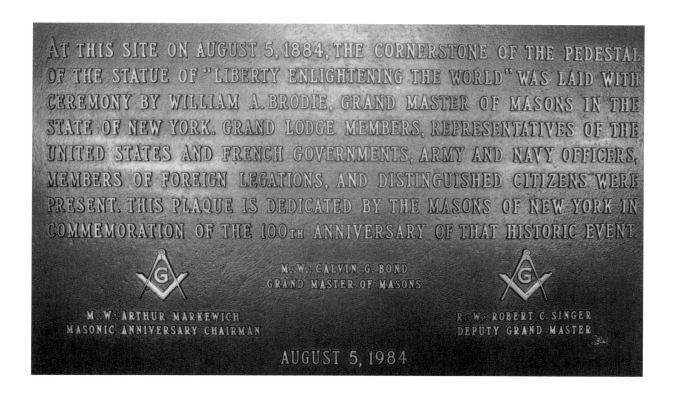

AT THIS SITE ON AUGUST 5, 1884, THE CORNERSTONE OF THE PEDESTAL OF THE STATUE OF "LIBERTY ENLIGHTENING THE WORLD" WAS LAID WITH CEREMONY BY WILLIAM A. BRODIE, GRAND MASTER OF MASONS IN THE STATE OF NEW YORK. GRAND LODGE MEMBERS, REPRESENTATIVES OF THE UNITED STATES AND FRENCH GOVERNMENTS, ARMY AND NAVY OFFICERS, MEMBERS OF FOREIGN LEGATIONS, AND DISTINGUISHED CITIZENS WERE PRESENT. THIS PLAQUE IS DEDICATED BY THE MASONS OF NEW YORK IN COMMEMORATION OF THE 100TH ANNIVERSARY OF THAT HISTORIC EVENT.

M∴W∴ CALVIN G. BOND
GRAND MASTER OF MASONS

M∴W∴ ARTHUR MARKEWICH
MASONIC ANNIVERSARY CHAIRMAN

R∴W∴ ROBERT C. SINGER
DEPUTY GRAND MASTER

AUGUST 5, 1984

FREEMASONRY AND THE STATUE OF LIBERTY

NEW YORK Freemasons, and members of the Masonic Fraternity everywhere, can claim a unique connection with Lady Liberty, 'The Lady in the Harbor'. Just 108 years ago, on August 5, 1884, the then Grand Master of Masons in New York, William A. Brodie, laid the cornerstone of the pedestal of the Statue of Liberty with full Masonic ceremony.

Hundreds of Masons, public officials, representatives of foreign countries, officers of the Army and Navy, and other distinguished citizens stood in the rain for the impressive ceremony, one similar to cornerstone layings at the Nation's Capitol (conducted by Worshipful George Washington, the first President of the United States), at the White House, the Washington Monument, Congressional buildings, and many state capitols and public buildings.

The Statue of 'Liberty Enlightening the World' was created by Frédéric Auguste Bartholdi, a Freemason, who was encouraged to do so by another French Mason, Henri Martin, and by a descendent of Lafayette, the American and French Revolutionary soldier (and Freemason). Both French and American Masons contributed to the campaign that raised funds to pay for the Statue and the pedestal.

In 1886, when the Statue was formally dedicated, thousands of Freemasons paraded in New York City, joined by President Grover Cleveland and many other dignitaries.

Lady Liberty was the focal point of waves of immigrants, who came (and still come) to the shores of the United States from all over the world. Their first glimpse of the Statue was one they never forgot, for it meant the end of poverty and oppression and the beginning of new hope. The 'melting pot' of America was created by millions of immigrants, who knew that freedom and opportunity were open to them in the new land, which they helped settle and build from the Atlantic to the Pacific.

In 1984, on the exact day that the cornerstone had been laid one hundred years before (and again in the rain!), several thousand Freemasons gathered beneath the Statue to rededicate themselves to freedom and liberty, and to commemorate the earlier ceremony. They also pledged to raise a substantial sum for the restoration project, and this eventually amounted to $2 million, one of the largest contributions by a non-governmental source. Every United States Grand Lodge took part in the successful two-year fundraising effort.

Today, a large plaque, adorned with the square and compasses, tells the millions of visitors to Liberty Island each year of Freemasonry's role in the creation and erection of this world-renowned symbol of freedom. It signifies to all the dedication of the Masonic Fraternity to keeping the torch of Liberty lighted for all mankind.

ROBERT C. SINGER,
PAST GRAND MASTER OF MASONS IN NEW YORK
AND PRESENT GRAND SECRETARY.

SOLDIERS AND STATESMEN

EIGHT years earlier, in 1876, Bartholdi's statue of the Marquis de Lafayette had been unveiled in New York. The statue symbolizes the figurative strength of Freemasonry, perfectly illustrating in this image of the heroic soldier a true Masonic combination of fortitude and idealism, strength of character, and physical courage. The same combination led General Washington to victory – when another Mason, Lord Charles Cornwallis (1738-1805) British General of the American Revolution, surrendered at Yorktown in 1781 – and brought freedom from British rule to America. In Europe the military success of Wellington, the 'Iron Duke' whose military success at Waterloo in 1815 brought peace to war-torn Europe, was matched by his political leadership, under which religious liberty was brought about in Britain through the emancipation of Catholics in 1829 – a true application of Masonic principles.

One of the greatest liberators in the history of South America was Simon Bolivar, whose military victories over Spain, (1819-1824) brought freedom to Colombia, Venezuela and Bolivia – named after him in his honour, in 1825. Among the thousands of Masonic soldiers and heroes of the United States of America, none have been more decorated for acts of heroism than Audie Murphy – he jumped on to a burning tank destroyer and used its machine gun to fend off more than fifty enemy troops – he received the Medal of Honour, the nation's highest award.

There are other examples of Masonic soldiers turned statesmen, including Theodore Roosevelt, who led his country after participating in the liberation of Cuba from Spain. Others, without political ambition, have helped bring nations to freedom or preserved hard-fought liberties. They include Field-Marshal Haig, Marshal Joffre, and General Pershing in World War One – Pershing, when entering Paris with the American troops in 1917, acknowledged his own country's earlier debt to France by addressing in spirit his great Masonic predecessor with the words, 'Lafayette, here we are' – Alexander and Douglas MacArthur, Omar Bradley, Mathew Ridgeway, and Henry 'Hap' Arnold in World War Two. But if peace can be attained through battle it must be maintained by the kind of statesmanship shown by Jan Masaryk, who, with his father, helped to create a new nation – Czechoslovakia – out of the ruins of the Austro-Hungarian Empire.

Left THE DUKE OF WELLINGTON (1769-1852), THE 'IRON DUKE' WHOSE MILITARY SUCCESS AT WATERLOO IN 1815 BROUGHT PEACE TO WAR-TORN EUROPE.

THE SURRENDER OF LORD CORNWALLIS TO GENERAL
WASHINGTON AT YORKTOWN, VIRGINIA IN 1781 WAS THE FINAL
BLOW THAT BROUGHT THE AMERICAN REVOLUTION TO AN END.

Left STATUE OF LAFAYETTE AND WASHINGTON BY BARTHOLDI, PARIS, FRANCE. LAFAYETTE IS HOLDING THE FLAGS OF THE TWO COUNTRIES IN HIS LEFT HAND AND WITH HIS RIGHT HAND OFFERS BOTH ENTHUSIASM AND SUPPORT TO WASHINGTON.

Right A LITHOGRAPH OF LAFAYETTE BEING WELCOMED BY THE FRENCH REVOLUTIONARIES OF 1830.

Below LAFAYETTE'S TOMB AT PICPUS CEMETERY, PARIS, FRANCE, ON WHICH THE FLAG OF THE UNITED STATES OF AMERICA IS PERMANENTLY DISPLAYED.

Simon Bolivar (1783-1830). He is called *El Libertador* (The Liberator)
and the 'George Washington of South America

AUDIE MURPHY (1924-1971), HE RECEIVED 24 MEDALS FROM THE U.S. GOVERNMENT, 3 FROM FRANCE, AND 1 FROM BELGIUM.

SMALLPOX, UNTIL RECENTLY ONE OF THE MAJOR KILLING DISEASES, – WAS ERADICATED BY THE UNIVERSAL USE OF VACCINATION. DISCOVERED BY EDWARD JENNER (1749-1823).

MEDICAL LIBERATORS

THE pursuit of Masonic ideals in the face of extreme adversity demands great courage and moral strength, while strength of another order can be seen in the determined labours of those who have striven in other ways to liberate mankind. Political freedom is of little value if life is constantly threatened by disease and starvation, and humanity owes an equal debt of gratitude to the long line of medical liberators.

One of the earliest of these was the English physician Edward Jenner, who, in 1796, first discovered the preventive power of vaccination (inoculation with cowpox – in Latin, *vaccinia*). The introduction of vaccination eventually led to the extinction of smallpox, epidemics of which had formerly killed or disfigured millions around the world.

Of equal importance was the more recent discovery in 1928, by the Scottish bacteriologist and Mason Alexander Fleming, of penicillin – the anti-bacterial agent present in green mould. When the chemical was finally isolated it was possible to use it in the treatment of wounds, and from 1943 onwards the lives of countless thousands of

BY HIS DISCOVERY OF PENICILLIN, ALEXANDER FLEMING (1881-1955)
OPENED A NEW ERA FOR MEDICINE.

Soldiers and civilians have been saved as a result. In 1945 Fleming with Florey and Chain, who had isolated penicillin, received the Nobel Prize for his discovery of what is still the most widely used antibiotic.

Among the most remarkable of these Masonic medical pioneers was the German physician Samuel Hahnemann (1755-1843), who developed the system of treatment known as homoeopathy. Exactly how this 'magic of the minimum dose' operates is still imperfectly understood, but its value lies in the alternative it offers to allopathy (the orthodox use of symptom-relieving drugs), and thus to drug dependence. Indeed, Hahnemann's concern to cure without harm has moral parallels with the many addictive drug rehabilitation programmes undertaken today by so many American Grand Lodges.

Other areas of social medicine are actively supported by the Craft. At Cambridge University in England a Chair of Gerontology (the study of human ageing) has recently been established and funded by the United Grand Lodge of England – a gesture that dovetails with the extensive and continuing support of the aged provided by the Grand Lodge. Many of the American Masonic philanthropies will be discussed in a later chapter

HOMOEOPATHY

OF all the medical innovations which have been made by Freemasons, the most original – and among the most fruitful, for the total absence of toxicity renders it virtually free from any risk of side-effects – is unquestionably homeopathy, the system of therapy developed by the German physician, Samuel Hahnemann.

Hahnemann was born at Meissen, Saxony, in 1755, and was initiated into the Craft in 1777, in the lodge St. Andreas Zu den drei Seeblättern, at Hermanstadt. He maintained his enthusiasm for Masonry throughout his life, putting its principles into practice in his life's work for humanity.

The basis of his system, which was first publicized in 1810 in his book *Organon of the Art of Healing*, is the Law of Similarity: 'Similia similibus curantur' ('Like is cured by like'). The theory is that a substance which can cause a given group of symptoms in the healthy can cure a similar set of symptoms in the sick, but in practice it is administered only in a highly diluted form after careful preparation.

Homoeopathic remedies are prepared from drugs that are mostly derived from plants, and the effects are determined by testing them (in doses below the toxic level) on healthy volunteers. For therapeutic purposes the drugs used are diluted by stages to an astounding degree – typically to much less than a millionth part of the original concentration – and at each stage they are violently shaken ('succussion') to bring about the process of 'dynamization'.

At this level of dilution there should be no trace of the original substance – but it still acts in the expected manner and patients are cured. And the cures are not due to a placebo effect, for clinical experiments in British and European hospitals have validated

STRENGTH

Left SAMUEL HAHNEMANN (COMMEMORATIVE PLAQUE BY DAVID D'ANGERS) GAVE UP
THE PRACTICE OF MEDICINE BECAUSE OF HIS UNHAPPINESS WITH THE TREATMENTS THEN IN VOGUE.
HE BECAME WELL-KNOWN AS A TEACHER OF CHEMISTRY, AND IT WAS DURING THIS TIME, IN 1784, THAT HE
FIRST BEGAN THE RESEARCHES THAT LED HIM TO DEVELOP HIS REVOLUTIONARY FORM OF THERAPY.

Above DR. MAX TETAU PARIS, FRANCE, CURRENTLY PRESIDES OVER 'HOMOEOPATHIA UNIVERSALIS' AND IT IS
A FITTING TRIBUTE TO THE CRAFT THAT HOMOEOPATHY, CREATED BY A MASON ALMOST
TWO HUNDRED YEARS AGO, SHOULD BE CARRIED FORWARD INTO THE NEXT CENTURY BY AN INITIATE.

homoeopathy as a viable form of therapy. Nor is the treatment confined to humans: veterinary homeopathy is proving to be increasingly successful in many countries around the world.

Today there is an increasing acceptance of homoeopathy by the medical profession. In Britain homoeopathic medicine is well established and is patronized by the Royal Family. There is a solid and continuing revival in the U.S.A., and in France 30% of the population receives homoeopathic treatment. There is a growing recognition of the importance of this form of therapy throughout Europe – including Russia – and it is widely practised in both India and Pakistan. Indeed, there are few countries where its benefits are not accepted.

But while it is effective in treating a very wide range of ailments – from headaches and high blood-pressure to allergies, asthma, bronchitis and rheumatism – it does not pretend to be a panacea. Severe illnesses that exceed the normal limits of natural resistance – Cancer, AIDS, and psychotic disorders, for example – are not treated by homoeopathy. But homoeopathic drugs can be prescribed to patients to combat the side-effects of chemotherapy, and where the dangers from toxicity are greatest (e.g. for newborn babies and expectant mothers) the use of homoeopathic remedies is especially valuable.

Responsible treatment, of course, demands careful training, and every year several thousand doctors are trained in homoeopathic medical schools around the world, under the aegis of a professional International Federation, 'Homoeopathia Universalis'. Already an important part of the medicine of today, homeopathy is surely destined to be the medicine of tomorrow.

DR. MAX TETAU

THE POIGNANT REMINDERS OF THE MILLIONS OF LIVES SACRIFICED IN
THE CAUSE OF FREEDOM SINCE 1914 WERE ESTABLISHED THROUGH THE EFFORTS OF
THE ENGLISH EDUCATIONALIST SIR FABIAN WARE (1869-1949).

DIGNITY IN DEATH

THE Craft also exhibits a concern to ensure that a dignified old age is succeeded by
dignity in death. For the Freemason, the certainty of the reality of eternal life relieves
death of much of its terror; but for those who remain to mourn, something more is
needed. This is especially so for widows and orphans of the millions who have died in
time of war, and it was their needs that were addressed by Sir Fabian Ware, whose work
led to the constitution of the Imperial War Graves Commission in 1917. The creation and
maintenance of cemeteries for the dead in all theatres of war since that time has been
due entirely to his energy and vision, and Masonic support for those permanent
memorials to the sacrifice of soldiers, sailors and airmen has been constant. Initially,
this support was channelled through the Builders of the Silent City Lodge, founded in
1927 by Rudyard Kipling (who provided the words for the inscription on the stone of
remembrance) and which Sir Fabian joined soon afterwards.

The purely practical problems of ensuring dignity in mourning were taken up by
George Shillibeer (1797-1866), who in the 1830s introduced the horse-drawn funeral
coach – a combination of hearse and mourning coach – that was the forerunner of the
modern hearse.

Left THE MENIN GATE MEMORIAL AT YPRES WAS ERECTED IN TRIBUTE TO THE HEROISM OF THE BRITISH EXPEDITIONARY FORCE OF 1914, AND COMMEMORATES ESPECIALLY THOSE BRITISH SOLDIERS WHO GAVE THEIR LIVES IN DEFENCE OF FREEDOM, BUT WHO HAVE NO KNOWN GRAVE.

Below THE GRAVES OF ALMOST THREE MILLION MEN AND WOMEN OF THE COMMONWEALTH FORCES WHO DIED IN TWO WORLD WARS ARE MARKED AND MAINTAINED BY THE COMMONWEALTH WAR GRAVES COMMISSION IN 2,500 WAR CEMETERIES AROUND THE WORLD.

TRANSPORT PIONEERS

SHILLIBEER was also concerned for the welfare of the living, pioneering the London omnibus (a name he coined), which became the basis of municipal transport systems around the world. Such systems were enabled to succeed by the complementary work of Shillibeer's fellow Mason, John Loudon Macadam (1756-1836), the surveyor who revolutionized road building by raising roads above ground level and rendering them impervious to water. As with the omnibus, the macadamized road is now found throughout the world, and the inventor's name has passed into the English language. (It is also worth mentioning here that Macadam's fellow pioneer in modern road building, the great engineer Thomas Telford, began his working life as an operative stonemason.)

The steamboat can certainly be claimed as a 'Masonic' invention. Robert Fulton (1765-1815), usually credited with inventing the first viable steamboat – the *Clermont*, 'the devil on his way to Albany in a sawmill', which steamed up the Hudson on 7 August 1807 – had as his sponsor in the Craft Robert Livingston (1746-1813), his financial partner. Livingston is better known in American history for administering the oath, sworn on the Bible of St. John's Lodge at New York, to George Washington on his inauguration as President in 1789. (The same Bible has been used on several occasions since, most recently at the inauguration of President Bush.)

Fulton went on to build a working submarine and the first steam-powered American warship, and he is justly remembered as a great engineer. But he was not in fact the first person to develop a steamboat. That distinction belongs to another American Mason, John Fitch (1743-1798) of Connecticut. Fitch first conceived the idea of a steam-powered vessel – and built his first model steamboat in 1785, shortly after his initiation into the Craft. His first full-size boat made a trial run in 1787, and three years later a larger version ran a regular summer service on the Delaware River. But during his lifetime Fitch was unable to gain official support for his invention (its importance and his own status as its inventor were not recognized until 1817) and bitterness and disappointment drove him to suicide in 1798. Despite the tragedy of Fitch's life, his work eventually led to a revolution in sea travel and to the building of ships large enough to carry millions of emigrants from Europe to America throughout the nineteenth century.

The two Montgolfier, brothers Joseph Michel and Jacques Etienne, both members of the *Loge des Neuf Soeurs* at Paris, were the inventors of the hot-air balloon, which made its first flight in 1783. Other, more efficient, hydrogen balloons followed but the Montgolfiers were the true pioneers. Some of the pioneers of aviation proper were also associated with the Craft: men such as Lieut. Arthur Brown, who piloted the first non-stop flight across the Atlantic in 1919, and Captain Edward Rickenbacker who, in 1917, commanded the first American aviation unit to see action on the Western Front and himself became the greatest American 'Ace' of the war. With the cessation of hostilities he went on to play a prominent role in developing America's civil aviation industry, which received further kudos from the flights of Charles Lindbergh that culminated in his solo crossing of the Atlantic in 1927.

GEORGE SHILLIBEER'S ORIGINAL OMNIBUS OF 1829. ALTHOUGH TEMPORARILY SUPERSEDED BY
THE RAILWAY TRAIN, THE MODERN DESCENDANTS OF SHILLIBEER'S UBIQUITOUS VEHICLE
NOW HOLD THE FIELD IN POPULAR TRANSPORT, AND THE NAME IS IMMORTALIZED IN
THE GENERIC TERM FOR POPULAR OPINION — THAT OF 'THE MAN ON THE CLAPHAM OMNIBUS'.

Eight of America's astronauts also have been inspired by the Craft, from John Glenn, who orbited the Earth in 1962, to Edwin 'Buzz' Aldrin, who first walked on the Moon with Neil Armstrong after the epoch-making voyage of Apollo II in 1969.

As railways developed, the lot of long-distance travellers was immeasurably improved by the efforts of George Pullman, who in 1863 built the prototype of the railway car that still bears his name. But as far as mass transport was concerned, the future lay elsewhere.

The development of a genuinely affordable automobile – the ubiquitous *Model-T* – was pioneered in America by Henry Ford, whose first vehicle of 1892 was followed in 1903 by the founding of the Ford Motor Company, which became the largest automobile producer in the world. Ford also initiated a profit-sharing plan for his workers as well as pioneering mass production techniques. Ford's innovations were mirrored in other countries – in France, for example, by André Citroen, who, like Ford, was an active Freemason. Nor was Ford alone in America: his fellow pioneer, Ransom Olds – after whom the *Oldsmobile* was named – and the contemporary automobile producer, Walter Chrysler, were both keen Masons.

Below THE RIVER STEAMER *MARK TWAIN* MOORED AT NEW ORLEANS. STERN-WHEEL PADDLE-STEAMERS – THE SYMBOL OF TRAVEL ON THE MISSISSIPPI – WERE MADE POSSIBLE BY THE LABOURS AND INVENTIVE GENIUS OF JOHN FITCH AND ROBERT FULTON AT THE TURN OF THE 19TH CENTURY.

Right IN RECENT YEARS HOT-AIR BALLOONING HAS BECOME AN INCREASINGLY POPULAR SPORT. THE PRINCIPLES ON WHICH THE BALLOONS OPERATE WERE FIRST PUT TO PRACTICAL USE IN 1783 BY THE MONTGOLFIER BROTHERS. THEIR BALLOON OF 1783 (*inset*) WAS THE FIRST TO CARRY HUMAN PASSENGERS.

Left CHARLES LINDBERGH'S EPIC SOLO CROSSING OF THE ATLANTIC OCEAN IN 1927, IN HIS AEROPLANE *THE SPIRIT OF ST. LOUIS*, CAPTURED THE IMAGINATION OF THE WORLD.

Below CAPTAIN 'EDDIE' RICKENBACKER DEVOTED HIS LIFE TO THE AIR. FROM FLYING THE NIEUPORT 28 IN THE 94TH AERO PURSUIT SQUADRON DURING WORLD WAR ONE TO BECOME AMERICA'S 'ACE OF ACES', HE TURNED TO CIVIL AVIATION, RETURNING TO THE MILITARY IN WORLD WAR TWO – TO RECEIVE THE HIGHEST AWARDS FOR BRAVERY IN THE SERVICE OF HIS COUNTRY.

STRENGTH

NOTHING MORE CLEARLY ILLUSTRATES THE RESTLESS ASPIRATION OF THE HUMAN SPIRIT
THAN THE DRIVE TO CONQUER SPACE – THE SUCCESSFUL CONQUEST OF WHICH IS ENCAPSULATED IN
THE IMAGE OF COL. EDWIN 'BUZZ' ALDRIN ON THE SURFACE OF THE MOON.

Left COMFORT IN RAILWAY TRAVEL IS VIRTUALLY SYNONYMOUS WITH THE NAME PULLMAN – NOT ONLY IN AMERICA, WHERE THE FIRST PULLMAN DINING CARS WERE BUILT IN 1868, BUT THROUGHOUT THE CIVILIZED WORLD.

Right and below ANDRÉ CITROEN, THE GREATEST OF EUROPEAN CAR-MAKERS, WAS KNOWN, FOR HIS COMMERCIAL FLAIR AND INVENTIVE GENIUS, AS 'THE FORD OF FRANCE'.

Above left HENRY FORD AT THE WHEEL OF AN EARLY MODEL A, WHICH IN 1903 BECAME HIS FIRST PRODUCTION CAR.

Left FORD WELCOMES ANDRÉ CITROEN ON HIS VISIT TO THE U.S.A. IN 1931.

Top A 1901-2 OLDS CURVED DASH, THE WORLD'S FIRST MASS-PRODUCED CAR.

Above A 1963 CHRYSLER IMPERIAL, WITH ITS V-8 ENGINE AND POWER-ASSISTED STEERING. IT WAS A VERY EASY AND PLEASANT CAR TO DRIVE.

A SECTION OF THE 800-MILE TRANS-ALASKA PIPELINE,
RAISED ABOVE GROUND TO TAKE ACCOUNT OF ENVIRONMENTAL NEEDS.

ENVIRONMENT AND EXPLORATION

THE dominance in the twentieth century of the motor car as a means of personal transport has led to the increasingly difficult search for oil, often in extremely inhospitable environments. One such area is Alaska, where the 800-mile trans-Alaska pipeline was opened in 1977, largely due to the vision of oilman and Freemason Charles Spahr. This was one of the first pipelines to take account of the broader environmental needs by being buried, except where the warm oil would cause the soil above to thaw and thus cause soil erosion.

Concern for the environment, of course, is not an exclusively Masonic virtue, but many members of the Craft have set fine examples for others to follow. One such was Cornelius Hedges (1831-1907), who in 1870 was a member of the expedition that first explored the area that was to become Yellowstone National Park. On the final day of the expedition Hedges insisted that the area should be 'set aside for the use and benefit of the people' – words that are carved into the park's granite entrance arch. Through his efforts, and those of Nathaniel Langford, one of the expedition's leaders and later the park's first superintendent, Yellowstone was established as the first of America's National Parks, in 1872.

Above THE SURVEY PARTY ENTERING YELLOWSTONE IN 1871.
Next page A STRIKING VIEW OF THE GRAND CANYON OF THE YELLOWSTONE,
THE FIRST NATIONAL PARK ESTABLISHED BY THE US CONGRESS IN 1872.

Among those who have opened up new continents to modern civilization, many of the most notable have been members of the Craft. North American exploration began in earnest with the three-year expedition, between 1803 and 1806, of Meriwether Lewis (1774-1809) and William Clark (1770-1838), who established a land route to the Pacific by travelling up the Missouri River to its source, then proceeding overland through the Rockies and ending with a descent of the Columbia River to the Pacific Ocean. At the same period Zebulon Pike (1779-1813) not only discovered the source of the Mississippi but also the spectacular mountain peak in Colorado that bears his name.

Other continents, too, were opened up by Masonic explorers. Perhaps the greatest explorer of the nineteenth century was Sir Richard Burton (1821-1890), whose gifts as a writer have given such exploits as his pilgrimage to Mecca in disguise and his discovery with Speke of the source of the Nile (the source of the Blue Nile having been traced in 1770 by another Mason, the Scottish explorer James Bruce), a lasting place in English literature.

In the present century polar exploration has been dominated by members of the Craft: Robert Peary, who first reached the North Pole in 1909; Sir Ernest Shackleton, the great Antarctic explorer; Captain Robert Falcon Scott, who lost the race to the South Pole in 1912 but whose expedition inspired the world by the dogged courage and gallantry of its members; and Admiral Richard Byrd, who flew over both Poles, in 1926 and 1929, and who dominated Antarctic exploration for thirty years.

A cartoon from the magazine *Vanity Fair* of Captain Robert Falcon Scott, 1868-1912.

INVENTION AND DISCOVERY

HEROIC deeds, of course, depend upon the less visible efforts of many, and often may require the inventive genius of others. To name but a few, Masonic inventors range from Samuel Colt, whose 'revolvers' and other firearms revolutionized war and colonial exploration alike, to King Gillette, inventor of the safety razor, and Frank G. Hoover – whose name is now synonymous with the vacuum cleaner he popularized, although he did not invent it. Minor technological inventions also owe an often unrecognized debt to the Craft. When the Statue of Liberty was being constructed, some of the funds required were raised by the sale of small-scale replicas, produced by the French manufacturer who cast the statue, M. Gaget, whose name has passed into English as the name for any small specialized mechanical device – gadget.

So it is that the strengths of the Craft, both literal and figurative, continue to benefit mankind in all fields of human endeavour.

THE MOST POTENT SYMBOL OF AMERICA'S 'WILD WEST' –
THE UBIQUITOUS COLT PEACEMAKER OF 1873.

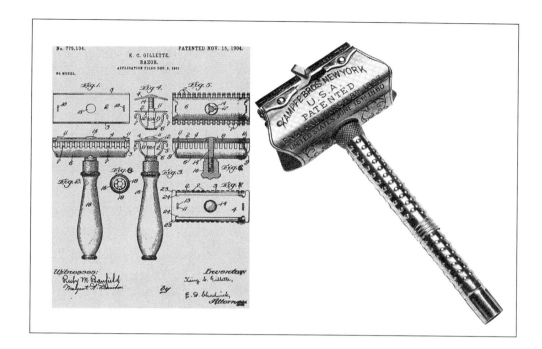

Left THE NAME GILLETTE IS SYNONYMOUS WITH THE SAFETY RAZOR AND THE DISPOSABLE RAZOR BLADE – INVENTED AND PATENTED IN 1901 BY KING CAMP GILLETTE, AND MARKETED BY THE AMERICAN SAFETY RAZOR COMPANY.

Below AN EARLY ADVERTISEMENT FOR THE GILLETTE RAZOR.

SPENCER DOUGLAS DAVID COMPTON,
7TH MARQUESS OF NORTHAMPTON AND HIS WIFE.
ACTIVE IN THE CRAFT FOR MANY YEARS, HE IS A PAST DEPUTY GRAND DIRECTOR OF CEREMONIES,
AND PAST ASSISTANT PROVINCIAL GRAND MASTER FOR NORTHAMPTONSHIRE &
HUNTINGDONSHIRE, UNDER THE UNITED GRAND LODGE OF ENGLAND.

BEAUTY

WHAT IS BEAUTY? 'TIS THE STAINLESS SOUL WITHIN THAT OUTSHINES THE FAIREST SHIN.

SIR AUBREY HUNT

THE third Pillar of Freemasonry, that of Beauty, represents the perfected Soul quality that every Mason should strive to manifest in himself and in every aspect of his life. The keywords for Beauty are Balance and Harmony. Balance between force and form, or masculine and feminine, coupled with awareness produces joy and fulfilment, or the spiritual experience of Beauty. Harmony, like Beauty, relies on the perfect proportions of its several parts – the whole Man – and leads to Unity.

In the Arts, Beauty is subjective, but conditional upon each individual's subsconscious understanding of the laws of Harmony and Proportion.

In speculative Masonry we use the model of King Solomon's Temple for our Lodges: we use the tools that built the Temple, allegorically to portray a system of morality, and we use symbols to illustrate the means by which a Mason may become more perfect. When a Mason enters the Porch of the Temple, balanced between the pillars of Strength and Wisdom, of force and form, he experiences the Pillar of Beauty in all its glory. He then becomes One with all those brethren who have already made the journey back to the Godhead. It is a living Temple built from the enlightened Souls of Man.

Masonry is the story of the transformation of the Soul, and the ritual of its ceremonies is an allegory of that journey that all Masons must make in order to achieve their highest potential.

The principles of the Craft have inspired men throughout the ages to become great artists, poets, musicians, architects and philosophers. The beauty that they have created is the natural effect of their journeys through this mortal existence. Soul qualities are not inherited, they are won by dogged persistence to the cause – which is Man's longing to return to his Creator.

There have been many systems tried by man over the past few thousand years, each new one building on the success of the former. The usages and customs of Masonry bear a close affinity to the precepts of the ancient Egyptians. The system of Pythagoras was also founded on a similar principle, as were many other systems of more recent times. We are told, however, that Masonry is not only the most ancient, but also the most honourable Society that has ever existed. Perhaps in time an even better system will grow out of Masonry, but at the present stage of mankind's evolution it will suffice, because it contains the perfect blueprint for Man on his journey back to the Source – which is Truth.

MARQUESS OF NORTHAMPTON.

THE GRACES CROWNING THE BUST OF RAPHAEL.
AN ENGRAVING BY FRANCESCO BARTOLOZZI, AFTER A DRAWING BY GIOVANI CIPRIANI.

THE VISUAL ARTS

THOUGH harmony is not uniquely a Masonic quality, it has yet led artists outside the Craft to seek for inspiration within it. William Blake (1757-1827) is a classic instance of someone who took the symbols of Freemasonry and used them to supreme effect within his own strange symbolic system. That Blake was influenced by Masonry is clear, for he worked with and for artists and engravers – like Basire, Cipriani, and Sandby – who were certainly members of the Craft. Better known artists, less idiosyncratic than Blake and more in the artistic mainstream, were also Masons – including Hogarth, Francesco Bartolozzi, Philip Loutherbourg, in all of whose work Masonic symbols and idioms are clearly present, and John Crome, and Jean-Baptiste Greuze, for whom the Craft was a more general support to their ideals of harmony and beauty.

More recent artists have also been members of the Craft. Alphonse Mucha (1860-1939), the Czech painter, designer, and illustrator, was one of the most notable European exponents of the 'Art Nouveau' movement whose poster designs in the 1890s included those for Sarah Bernhardt. He was also a prominent Mason, being elected Sovereign Grand Commander of the Czech Supreme Council (A. A. S. R.) in 1923. More influential than Mucha was Juan Gris (1887-1927), the Spanish painter whose personal form of Synthetic Cubism places him on the level of Picasso and Braque as one of the greatest and most original artists of the Cubist movement.

The highly original paintings of Marc Chagall (1887-1985) show the influence of many modern movements while maintaining a unique quality of their own. Chagall drew much of his inspiration from the Bible, every aspect of which – from the Creation story to the poetical books – he saw as conveying the constant message of the love of God in all things. Thus, while much of his work contains themes drawn from the Hasidic Judaism of his native Russia, it also expresses a universal faith and transcends sectarian divisions.

Artistic ideals have also been applied in the material world by Masonic craftsmen. The ornate interior designs of William Burges (1827-81), such as those of Castell Coch near Cardiff, or the Tower House in Kensington, London, complemented by an exquisite range of furniture, are unique in the whole range of Victorian applied art. Although none of his interiors were designed purely for Masonic purposes they nearly always contain Masonic motifs, in recognition of the Craft whose principles inspired him. Burges pro-vided a perfect example for many other artists and craftsmen who have subsequently sought to apply the skills of the operative art to the temples of the speculative craft.

The dedication of such men both to the artistic ideals and to the service of their brethren can be seen not only in such spectacular creations as Freemasons' Hall in London, where the massive grandeur of the exterior conceals the elegant beauty of its Art Deco interior, and in the Masonic Temple in Philadelphia. The glorious interior of New York's Masonic Temple has recently been magnificently restored, bringing back the rich colours of the striking original decoration, but also in the superb craftsmanship they have brought to every minute detail of their work. The Philadelphia Temple is perhaps the most elaborate in the United States.

Thus Freemasons who have also been silversmiths, furniture makers, potters, clockmakers or bookbinders have brought the principles of the Craft to their artistic activities – to the general enrichment of the world's artistic heritage. Examples abound: the rich and subtle tooling on books bound by John Lovejoy in the eighteenth century; the charming porcelain figures modelled by Johann Kaendler at Meissen; and while Paul Revere is justly remembered for his famous ride from Boston to Lexington, it should not eclipse his superlative skill as a silversmith and engraver. Nor should such a parade of famous men entirely overshadow the work of more humble, and sometimes unknown, craftsmen of the past whose handiwork is still used by their brethren of today or is on display in the world's museums and art galleries.

There have been Freemasons prominent in the field of visual satire. William Hogarth is renowned for the biting wit of his brilliant satirical engravings, into several of which he introduced Masonic themes. However, there is no Masonic content in the trenchant political cartoons of Paul Revere, nor in the work of H. M. Bateman. His visual portrayals of the dire consequences of social gaffes possess both a period charm and an innocence that renders them timeless; and, true to the principles of the Craft, they are entirely free of malice.

Above 'An Avalanche in the Alps' painted in 1803 by Philip Loutherbourg.

Right A poster by Alphonse Mucha
for the International and Universal Exhibition of St. Louis, USA, 1904.

Left 'NATURE MORTE AUX POIRES' *(PEARS AND GRAPES ON A TABLE)*, A PAINTING BY JUAN GRIS, 1913, SOLD IN NEW YORK CITY BY CHRISTIE'S, NOVEMBER 5, 1991.

Below 'GRIS BY GRIS', 1911.

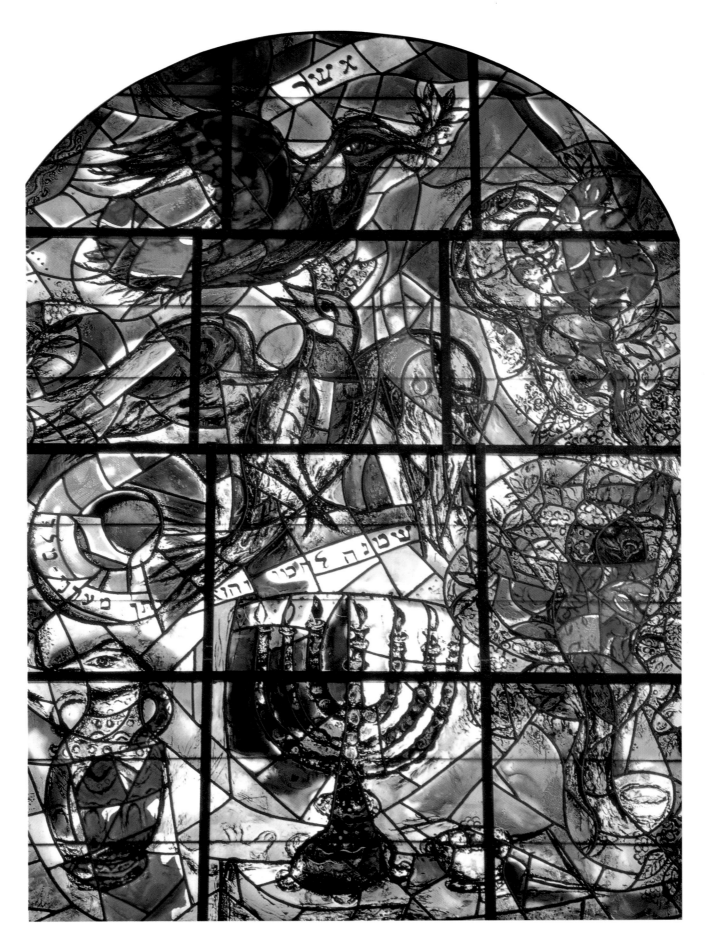

Above MARC CHAGALL AT WORK ON ONE OF HIS PAINTINGS.

Left A STAINED-GLASS WINDOW CREATED BY MARC CHAGALL FOR THE SYNAGOGUE AT THE HADASSAH-HEBREW UNIVERSITY MEDICAL CENTRE IN JERUSALEM, ISRAEL.

BEAUTY

Above left INSIDE OF THE TEMPLE ROOM OF THE HOUSE OF THE TEMPLE IN WASHINGTON, D.C.
Below left EVENING VIEW OF THE REAR OF THE HOUSE.
Above THE GOTHIC ROOM IN MASONIC HALL, HEADQUARTERS OF THE GRAND LODGE OF
FREE AND ACCEPTED MASONS OF THE STATE OF NEW YORK.

THE GRAND TEMPLE CEILING IN FREEMASONS' HALL, LONDON, ENGLAND

Masonic Philately

Because of the universality of their achievements, prominent Freemasons have been commemorated on postage stamps of most countries of the world. (The first stamps issued by the U.S. Post Office in 1847 bore the portraits of George Washington and Benjamin Franklin, both Masons.)

Left GUTZON BORGLUM, SCULPTOR OF MOUNT RUSHMORE MEMORIAL

Below GUTZON AND HIS ASSISTANT AT WORK IN HIS STUDIO ON A ONE-TWELTH ACTUAL SIZE MODEL.

Right MOUNT RUSHMORE HEADS OF, *left to right*, GEORGE WASHINGTON, THOMAS JEFFERSON, THEODORE ROOSEVELT, AND ABRAHAM LINCOLN. IT HAS THE LARGEST FIGURES OF ANY STATUE IN THE WORLD.

CREDULITY, SUPERSTITION, and FANATICISM.

A MEDLEY.

Believe not every Spirit, but try the Spirits whether they are of God, because many false Prophets are gone out into the World.
1 John C:4.V:1.

Designd and Engravd by Wm. Hogarth.   Publish'd as the Act directs March ye 15th 1762.

Above PORTRAIT BY JEAN BAPTISTE GREUZE OF DENIS DIDEROT (1713-1784),
THE PHILOSOPHER AND DIRECTOR OF *L'ENCYCLOPÉDIE*, ONE OF THE GREAT LITERARY MONUMENTS OF
THE EIGHTEENTH CENTURY, DIDEROT PRAISED THE WORK OF GREUZE AS 'MORALITY IN PAINT'.

Left CREDULITY, *SOPERSTITION AND FANATICISM*, WILLIAM HOGARTH'S ENGRAVING OF 1762,
SATIRIZED THE BIGOTRY AND INTOLERANCE OF RELIGIOUS FANATICS OF HIS DAY.

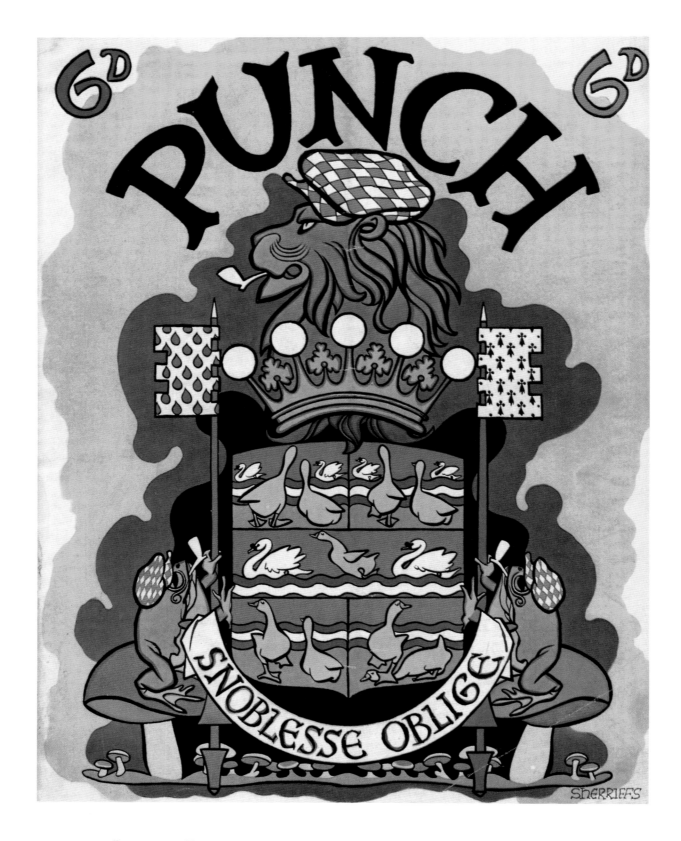

PUNCH, THE ENGLISH HUMOROUS MAGAZINE FOUNDED IN 1841 BY MARK LEMON,
WAS PUBLISHED FOR 150 YEARS WITHOUT A BREAK.

AMONG THE MOST FAMOUS CONTRIBUTORS TO PUNCH WAS ENGLISH CARICATURIST PHIL MAY (1863-1903)
WHO WAS BEST KNOWN FOR HIS HUMOROUS DRAWINGS OF LONDON COCKNEY STREET LIFE.

AN UNFINISHED PORTRAIT BY JOSEPH LANGE OF MOZART (1756-1791), IN THE YEAR OF HIS DEATH.

THE PERFORMING ARTS

BEAUTY and harmony, of course, can be conveyed through all the senses. Through the ear alone we can appreciate the pure pleasure of music, or unite it with our visual sense in the enjoyment of opera, ballet, and all the performance arts – ranging from theatre and cinema to great sporting spectacles. And, finally, we can experience the intellectual and imaginative pleasures of the written word. In all these expressions of beauty the Craft has played its part.

In the field of music many Freemasons have risen to prominence and have openly acknowledged the role played by the Craft in their lives. Thus Mozart, the supreme musical genius of the Enlightenment, saw Freemasonry as an essential part of his life in Vienna. Indeed, it may be argued that for the last – and most productive – seven years of his short career, the Craft was the pivot around which his social and cultural life revolved.

Mozart's work includes at least a dozen items composed for, or performed at, specific occasions – in addition to his last, and greatest, opera, the Masonically inspired *The Magic Flute* (whose libretto was the work of Mozart's fellow Mason,

Emmanuel Schikaneder. In 1785 Mozart encouraged his friend Joseph Haydn to enter the Craft, which he duly did; and in the last two hundred years Western music, in all its forms, has continued to be enriched by the work of Masonic musicians, both performers and composers.

The roll-call of Masonic musicians is a long one; from Thomas Arne, who arranged the British national anthem, and Rouget de Lisle, who composed *La Marseillaise*, to great jazzmen such as Count Basie, Duke Ellington and Lionel Hampton. It includes composers (Liszt, Meyerbeer, Sousa, Sibelius), creators of popular opera (Gilbert and Sullivan, Lionel Monckton), songwriters (Irving Berlin), and singers (Al Jolson, Nat 'King' Cole). All of them were proud to be members of the Craft.

The inspiration of Masonic principles can be seen alike in the exposure of hypocrisy that is a persistent theme of the Savoy Operas and in the patriotic themes that pervade the music of Sibelius – perhaps the greatest Masonic composer since Mozart. His music can with justice be said to have inspired a whole nation and, by its spiritual strength, to have aided materially the heroic defence of Finland against Stalin's armies during the 'Winter War' of 1939.

It is, perhaps, the result of a desire to bring joy to the world that has led Freemasons to be especially active in the field of popular entertainment – whether one thinks of Adolphe Sax, inventor of the saxophone, or impresarios like Carl Rosa, and Florenz Ziegfeld.

In many ways the Masonic ceremonies themselves can be seen as a form of theatre, and it should not surprise us to find that the Craft has had a natural appeal for actors down the ages. Fame on the stage is notoriously ephemeral, but among the many Masonic actors are several whose names will never be forgotten, including David Garrick, Edmund Kean, Sir Henry Irving, and Beerbohm Tree. In the earliest days of cinema many of its prominent figures entered the Craft. The diverse comic talents of Harold Lloyd, W. C. Fields, and Oliver Hardy – so different in style and form – have delighted millions; so, in different ways, have the acting skills of such actors as Douglas Fairbanks, Clark Gable, Ernest Borgnine, and John Wayne as well as cowboy stars Gene Autry and Roy Rogers. Among producers and directors may be mentioned Jack Warner, Louis Mayer, D. W. Griffith, and Cecil B. De Mille, as well as the virtual 'Czar' of Hollywood in its golden age, Will Hays, whose direction of the industry over a 25-year period kept it free from government interference.

In the related, but more intimate, field of circus and music-hall we find performers as varied as Gen. Tom Thumb (Charles S. Stratton), Grock the clown (Adrian Wettach), the conjurer Harry Houdini, the Scottish singer Sir Harry Lauder, Bert Williams, 'Buffalo Bill' Cody, and the Ringling Brothers.

William F. Cody was among the greatest of American showmen who based his famous 'Wild West Show' on his exploits as a Pony Express rider, scout, and Indian fighter – the re-creation of his epic fight with the Cheyenne chief, Yellow Hand, formed the centrepiece of his show. He also honoured the feats of his fellow frontiersman, and fellow Mason, 'Kit' Carson.

Cody's show was as much a sporting performance as anything else, and in sport Masons have also played their part. Jack Dempsey, Jack Johnson and, Sugar Ray Robinson were among the greatest boxing champions of the world; 'Captain' Matthew Webb, the first person to swim the English Channel; Sir Malcolm Campbell, who broke the land speed record; Sir Alec Rose, the lone round-the-world yachtsman; and 'Ty' Cobb, one the greatest baseball players of all time. The common factor linking these men so diverse in their personalities, backgrounds, and achievements, was their membership of the Craft and the inspiration it gave to each of them. The same inspiration and dedication can be seen also in the work of sporting administrators such as Avery Brundage, for twenty years, until 1972, the President of the International Olympic Committee.

Left THIS GROUP OF STATUES ON THE ARC DE TRIOMPHE IN PARIS, FRANCE, IMMORTALISES THE NATIONAL ANTHEM *LA MARSEILLAISE* COMPOSED BY ROUGET DE LISLE.

Above A PORTRAIT OF HAYDN, COMPOSER AND FRIEND OF MOZART.

Left DUKE ELLINGTON, COMPOSER, ARRANGER, AND STYLIST

Right COUNT BASIE, JAZZ MUSICIAN AND
BANDLEADER.

Left NAT 'KING' COLE, ONE OF THE
GREAT BALLAD SINGERS OF ALL TIME.

Right IRVIN BERLIN, COMPOSED MANY
FAMOUS AMERICAN POPULAR SONGS.
ONE OF HIS BEST-KNOWN SONGS IS
WHITE CHRISTMAS

SIBELIUS, SEEN HERE WITH HIS WIFE, WAS FINLAND'S GREATEST COMPOSER, AND WAS THE GREATEST MASONIC COMPOSER SINCE MOZART.

LOUIS ARMSTRONG, FIRST INTERNATIONALLY FAMOUS SOLOIST IN JAZZ

Above THE ZIEGFELD FOLLIES FEATURED BEAUTIFUL WOMEN IN EXTRAVAGANT COSTUMES PERFORMING IN FLAMBOYANT STAGE SETTINGS. MUCH OF THE MUSIC WAS COMPOSED BY IRVING BERLIN, AND JEROME KERN, (*left*) BOTH OF THEM MASONS.

Left Peter Sellers, in one of his best-known roles as the idealistic doctor in *'The Millionairess'* (1961) with Sophia Loren.

Right Oliver Hardy created, with his English partner Stan Laurel, one of the best loved screen comedy duos.

Right below The idiosyncratic American comedian W.C. Fields – seen here with Mae West in *'My Little Chickadee'* (1940) – appeared in some forty films between 1915 and 1944.

Right Harold Lloyd was one of the greatest of comic actors on the silent screen, making eighteen feature films and some hundreds of 'two reelers'.

Right CLARK GABLE, 'THE KING OF HOLLYWOOD' FOR MORE THAN TWO DECADES. HIS FILM *GONE WITH THE WIND* IS RANKED AS ONE OF THE GREATEST CLASSICS OF THE CINEMA.

Left DOUGLAS FAIRBANKS SR, THE ORIGINAL SWASHBUCKLING ACTOR OF THE SILENT SCREEN.

Below TOM MIX, THE REAL-LIFE U.S. MARSHAL WHO BECAME AN ACTOR AND STARRED IN OVER FOUR HUNDRED 'WESTERN' FILMS.

'BUFFALO BILL' CODY WAS A TRUE FRIEND OF THE AMERICAN INDIAN, MAINTAINING ALWAYS A MUTUAL TRUST AND RESPECT. WHEN HE WAS ASKED FOR HIS SOLUTION TO THE INDIAN 'PROBLEM,' HE REPLIED, 'NEVER MAKE A SINGLE PROMISE TO THE INDIANS THAT IS NOT FULFILLED.'

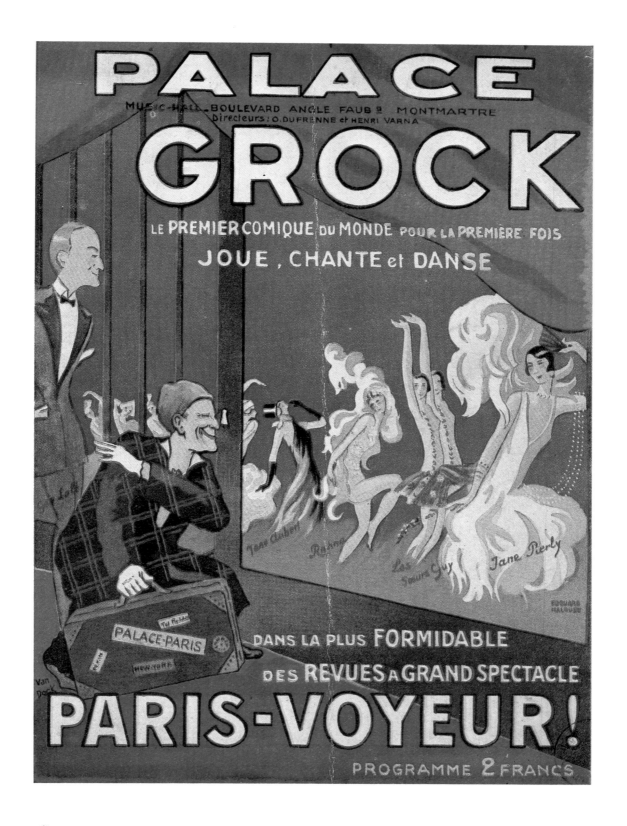

GROCK, MOSTLY REMEMBERED AS A CLOWN ON STAGE, WAS IN FACT A MAN OF MANY REMARKABLE
TALENTS. THIS PROGRAMME ANNOUNCES HIS ACTING, SINGING, AND DANCING ABILITIES

JOHN WAYNE MADE MORE THAN 175 MOVIES.
HE WON AN OSCAR IN 1969 FOR HIS STARRING ROLE IN THE FILM *TRUE GRIT*.

Top ERNEST BORGNINE WON AN OSCAR FOR HIS PERFORMANCE IN *MARTY* IN 1956.
Above BORGNINE IN HIS MEMORABLE ROLE AS 'DUTCH' IN *THE WILD BUNCH*.

Right A SCENE FROM THE FIRST BIBLICAL SPECTACULAR FILM BY CECIL B. DEMILLE, *THE TEN COMMANDMENTS*.

Below CECIL B. DEMILLE ON SET.

HARRY HOUDINI, THE MOST REMARKABLE AMERICAN STAGE MAGICIAN OF HIS DAY (SHOWN HERE ON THE COVER OF AN ISSUE OF THE MAGAZINE 'THE SPHINX'), WAS HELD IN HIGH ESTEEM BY HIS FELLOW PROFESSIONALS.

Below JACK DEMPSEY WAS ONE OF THE MOST POPULAR HEAVYWEIGHT BOXING CHAMPIONS OF ALL TIME.

Above TY COBB WAS ONE OF THE GREATEST PLAYERS IN BASEBALL HISTORY

Scientific and Literary Creativity

THE beauty of superlative performance – whether musical, theatrical or sporting – can be easily appreciated by all. But there are also more subtle beauties, no less exquisite, that arise out of human creativity, whether artistic, literary or scientific. This is, of course, also the province of Wisdom, and the dividing line between Beauty and Wisdom in the field of creativity is fine indeed. For the creative mind such a line may be impossible to draw, especially when as in the case of Goethe – it encompasses both art and science. But perhaps it may be said that in purely scientific creativity, beauty lies in the inspiration, and wisdom in its practical application.

Thus there is essential beauty, as well as wisdom, in the work of the truly great scientist who penetrates to the heart of the 'Hidden Mysteries of Nature and Science' to draw out the laws of nature that govern our physical existence. And because all true scientists recognize the working of a creative power in the universe, and as their work is directed towards the good of humanity, many of them since the days of Desaguliers and Benjamin Franklin have been glad to enter the Craft and to adopt its principles.

Some, as we have already seen, turned their inventive genius to the immediate task of benefiting their fellow men, through technological innovations. Others engaged themselves in pure research, gaining international recognition of their work. Among the earliest of these was Franklin himself, whose demonstration that lightning was atmospheric electricity led to his invention of the lightning rod. In recognition of this Franklin was elected a Fellow of the Royal Society and was received with adulation in France, where his celebrity greatly increased French support for the American cause.

One of Franklin's contemporaries, fellow American and Freemason Sir Benjamin Thompson, Count Rumford (1753-1814), also gained international recognition as a scientist. He was born in Massachusetts, but being a Loyalist he left America at the time of the Revolution and spent the rest of his life in England and Europe. In Germany, where he was the first to introduce the steam engine, Rumford continued his research into heat and became the first to prove that heat is a mode of motion. For this, and other discoveries, he too was elected to the Royal Society. Rumford was also active in helping to bring about social reform – especially the setting up of soup kitchens for the poor – and encouraged the development of science by establishing the Rumford Medal for the Royal Society and by endowing a Chair of Applied Science at Harvard.

But perhaps Rumford's most important achievement was the foundation, in 1799, of the Royal Institution, which ever since has provided an unrivalled means of encouraging enthusiasm for science in the young. In this far-sighted enterprise he was aided by another member of the Craft, Sir Joseph Banks, the botanist, founder of Kew Gardens at London, and President of the Royal Society.

The tradition of Masonic scientists continues, from Hans Christian Oersted, the father of electromagnetism, to the pioneering botanist Luther Burbank and a distinguished line of Nobel Prize winners. The first of these was Albert Michelson, the co-discoverer of the speed of light, who gained the prize for physics in 1907. Two years later Wilhelm Ostwald received the prize for his work in chemistry, though he is better known for his research in colour theory. Indeed, given the Masonic desire for 'Light' it is very appropriate that so many Masonic scientists – from Goethe to Ronald Norrish, who shared the Nobel Prize for chemistry in 1967 for his work on flash photolysis (by which chemical changes taking place in one-billionth of a second can be studied) – have been concerned with light and colour. Analogous to these researches into light is the discovery by another Masonic physicist, Sir Edward Appleton, of the layers of charged particles known as the ionosphere. In 1947 Appleton received the Nobel Prize in physics in recognition of his work.

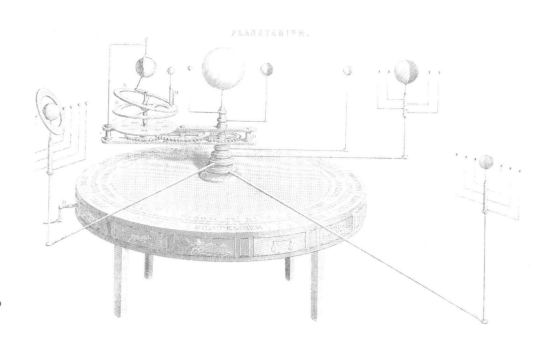

Right THE PLANETARIUM, IN ITS ORIGINAL FORM AS A MODEL OF THE SOLAR SYSTEM, WAS THE INVENTION OF JOHN THEOPHILUS DESAGULIERS – THE ANGLO-FRENCH SCIENTIST.

Below RICHARD HOE'S 'FAST 10-FEEDER AMERICAN PRINTING MACHINE', A DEVELOPMENT OF HIS EARLIER INVENTIONS – THE ROTARY PRESS AND THE WEB PRESS – THAT REVOLUTIONIZED NEWSPAPER PRINTING.

THE ROYAL BOTANICAL GARDENS

THE Royal Botanic Gardens at Kew, London England were laid out in 1759 and extended in 1772 when Sir Joseph Banks returned from his voyage around the world with Captain Cook and became the unofficial director. Under his guidance collections of plants from many parts of the world were carefully built up, and by the time of his death in 1820, the gardens had become internationally famous.

During the last hundred years the gardens have gone from strength to strength, and with its established library and laboratory for plant research, it is now recognised as one of the world's most beautiful botanical gardens, synonomous with all that is best in botanical research.

Left SIR JOSEPH BANKS (1743-1820).
Below left ONE OF THE BEST-LOVED FEATURES OF KEW GARDENS IS DECIMUS BURTON'S GREAT PALM HOUSE OF 1845, SEEN HERE IN A CONTEMPORARY PRINT.
Below THE NEW SIR JOSEPHS BANKS BUILDING HOUSES THE LIBRARY AND THE OUTSTANDING ECONOMIC BOTANY COLLECTION, TOGETHER WITH THE MAGNIFICENT PERMANENT EXHIBITIONS.

Above ROBERT BURNS – THE NATIONAL POET OF SCOTLAND, AND 'POET LAUREATE' OF FREEMASONRY.

Right SIR ARTHUR CONAN DOYLE (INSET) GAINED LASTING FAME BY HIS CREATION OF ONE OF THE BEST KNOWN AND BEST LOVED DETECTIVE CHARACTERS IN LITERATURE – THE IMMORTAL SHERLOCK HOLMES (PLAYED HERE BY ENGLISH ACTOR BASIL RATHBONE).

THAT most remarkable Mason, Sir Arthur Conan Doyle (1859-1930), bridged the worlds of science and art. Having qualified as a doctor, he gave up his medical career to devote himself to writing. The astonishing and immediate success of his most famous character, Sherlock Holmes, also assured the immortality of his creator. Holmes has become one of the most ubiquitous cultural icons of all time. It is Holmes's constant quest for truth, and superlative skill that raises him above the ranks of other fictional detectives: it is also his passionate struggles against injustice, and the entire absence of selfish motives in his work that distinguish him and define his greatness. All these qualities can be seen as Masonic principles in action, and it is no accident that when he is led by his creator to refer to the Craft his comments are always favourable.

Not all literary Freemasons bring the Craft into their work. The beauty of their writing, whether in poetry or prose, does not depend on its Masonic content; but a passion for truth – an essential Masonic quality – is often found, as in the paradoxical poetry of Robert Burns, which is at once parochial and universal:

What tho' on hamely fare we dine,
Wear hodden-grey, and a' that ;
Gie fools their silks, and knaves their wine,
A man is a man for a' that
For a'that, and a' that,
Their tinsel show and a' that
The honest man, tho' e' er sae poor,
Is King o' men for a' that.

The search for truth, too, lies at the heart of the children's classic, *Pinocchio*, the tale of a puppet who finally gains the humanity through the practice of selfless 'brotherly love'. Its author, Carlo Collodi (Carlo Lorenzini), was a follower of Mazzini, whose struggle for political freedom helped inspire the Belgian novelist and Freemason, Charles De Coster. In his masterpiece, *Les Aventures de Tyl Ulenspiegel*, De Coster skillfully utilized a folklore hero as a vehicle for an impassioned defence of liberty against political and religious despotism. Ulenspiegel's motto could ultimately be taken up by all Freemasons: 'I am not body but spirit'.

The same motto might also be given to another Masonic creation for children, in the sense that its essence continues to outlive its multitude of physical forms; as ubiquitous and enduring as any literary creation and without question an object of more love and affection for children than any book ever written: the Teddy Bear.

In November 1902 President Theodore Roosevelt was in the southern States to settle a boundary dispute between Mississippi and Louisiana. As a keen sportsman, he also spent ten days hunting, though he failed to find a single bear. But when, in desperation, his hosts set up a small tethered bear-cub as a target, Roosevelt refused to shoot it, saying: 'I draw the line. If I shot that little fellow I couldn't look my own boys in the face again.'

The incident might have passed unrecorded had it not been for the presence of Clifford Berryman, the foremost political cartoonist of the day, who preserved it for posterity with his cartoon 'Drawing the Line in Mississippi'. Immediately that pitiful little cartoon bear – and the toy bears that became instantly popular as a consequence – became known as the 'Teddy Bear'.

Roosevelt's chivalry was part of his character, but also mirrored the Masonic principles by which he lived. But Berryman was also a Mason, and it is a measure of his altruism that he refused to copyright his creation. His reward came in another way: 'I have made thousands of children happy,' he said, 'that is enough for me.' Beyond all question, the Teddy bear, beautiful or not, is a joy for ever.

Wisdom might epitomize the purpose of Freemasonry, and Strength might emphasize the sureness of its foundations; but more than these, Beauty – elusive as it is – represents the true Spirit of Masonry. Through its infinite variety of human expression it encapsulates in abstract form the essence of the great Masonic principles of Brotherly Love, Relief, and Truth, and in so doing presents to the world at large the true face of the Craft.

'WITH OUTSTRETCHED HAND AND SMILING FACE, HE GAVE THEM WELCOME TO THE PLACE'.
AN ILLUSTRATION BY R. K. CULVER FROM SEYMOUR EATON'S
MORE ABOUT THE ROOSEVELT BEARS (1907)

Above One of the best loved children's classic puppet stories, *Pinocchio*, was the creation of the Italian journalist and writer C. Collode. *Above right* From 1893 Alexander Horlick helped to make 'Horlicks Malted Milk' one of the most famous nutritional drinks in the world. *Right below* The orphaned deer Bambi immortalized by Walt Disney was the creation of Felix Salten.

ON THE WINGS OF WORDS, A FILM ABOUT THE CHILDHOOD LANGUAGE AND LEARNING PROGRAM OF THE SUPREME COUNCIL, SOUTHERN JURISDICTION, U.S.A., NARRATED BY ERNEST BORGNINE.

THE FIVE VIRTUES

'CONSIDER YOUR ORIGINS: YOU WERE NOT MADE THAT YOU MIGHT LIVE AS BRUTES,
BUT SO AS TO FOLLOW VIRTUE AND KNOWLEDGE'

DANTÉ

ALL too often Freemasonry is portrayed as something apart, an activity carried out in private by an elite group bonded together by motives of self-interest. But nothing could be further from the truth, for the Freemason is above all a citizen of the world whose duty (as the Craft ceremonies continually remind him) is not to the self, but to his family, his country and his fellow-men.

The true Freemason builds his life around the moral principles that lie at the heart of the Craft, and becomes in his every word and deed the epitome of Brotherly Love, Relief and Truth. He will thus respect the rights of others to hold beliefs and attitudes that differ radically from his own, for he knows that tolerance is an essential part of Brotherly Love.

But justice demands that tolerance does not become licence, and all Masons strive to uphold the law of the land as laid down by legitimate civil authority. Equally, Masons have always been faithful to the cause of freedom, and have resisted tyranny in all its forms political, social and religious – as the very antithesis of all that the Craft represents.

Vigilance in defence of personal and national freedom is not, of course, the sole preserve of the Freemason, but he more than most is constantly reminded, by his work in the lodge, of the great principles that underpin that freedom. And in striving to lead a life based upon those principles he seeks to turn his achievements in every field of human endeavour to the good of all his fellow men.

All those Masons whose life's work has improved the lot of Man – whether by bringing freedom from oppression, by liberating the human spirit, by ennobling human thought, by the example of personal prowess, of by enhancing the cultural life of society have been inspired by the same principles and in the same way. Through his initiation into the Craft each one of them has gained an insight into the meaning of life that has enabled him to go out and give practical expression to the principles of Masonry, and by the exercise of his unique talents to enrich the lives of many.

Nor is this stimulus confined to the Great and the Good. Every Mason, however mundane his outer life may seem to be, is inspired in a like manner, and by making the practice of Tolerance, Charity, Integrity and Fidelity an essential part of his everyday dealings with others, his achievements will help to build a better future for human-kind.

1
TOLERANCE

'I GREET YOU AS A BROTHER.'

TOLERANCE is one of Freemasonry's watchwords. In a world where the natural sense of the brotherhood of man is often submerged beneath the oppressive weight of sectarian intolerance, or of the kind of strident nationalism that is the reverse of true patriotism, it is heartening to remind ourselves that no distinction of colour, religion or social class is of any consequence to the true Freemason in his dealings with his brothers. Just as all men are equal in the sight of God, so they are to Masonic eyes. The true Freemason will always be innocent of either racial or religious hatred.

From the earliest days of the speculative Craft, political and religious disputes among Masons have been forbidden and partisan attitudes, to either politics or religion, discouraged; for, in the words of the ancient Charges, these 'never yet conduc'd to the welfare of the Lodges, nor ever will'. Because of these wise rulings, men of every shade of political and religious opinion can meet as friends, their differences of belief set aside, and work together to advance their own moral well-being and to promote the public good.

These virtues of tolerance and brotherly love are, and always have been, universally present within Freemasonry. As well as motivating that charity for which the Craft is justly renowned, their practice in time of war has saved countless lives, restored liberty, and, where liberation has proved impossible, has eased the lot of prisoners-of-war.

Some of the earliest and most famous instances of

such compassion at work were the actions, during the American Revolution, of the Mohawk Indian chief, Joseph Brant, who had been made a Mason in London in 1776 – the first native American to enter the Craft. A remarkable man by any standards, Brant distinguished himself in the wars against the French. He became principal chief of the Six Nations in 1771 at the age of 29 and went on to command the Indian troops under the Crown during the Revolutionary War. But while his Mohawks were feared for their savagery, Brant himself saved the lives of Col. John McKinstry and at least three other American officers.

Perhaps even more significant than Brant's intervention over the Mohawk captives was his work to bring Christianity to the Six Nations, and thus help integrate the Indian tribes into a wider American culture. Fragmentary selections of biblical texts in Mohawk were available in the early 1770s, but Brant set about producing full translations of his own. His version of St. Mark's Gospel appeared in 1787 – a pioneering step towards the creation of a Mohawk New Testament.

As well as following in Brant's literary footsteps, other Indians also copied his example and became members of the Craft. As Freemasonry expanded with the growth of European trade and colonization, indigenous peoples elsewhere embraced the Craft, which began to take up men of every race and religion. This universal aspect of Masonry was celebrated in Kipling's poem 'The Mother-Lodge', when the narrator recalls that:

JOSEPH BRANT, CHIEF OF THE MOHAWKS, 1742-1807

We'd Bola Nath, Accountant,
An' Saul the Aden Jew,
An' Din Mohammed, draughtsman,
Of the Survey Office too;
There was Babu Chuckerbutty,
An' Amir Singh the Sikh,
An Castro from the fittin' sheds,
The Roman Catholick !

It must be admitted, however, that the harmony eulogized by Kipling did not prevail in the early days of the Craft in India. The first Indian Mason, Omrat-ul-Omrah, Nabob ot the Carnatic, was initiated in 1775, but few others followed him (and those that did were Muslims) until the middle of the nineteenth century, when religious and social barriers began to break down. There was also a tendency among some Masons to view the Craft as a purely Christian institution, despite the Charge to 'let a man's religion or mode of worship be what it may'. As we have already seen, this mistaken notion was finally, and decisively, rejected by the Duke of Sussex, who, after the Union of the Grand Lodges in 1813, determined to make Freemasonry a genuinely universal brotherhood. In spite of this, it yet required a better understanding of the true nature of Hinduism before European Masons fully accepted that Hindus could quite properly admit to a belief in God, and thus join Muslims, Parsees, Sikhs and Jains within the bounds of Freemasonry. But that understanding eventually came, and today they meet with Hindus in perfect harmony.

The non-sectarian nature of the Craft should have been obvious by its admission of Jews from at least 1721 (when practising Jews are known to have been initiated at London in the Goose and Gridiron Lodge, one of the four lodges that constituted the Premier Grand Lodge) and by the regular election of Jews as Grand Lodge officers from 1760 onwards. In general, the Craft has been free from the virus of anti-semitism, and when such sentiments have appeared (as they did occasionally in Germany during the nineteenth century) they have usually been as a result of the misguided belief that Freemasonry was the exclusive preserve of professing Christians. But such attitudes were not typical of Freemasonry as a whole and, as with the admission of Hindus, racial and religious intolerance has long been eradicated from the Craft worldwide.

Indeed, it has been the opponents of Freemasonry who have consistently demonstrated intolerance, whether motivated by political or religious antagonism, or both: from the bigotry of the Inquisition and of the fanatics who fuelled the fantasies of the William Morgan affair (see p. 43) to the current crop of baseless but widely circulated attacks on the Craft in England, Continental Europe and North America. Wisely, Freemasons have responded to such attacks with reason and restraint. But the need for vigilance in the defence of human liberty is as great within the Craft as in society in general: when assaults upon freedom of conscience have been ignored, evil has been allowed to triumph.

During the era of dictatorships, both fascist and communist, the fate of the Craft epitomized that of nations. Ancient lies claiming that Freemasonry was a satanic organization were resurrected, and the Craft was also linked to spurious scenarios involving Jewish conspiracies to overthrow Christian civilization. As a result, Freemasons – like Jews, gypsies, patriots and democrats – became victims of the organized state terror of both Hitler and Stalin. Yet even in the Nazi concentration camps the ideals of the Craft were sustained through unspeakable horrors. Masonic meetings were regularly held in Buchenwald; imprisoned Belgian Masons formed their own underground lodge, while at the concentration camp of Compiègne Masonic meetings were held weekly at the same time as the Catholic mass.

Such unity in adversity underlined the fact that there was no essential hostility between Catholicism and Freemasonry, and in the decades following World War Two – particularly during the 1960s – there was a gradual relaxation of the Catholic's opposition to Freemasonry resulting from a growing recognition that the anti-clericalism of the irregular Grand Orient of France had no place among true Freemasons. More recently, however, the Church has attempted to reimpose its ban on membership of the Craft, even though regular Freemasonry has never opposed the admission of Roman Catholics and despite the fact that in the past and even today there are many active Masons all over the world who remain loyal members or their Church.

The Craft's religious tolerance in peace has been complemented by practical acts of compassion towards political enemies in wartime – shown especially in the long tradition of Masonic support for prisoners-of-war. Ever since the Seven Years War (1756-63), when French prisoners formed lodges during captivity in England, friendship and charity have been extended to brethren who are, technically, 'enemies'. During the Napoleonic Wars, for example, the plight of both British prisoners in Europe and French prisoners in Britain was made easier through the aid provided by all three of the British Grand Lodges. A similar charity was also found during the American Civil War. At Johnson's Island on Sandusky Bay in Lake Erie, Confederate prisoners were able to hold regular Masonic meetings, often attended by their Yankee guards, and generous care was extended to Masonic prisoners. This expression of brotherly love was also reciprocated. When prisoners attended Masonic burials they gave their word not to attempt to escape – and that trust was never broken.

In the twentieth century British Freemasons interned in 1914 at Ruhleben were sustained by mutual support while the Grand Orient of the Netherlands (a neutral country during World War One (1914-1918) actively helped interned servicemen to found lodges of their own. Other examples include prisoners-of-war at Yozgat in Turkey, who not only founded their own lodge (named Cappadocia) in 1918 but also raised money for the benefit of starving Armenian women and children in the district.

During World War Two (1939-1945) Freemasonry faced far greater opposition from both the Nazis and the Japanese. Even so, Masonic activities were maintained in at least fourteen prisoner-of-war camps in Germany – with lodges being established in three of them, including Oflag 79 at Brunswick, where the membership included Masons from England, Scotland, Australia, Canada, India, New Zealand, South Africa and the United States. In the Far East the situation was far more diffcult; but despite almost intolerable stress, and in the face of the deliberate torture of known Freemasons, Masonic fellowship was sustained in such places as the notorious Changi camp and jail in Singapore, Sumatra, Hong Kong, and Shanghai.

Since the end of World War Two, Japan has joined the long list of nations in which the Craft has flourished. The Grand Lodge of Japan was founded in 1957 and Freemasonry has now become an accepted part of Japanese life, as it has in Germany and in the new democracies of Eastern Europe.

In Africa, Freemasonry has been established for some two centuries, and it is only in the militantly Muslim states of North Africa that its practice is prohibited. In former British and French colonies, brethren of different races and religions have been meeting in harmony for many years, and have included in their number such well-known figures as the Algerian Abd-el-Kader (1807-1883); Felix Eboué, the first black Governor-General of a French colony, who rallied Congo to the Free French Forces in 1940; and two Presidents of the Republic of Gabon, Leon M'Ba and Omar Bongo. Sadly, by an accident of history most black Freemasons are members of the presently unrecognized Prince Hall Lodges (see p. 42), and thus cannot meet their black and white brothers Masonically, although they maintain friendly and harmonious relations in the world at large.

ROGER NATHAN-MURAT – A SOLDIER OF TOLERANCE

IN June 1940 France capitulated to the Nazi invaders, and the country was divided into an occupied zone and a nominally independent area under a puppet government. In both areas anti-Jewish and anti-Masonic laws were enacted almost immediately: 'secret societies' were outlawed and no Mason could be a civil servant or hold any official position. Lists of known Masons were published (although they were both incomplete and inaccurate), and every citizen had to register with the police and to declare their religion. In this way Jewish families were identified: to be both a Mason and a Jew was to face persecution and death.

And so it was with Roger Nathan. He came from a prominent Jewish family at Marseilles, where he won renown in the 1930s as a keen sportsman and champion swimmer. He was also an enthusiatic Mason; initiated in 1934 in Lodge No. 104 EGALITE-JUSTICE, under the Grand Lodge of France, he later became Orator (Chaplain) of the Lodge. At the outbreak of war Nathan was drafted to the Middle East, but as a true patriot he refused to abandon his country, and despite a real risk to his own and his wife's lives (their family was arrested and all of them were finally killed at Auschwitz), they returned to France and joined the Resistance.

In December 1940 Nathan, now nicknamed 'Murat', founded LIBERTE, as Resistance network in south-eastern France. This group issued its own clandestine newspaper – the first to appear in Vichy France – which was both printed and distributed by Freemasons. The network was also active in manufactureing forged identity cards (Nathan assumed the identity of a dead friend, Raymond Noury) and in sabotaging the Nazi war machine. Inevitably the risk of arrest and imprisonment grew. With the help of a Masonic friend, who was a policeman, Nathan-Murat narrowly avoided arrest at Marseilles in 1942, and left for Lyon. Here he was eventually arrested by the Gestapo, although not until his wife and daughter had succeeded in escaping to Switzerland.

He was sent first to the camp at Compiègne, where he met Gaston Weill, Worshipful Master of the Grand Lodge of France, and took part in Masonic meetings each Sunday. But in January 1944, Nathan-Murat, Weill and other Masons were moved to the Concentration Camp of Buchenwald. Even here, in the face of enormous hardship, they contrived to continue their Masonic meetings – ignoring the differences between the various Constitutions – and, despite the absence of the symbolic Working Tools, they even managed to initiate a fellow prisoner (who later became a medical practitioner at Marseilles). From Buchenwald the prisoners were moved to extermination camps, but Nathan-Murat, who was sent to Ohrdruff S3, managed to survive – partly because his basic physical strength enabled him to resist the terrible privations of the Camp, and in equal part through the inner strength he gained from his deep commitment to Masonic principles.

As the Allied armies closed in on Buchenwald, in April 1945, Nathan-Murat escaped from the camp with two fellow prisoners, and met the advancing American troops – handing over as prisoners of war five German soldiers they had captured in the course of their escape.

After the war, Nathan-Murat returned to his native city and resumed his Masonic activities, becoming especially active in the relief of those brethren who had suffered in captivity, and who had lost homes, jobs and families during the occupation. Thus in peace as in war, Roger Nathan-Murat demonstrated, as he continues to do, the true humanity of the Freemason.

ROGER NATHAN-MURAT, ONE THE LAST SURVIVORS OF THE 5,000 FRENCH FREEMASONS IMPRISONED IN CONCENTRATION CAMPS DURING THE NAZI OCCUPATION OF 1940-1945. STILL ACTIVE AT 85 YEARS OF AGE, NATHAN-MURAT ENJOYS BOTH HIS FAMILY AND HIS WORK AS A FREEMASON.

2
ACHIEVEMENTS

'I WILL SUPPORT YOU IN ALL YOUR LAUDABLE UNDERTAKINGS.'

THIS Masonic commitment to human improvement finds many practical expressions – not only in charitable works, but also in educational projects and enterprises that aim to further mutual understanding between men and between nations, such as Rotary International.

Education, in its broadest sense, has always been actively supported by the Craft – as we have seen in a previous chapter. Besides founding schools and colleges, Freemasonry has continuously played a leading role in endowing and maintaining libraries, both in England and the United States.

The Public Library movement effectively began in England with the work of the great reformer Henry Brougham (1778-1868) – one of the few public men of his day to give freely of his time and energy in the advancement of universal adult education. In 1825 he founded the Society for the Diffusion of Useful Knowledge, which was dedicated to publishing literature for working men. He was also instrumental in setting up Mechanics' Institutes containing libraries. In time this movement led to the establishment of free public libraries throughout the country, with the greatest impetus coming in the 1890s from the generosity of newspaperman and Freemason John Passmore Edwards, who was personally responsible for founding and endowing 25 libraries.

Today, free libraries are a cultural norm in the West, but many of them are maintained directly through the efforts of Craft members. They include all the great Masonic libraries of the world – which are mostly open to all, whether Masons or not, and which by no means confine themselves to holdings of Masonic material. The Scottish Rite Library at Waco in Texas, for instance, contains a magnificent collection of Texicana, while among the many thousands of volumes of the Scottish Rite Southern Jurisdiction at the House of the Temple in Washington, is the finest collection of books in the world devoted to the life and work of Robert Burns. Of more specific Masonic interest, though equally significant for American history, is the Albert Pike collection also housed at the House of the Temple. Other vast collections are maintained by the Grand Lodges of New York, Pennsylvania and Massachusetts as well as the extensive Scottish Rite Library at Lexington, Massachusetts.

Similar collections enrich the holdings of many Masonic libraries in Europe and America, and as the importance of Freemasonry in the social and cultural history of the last three hundred years is being increasingly acknowledged by historians, the research potential of such libraries is being widely recognized.

As well as libraries and institutes of higher education, Freemasons around the world have been active in sponsoring scholarships, schools and colleges. One of the first Masonic schools was the Royal Cumberland Free Masons' School, founded in 1788 (when female education was rare) for the daughters of Freemasons. It continues to thrive today as the Rickmansworth Masonic School, an independent school for girls, open to all, but still supported by the English Craft.

JOHN W. TEETS

ACHIEVEMENTS IN EVERY FIELD OF HUMAN ENDEAVOUR THAT BENEFIT ALL MANKIND ARE NOT ONLY REWARDING FEATURES OF MASONRY. EQUALLY IMPORTANT ARE THE EFFECTS OF MASONIC IDEALS ON THE LIVES OF INDIVIDUAL MASONS. THE TENETS OF THE CRAFT CAN AND DO INSPIRE AND ENRICH A MASON'S WHOLE LIFE — AS IS PERFECTLY EXEMPLIFIED IN THE CAREER OF JOHN TEETS, CHAIRMAN AND PRESIDENT OF AMERICA'S DIAL CORPORATION.

IN 1963 JOHN TEETS SUFFERED BOTH TRAGIC FAMILY LOSS, AND THE DESTRUCTION OF HIS THRIVING RETAIL BUSINESS. 'SUDDENLY,' HE RECALLED, 'AT AGE 30, I WAS A WIDOWED FATHER WITH TWO YOUNG DAUGHTERS AND OUT OF BUSINESS. IF EVER, HERE WAS A TRUE TEST FOR ONE'S EMOTIONAL AND SPIRITUAL FOUNDATIONS.' BUT HIS DEEP MASONIC COMMITMENT HELPED HIM TO REBUILD HIS LIFE. 'I'VE COME TO BELIEVE,' HE SAID, 'THAT MY PERSONAL TRIALS, ALONG WITH THE SENSE OF INDIVIDUAL RESPONSIBILITY INHERITED FROM MY FATHER AND TEMPERED THROUGH FREE-MASONRY, GAVE ME INNER STRENGTHS THAT PREPARED ME TO LEAD ONE OF AMERICA'S FORTUNE 500 FIRMS.'

The Duke of Edinburgh's Award Scheme was the brainchild of Prince Philip, Duke of Edinburgh (a member of the Craft for many years), who established the scheme in 1956 to foster the values of self-reliance and personal integrity in the young and to encourage their attainment. The Award Scheme is designed to challenge young people to realize their full potential and to guide those individuals and organizations engaged in the physical, social and moral development of the young. This programme 'encourages young people between the ages of 14 and 25 to serve others, to explore and adventure, to expand their interests and enjoy some form of sport or recreation'. The scheme also aims to integrate the whole community by giving older people the opportunity to share their talents, skills and enthusiasm with the young – all of which constitutes a fine example of Masonic ideals in action.

Specifically Masonic organizations for young people are largely confined to the United States. Prominent among them is the Order of DeMolay, founded in 1919 by Frank S. Land, a young Mason from Kansas City, 'to meet the need for a better organized, more elevating social life for boys nearing the age of manhood'. The name of the Order is taken from Jacques de Molay, the last Grand Master of the Templars (see p. 15), who exemplified stoic fortitude and heroic integrity in his martyrdom. Membership of the Order is confined to young men, many of which are sons of Masons, and each of its Chapters is Masonically sponsored. It is not in any sense a means of recruiting future Masons, although many DeMolay members do go on to enter the Craft. DeMolay has also branched out to Canada, Brazil and Germany.

Parallel to the Order of DeMolay are the Order of Rainbow for Girls and the International Order of Job's Daughters, both organized in a similar way. These are also associated with the most widespread of Masonically inspired Orders for women: Order of the Eastern Star.

The larger question of women in Freemasonry is an extremely vexed one. Concerning Eastern Star there is no dispute. Although not a Masonic Order, it has a ritual based (on the lives of five biblical heroines), this has no

Masonic content. The Order was founded in 1850 by the prolific Masonic author Rob Morris for the allegorical teaching of moral precepts to the female relatives of Masons (although no Eastern Star Chapter can work without two male officers, Worthy Patron and Worthy Treasurer, both of whom must be Master Masons). By 1876 the General Grand Chapter, which governs the Eastern Star throughout most of North America, was established, and today the Order is widespread throughout the United States, Canada and Australia. Because of its charitable and social work in the local community, it has become a valuable part of both urban and rural society in those countries.

Other Orders for women associated with male Freemasonry – such as the Daughters of the Nile, which is linked to the Shriners – also place public benevolence at the head of their objectives; but none of them is truly Masonic in character, although all of them have their roots in what is known as 'Adoptive Masonry'.

From the foundation of the Premier Grand Lodge in 1717, women have never been admitted to regular Freemasonry, in accordance with the third of the *Old Charges* reproduced in Anderson's *Constitutions* of 1723 which states categorically that

> 'The Persons admitted Members of
> a *Lodge* must be good and true
> Men, free born, and of mature and
> discreet Age, no Bond Men, no
> Women, no immoral or scandalous
> Men, but of good Report.'

But while this rule was rigidly applied in the British Isles, in Europe matters took a different course. By the 1740s a number of curious Orders had sprung up in France and Germany that admitted both men and women and professed to confer quasi-Masonic initiation. Initially, these Orders were rather superficial in character, but a more serious moralizing element gradually emerged, and by 1774 the Grand Orient of France had formally adopted the 'Rite d' Adoption'.

These pseudo-Masonic Adoptive Lodges were designed to provide an analogue of Masonry for women. However, they were not exclusively female. Each one was attached to a regular Masonic lodge, whose Master also presided over the female lodge, assisted by a female President, or Mistress. His two Wardens also worked in tandem with two female officers: an Inspectress and a Depositrix. The Adoptive Lodges worked four degrees (of Apprentice, Companion, Mistress and Perfect Mistress) through rituals whose symbolism derived from biblical legends: from the Fall and the Flood to the Tower of Babel, Jacob's Ladder, and the wanderings of the Israe-

lites in the wilderness. During the French Revolution the 'Adoptive Rite' closed down along with the rest of Freemasonry, but the Empress Josephine (Napoleon I's first wife), who was an active member, helped to revive it, and it survived in France for some of the nineteenth century. In 1866 Albert Pike published a revised translation of the rituals,in the United States but the Rite was not taken up as the demand for a female Order had been fully met by the Order of the Eastern Star.

Because of this, the irregular Masonic Orders that do admit women have never established themselves in America, although they thrive in England and Europe – albeit unrecognized by any Grand Lodge. Almost without exception, modern female Freemasonry derives from the actions of a French lodge, Les Libres Penseurs (The Free-Thinkers) that had broken away from the Grande Loge Symbolique Ecossaise. Three years later its members initiated, passed and raised a prominent feminist, Maria Desraismes (1828-1894) – more a gesture of support for women's rights than with any intention of founding a new Order. However, in 1893, Mlle Desraismes joined forces with a Parisian physician, Dr Georges Martin (1844-1916), and initiated sixteen women as the first step towards establishing a 'mixed' lodge for both men and women.

The first Parisian lodge, called *Le Droit Humain*, was soon followed by others, while the name of the Order was eventually changed to 'Universal Co-Masonry'. When in 1902 Mixed Masonry arrived in England, the first lodge took the name of 'Human Duty'. The members were drawn largely from the Theosophical Society, and from the beginning it was under the control of Annie Besant, President of that Society. As the Theosophical Society went through various crises, so Co-Masonry divided – in 1908, 1913 and 1925. Of the various breakaway Orders, only one (the Order of Ancient, Free and Accepted Masonry) remains open to both sexes. The others as rigidly exclude men as the regular Grand Lodges exclude women. Most of them follow the example of the Order of Women Freemasons in working standard Masonic ceremonies, and they also have full programmes of charitable work. Even so, they are unrecognized by every regular Grand Lodge.

Such women's Orders are now well established in Britain and in many European countries and draw their membership largely from Masonic wives and daughters. They have made little progress in America, perhaps because of the close relationship between regular Masonry and the Eastern Star. This also applies to Prince Hall Masonry, which has its own highly successful equivalents of the Eastern Star.

It is most unlikely that the regular Grand Lodges will alter their stance and recognize any of the women's Orders – at least in the foreseeable future

ROYAL NATIONAL LIFEBOAT INSTITUTION

SINCE the foundation of the Royal National Lifeboat Institution in 1824, its volunteer lifeboat crews have saved nearly 130,000 lives.

There are lifeboat stations at 209 locations around the coastline of the United Kingdom and the Republic of Ireland, with 268 lifeboats at these stations and over 100 in the Institution's relief fleet. The overall running cost each year of the RNLI is approximately £48 million. The *Duchess of Kent*, funded by the United Grand Lodge of England and named in April 1982 by The Duchess of Kent, is one of the latest relief lifeboats.

The *Duchess of Kent* is a 52-foot long, all-weather lifeboat, capable of 18 knots, able to operate up to 50 miles offshore, and cost upwards of £650,000 to build. Since entering service she has seen action at stations as far afield as Scotland, Wales, Cornwall, the Isle of Man and the Isles of Scilly, saving 45 lives.

Freemasons have shown support for the RNLI over many years with 11 lifeboats funded by them since the Institution was founded. The Grand Master of the United Grand Lodge of England, The Duke of Kent, is also President of the RNLI.

LIEUT. COMMANDER B. MILES, RD FNI RNR
RNLI DIRECTOR

THE RNLI LIFEBOAT *DUCHESS OF KENT*.

3
CHARITY

'THE POSTURE OF MY DAILY SUPPLICATIONS SHALL REMIND ME OF YOUR WANTS.'

IF those outside the Craft are unsure of what Freemasonry actually is, they usually have a much clearer picture of what it does. Its charitable work is well known, and while the needs of brethren in distress have always been a priority for the Craft, Masonic charity has never been restricted to Freemasons alone. Indeed, the vital importance of charity is emphasized to the newly-made Mason during the course of his initiation, and although the first Charity Committee, set up in 1724, was designed for the 'Relief of distress'd Brethren', Masons were giving generously to wider charities from the first days of the speculative Craft.

When General Oglethorpe (1696-1785) began his settlement of the Colony of Georgia in 1732 he received the active support of the Craft, whose members raised a collection 'to send distressed persons to Georgia where they may be comfortably provided for'. Thus began a long and noble tradition of relief, wherever and whenever the need arose, with no distinction made between Mason and non-Mason.

The duty of Masons to 'give in the cause of charity' was stressed by William Preston in his *Illustrations of Masonry* (1772) He laid it down as axiomatic that

'To relieve the distressed is a duty incumbent on all men, but particularly on Freemasons, who are linked together by an indissoluble chain of sincere affection. To soothe the unhappy, to sympathize with their misfortunes, to compassionate their miseries, and to restore their troubled minds, is the great aim we have in view'

Since Preston's time, Masonic charities have been active in the relief of human suffering in almost every country of the world.

Today some hundreds of millions of dollars are distributed every year by Masonic bodies worldwide: for medical care and research; for social and cultural welfare; and for the relief of the victims of both natural and man-made disasters. There is, of course, considerable support for Masonic hospitals in many countries, for institutional homes for elderly Masons and their dependents, and for Masonic widows and orphans. But this is not at the expense of non-Masonic charities and it is perhaps too little recognized that the relief of Masons by fellow Masons removes a considerable financial burden from the community at large and releases funds to meet the needs of others.

Natural disasters strike without warning, and for over 150 years the Craft has responded swiftly to meet the immediate and subsequent needs of victims. From the Hanover floods of 1825 to the Armenian earthquake of 1988 and the hurricane that swept through the West Indies in 1939, Masonic charities have been among the first to offer financial aid.

The needs of other victims, whether of war, man-made disasters, or of poverty, have also been met. Freemasons throughout the world sent help after the Chicago fire of 1871, as they did to aid those whose children died in a school which was overwhelmed by the avalanche of a 'slag heap' (coal waste tip) in Aberfan, Wales, in 1966 and the victims of the poison gas cloud at Bhopal in 1985. Two years later the United Grand Lodge of England gave £250,000 for the charity Shelter's Crisis at Christmas appeal, and other projects are regularly supported on the same scale by the Craft in the United States and around the world. In wartime the sufferings of combatants and civilians alike have been relieved – air-raid victims in World War Two, support for the South Atlantic Fund following the Falklands conflict in 1983, and, in 1991, contributions to the Desert Outreach Program for troops involved in the Gulf War.

Extending its charity to causes other than the relief of suffering, the Craft also remembers its operative roots. In recent years the United Grand Lodge of England has supported the restoration funds of every cathedral in England and Wales. On a more practical level, it has given grants to assist the stonemasons' yards at the cathedrals of Canterbury, Gloucester and Winchester, and also at Selby Abbey.

Important though all these causes are, the most visible and significant Masonic charities are those devoted to medical and community care. Of the £18 million disbursed by Masonic charities in England in 1990, and the $525 million raised by the American Masonic philanthropy in the same year, the largest proportions were allotted to aiding the sick and the elderly through a remarkably diverse range of research and support programmes.

In Britain, three-quarters of a million pounds has been given since 1984 to hospices for the terminally ill. In 1967 a trust fund of more than £600,000 was established to support research projects by the Royal College of Surgeons – matched over the past decade by aid given to other university and hospital based medical research: at Nottingham, Liverpool, the University of Wales and at the Royal Maudsley and Great Ormond Street Children's Hospitals.

Even more extensive is the support given to hospitals and research programmes in the United States. The first Hospital for Crippled Children was founded by the Shriners (the Ancient and Arabic Order Nobles of the Mystic Shrine) at Shreveport, Louisiana, in 1922. There are now nineteen such hospitals, open to any child needing their help, together with three Burns Institutes also funded by the Shriners. In addition, most Grand Lodges in America provide for orphans, while at Baton Rouge, Louisiana, the Prince Hall Masons have set up Camp Chicota as a summer camp for underprivileged children.

The many Masonic bodies in the United States also support a wide range of research programmes. These include the Kansas Masonic Oncology Center, the auditory research funded by the Royal Arch Research Assistance Program, and the work on arteriosclerosis of the Cryptic Masons Medical Research Foundation.

Charitable provision for the elderly has always been an important Masonic concern, reflected in the homes for the aged Masons in Britain, Australia, the United States, and in many other parts of the world. Mental health has also been a priority. For more than fifty years the Scottish Rite, Northern Jurisdiction, has maintained an extensive research programme into the causes of schizophrenia, while the practical problems of mental disorders have been addressed by grants approved for the 275th anniversary of the Grand Lodge of England. These total more than £2 million to be used for community homes and work projects for the mentally handicapped. Significant support is given to research into drug abuse, both by the United Grand Lodge of England and by the Conference of Grand Masters in America, which established the National Masonic Foundation for the Prevention of Drug and Alcohol Abuse.

The wider aspect of Masonic charity is demonstrated in the life's work of the English industrialist William Lever (1851-1925), first Viscount Leverhulme and founder of the famous soap company, Lever Brothers Ltd. His career as a public benefactor began in 1888 with the building of the model village of Port Sunlight on the Mersey estuary. He followed this by setting up a profit-sharing plan for his workers – one of the first of its kind. The Lady Lever Art Gallery was his gift to the public in memory of his wife, and the Leverhulme Trust grants very substantial sums each year to both academic research and educational projects.

In America there are many Masonic educational programmes, from the Scottish Rite Abbott Scholarships for undergraduates and the Illinois Scottish Rite Nursing Scholarships, to the national museums and libraries at Lexington, Massachusetts, Washington D. C., and elsewhere. For instance, the George Washington Masonic National Memorial is, through its collections, a valuable resource for students of American history. Among the most important of such foundations is the Scottish Rite Masonic Museum of Our National Heritage at Lexington, which contains changing exhibitions on many aspects of American and Masonic history, as well as a magnificent library, and runs a wide range of stimulating educational programmes. It is also developing one of the most extensive collections of Masonic artifacts in the world.

CHARITY IN ACTION

AND NOW ABIDETH FAITH, HOPE, CHARITY, THESE THREE; BUT THE GREATEST OF THESE IS CHARITY.

1 CORINTHIAN 13:13

PHILANTHROPY is an inseparable part of the Masonic Fraternity in every land, but it is most prevalent in America.

Whether they are local luncheon clubs with a few dozen participants or national groups with memberships in the hundreds of thousands, an almost universal feature of Masonic organizations is their sense of duty in supporting charity. A study of American Masonic charities is essentially a study of the evolving needs of western society. When food and shelter were both immediate and regular concerns, Masons responded with firewood and the fruits of the harvests. When care of widows, the aged and orphans were worries, Masons erected retirement homes and orphanages. When education was needed, Masons built schools and established scholarships, and, as these requirements became improved upon, Masons turned their philanthropy to more specific needs within the community: to crippled children; cancer patients; burn victims; those whose speech, language, sight or hearing is impaired; the homeless; the mentally ill; and many others.

Why Masons are so concerned with Philanthropy can be explained by considering what Masonry *is*. While there is no agreement on the actual origins of Freemasonry, the nature of the Order that has grown from the first Grand Lodge of 1717 is clear: it has become a worldwide Fraternity teaching universal principles of Brotherly Love, Relief and Truth. In a broader sense it teaches and promotes borderless brotherhood, moral improvement, mutual support, religious toleration, civic betterment, freedom of thought, and universal charity. The latter, as if echoing the words of St. Paul to the Corinthians 'the greatest of these is charity' is undeniably the most noticeable activity. Certainly, Freemasonry without Charity could never be.

Even when Masonry was a much smaller organization than it is today, its charitable work was both public and generous – as with the 'distressed brethren', who in 1733 were helped to start a new life in the newly founded Colony of Georgia. Similarly, the Masons of the newly founded Grand Lodge of Rhode Island put Charity to the fore in 1791 when one of the first actions was, 'a collection made of £11.9.4 Law Money, to be invested into Wood & distributed to the Poor of this Town the ensuing Winter.'

The growth of Masonic Philanthropy has been governed by the gradual development of the Craft. Masonry is not static, and just as society changed its structures as it evolved, so did Freemasonry. Throughout the eighteenth century, and for much of the nineteenth, its evolution in America followed the pattern set in Britain and in Europe, although the final shape of American Masonry was determined much more by the very different political and cultural conditions of a new, pioneering country.

The westward expansion of America was accompanied by the growth and maturation of its institutions. The social organizations that served the first colonists were not well suited for towns, and those appropriate for small farming villages did not meet the needs of industrial cities. The Masonic Fraternity was subject to the same social pressures for change, but it followed a unique evolutionary path. Rather than change its basic organizational unit, the local Lodge, Freemasonry spun off a constellation of collateral organizations, each meeting different needs that arose at different times.

After expanding in organizational and symbolic complexity, American Masons sought to bring women within their sphere. This aim was achieved with the foundation of the Eastern Star in 1855, the Amaranth in 1873, and the White Shrine of Jerusalem in 1894. Both men and women belong to these groups, and to many others of a similar nature – all of which are associated with the Masonic Order by fraternal and family ties. A similar tie binds Masonically sponsored youth groups to the Craft. They were founded much later than the Orders for women – Order of DeMolay in 1919, Job's Daughters in 1920, and the Order of Rainbow for Girls in 1922 – but they are no less important.

The next growth in Masonry was away from the seriousness and rather solemn morality of the Lodge and towards more lively enjoyment of social pleasures. With this approach in view, Orders were founded such as the Shrine (1872), the Grotto (1889), and the Tall Cedars of Lebanon (1902). They are, in a sense, peculiarly American, for such bodies have become much more deeply entrenched in America than in Britain and Europe – where philosophically speculative Orders rather than socially active ones have become the norm.

This brief outline of the gradual evolution into the complex structure that is Freemasonry today indicates the organizational adaptations Masonry has made to continue to meet the needs of its members. It serves to show also how the development of Masonic Philanthropy has been determined by positive changes within Masonry as much as by the changing needs of society – for every Masonic body has its own part to play in the charitable work of the Craft.

Individual cases of distress are often still met by a local Lodge or Chapter, but the evolution of American society and the geographic dispersal of Lodge members have made such needs less common and less easily recognized. To meet these changes, American Masons have turned to more organized forms of relief. A Masonic Home for widows and orphans was founded, in Kentucky, as early as 1866. This action was followed by the Grand Lodge of North Carolina in 1872 and since then by most other states: thirty-nine state Grand Lodges maintain homes for aged Masons and their widows and eleven still have orphanages, but the need for the latter has diminished over the years.

The existence of such homes has been used to argue that Masonic Philanthropy is directed principally towards its own members, but this charge cannot stand up. According to a 1991 by Brent Morris over half of the money given by American Masons for charity benefits society at large: today, more than 58% of Masonic Philanthropy is directly spent on the American public. The list seems endless, but includes clinics devoted to childhood speech, language and learning disorders; the Museum of Our National Heritage in Lexington, Massachusetts; the Peace Chapel and Auditorium at the International Peace Garden on the U.S.-Canadian border in North Dakota; a foundation paying for sight-saving eye surgery; dental care for the handicapped; and medical research in cancer, schizophrenia, arteriosclerosis, aphasia, and muscular dystrophy.

This partial list only scratches the surface, but the point it makes is deep: Freemasons are dedicated to the relief of mankind, and their works are a living testimony to their ideals.

Masonic Philanthropy is well organized and the vast sums raised for charitable purposes are carefully distributed, but nationally organized activities are only a part of the story: each local Lodge and Chapter has its own philanthropic work which is carried on without fuss and is rarely known to the public. Nor is such philanthropy limited to financial giving. For example, the Masonic Service Association quietly oversees a Hospital Visitation Program with a goal that every V. A. Hospital in the United States has a Masonic volunteer working with patients. How can a financial value be placed on the more than 500,000 hours a year spent on this work?

The most visible part of Masonic Philanthropy, however, is the provision of hospitals, health care and medical research. This work involves huge budgets, as with the Shrine which expended almost $325 million during 1991, and it is easy to point with pride to the Shriners' Hospitals and to the sublime simplicity that motivates the philanthropy behind them: if a patient can be helped, the services are provided – cost is never a consideration. Basic medical research, on the other hand, has a lower public profile, for it is not as photogenic as large hospitals and smiling patients, but its results are every bit as important and they illustrate perfectly the universality of Masonic giving, for they benefit all mankind.

It is a relatively simple matter to calculate the extent of Masonic Philanthropy in the areas of health, education and institutional support of the elderly, and to set out significant contributions to non-Masonic national charities; for example, special support is given to the Muscular Dystrophy Association by the Tall Cedars of Lebanon, and to the American Diabetes Association by the Amaranth Diabetes Foundation. But it is far more difficult to calculate the increased community activity by individual Masons who have been inspired to greater service by the teachings of their Craft.

This inspiration is, perhaps, best seen in the Masonic contributions to the International Peace Garden straddling the border between North Dakota and Manitoba. Every year an International Music Camp is held in the Garden, with performances often presented in a unique 2,000 seat auditorium built in 1981 by the Masons of North Dakota and Manitoba and shaped like the Masonic Square and Compasses. This Masonic Memorial Auditorium was a gift from American and Canadian Masonry to the Peace Garden, just as the Peace Chapel, built in 1970, was provided and is maintained by the General Grand Chapter of the Order of the Eastern Star as a gift to all people who seek world peace through divine guidance.

In these and in many other ways, Masonic Philanthropy, which is truly international in scope, reaches every walk of human life. It is maintained and applied by Masons in every country where Freemasonry is established. For Masons everywhere it can justly be said that Charity *is* their Way of Life.

S. BRENT MORRIS

TEXAS SCOTTISH RITE
HOSPITAL FOR CHILDREN

FOUNDED by Scottish Rite Masons in 1921 to provide medical help for children with polio, the Hospital now treats children from almost every county in Texas for a variety of orthopedic, neurological and learning disabilities. The Hospital accepts infants and children up through 18 years of age without regard to race, creed, color or financial eligibility, as there is no charge for treatment at the Hospital. Funding comes solely from private donations. The Hospital receives no government funding or dues paid by any Masonic order. Texas Scottish Rite Hospital for Children operates as a non-profit corporation under a charter granted by the State of Texas. Volunteers contribute a large part of the Hospital's effort, with 650 individuals donating 88,894 hours this past fiscal Year. The governing board is composed of elected representatives from the nine Scottish Rite Valleys in Texas.

Located on fourteen acres of wooded property, convenient to downtown Dallas, the present facility was completed in late 1977. Currently, more than 10,000 children are seen as active patients. Most are treated on an outpatient basis. No family has ever been charged for treatment. In fiscal '90, the Hospital scheduled 34,141 outpatient visits and performed 3,731 surgical procedures.

Texas Scottish Rite Hospital for Children is recognized nationwide for its research programs, particularly in spinal instrumentation for the correction of scoliosis and in gait analysis. Students come from across America to receive professional training and leading universities are affiliated with the educational programs which ultimately benefit the children seen as patients.

'...THAT AMONG THESE ARE LIFE, LIBERTY, AND THE PURSUIT OF HAPPINESS.'

Left TEXAS SCOTTISH RITE HOSPITAL FOR CHILDREN, LOCATED ON FOURTEEN ACRES OF WOODED LAND.

THE MASONIC SERVICE ASSOCIATION

FREEMASONRY was formed in the United States as a series of independent Grand Lodges. The normal geographic location would be the State within which the Grand Lodge was located, so the United States does not have a National Grand Lodge, but rather fifty-one independent and sovereign Grand Lodges.

During World War One the Grand Lodges of the United States, who had a significant number of Masons in the Armed Forces, wished to do something to help the servicemen. The Federal Government had said they would not deal with separate Grand Lodges. but if the Freemasons were able to provide one organization with whom the Federal Government could work, they would be delighted to have Masonic assistance. So, with that experience still in mind, in 1919 the Grand Lodges of the United States met and formed what is now called the Masonic Service Association of the United States. Originally, we were formed as a vehicle for providing aid to servicemen. However, it soon became evident that there were many other things that an organization such as ours could do.

Specifically, in January 1923, we started publishing a monthly pamphlet entitled 'The Short Talk Bulletin'. and since that time over 800 of them have appeared in print. They cover a wide variety of Masonic subjects and have proven to be very popular. MSA also produces digests, statistical information, informational lists, and acts as a clearing house for Masonic information.

We also have a Disaster Relief Program, whereby if a natural catastrophe occurs within a Grand Jurisdiction, an appeal for assistance can be put out to aid that Jurisdiction. For example, in recent years we have had appeals on behalf of the Grand Lodges of South Carolina and Puerto Rico for damage caused by Hurricane Hugo, by the Grand Lodge of California for earthquake damage, and by the Grand Lodge of the Philippines who have had numerous natural catastrophes within the last three years. An appeal is made to each Grand Lodge, who then make the request known within their Grand Jurisdiction. We receive funds from individuals, Lodges, Appendant Masonic Bodies, and Grand Lodges. All of these monies are accumulated, and then forwarded to the Grand Lodge on whose behalf the appeal was made. No charges are made for administrative costs, and 100% of the monies collected are sent to the Grand Lodge involved.

The third aspect of the MSA is our Hospital Visitation Program. This is an outgrowth of the original reason we were founded, that is to provide aid to military personnel. During World War Two, this was in the form of Masonic Service Centers, which functioned much like a USO. After World War Two there was no further need for this type of service as it was being provided by others, so the MSA concentrated on a system of Hospital Visitors within each Veterans' Administration Hospital around the United States. We also have Visitors in State Veterans' Homes, and in two cases in public hospitals. Those are the Medical Center Hospital of Vermont, and the Mayo Clinic in Rochester, Minnesota.

These visitors – who are actually Volunteers contributing countless hours of service – do many things for the patients that they are unable to do for themselves. For instance, they may read to them, write letters for them, do personal errands, take them to Chapel Service, or take them to other parts of the Hospital where testing or treatment is to be provided.

In short, our role is to be humanitarian, and to remember that many veterans have no family or friends, and they are all alone. We provide a personal touch to help spark a smile or a ray of hope in a segment of the population that all too often is forgotten.

The Masonic Service Association now provides services to Grand Lodges, not only in the United States, but in Canada and other parts of the world as well. It has been said of us that when it appears that nobody cares, the MSA is there to show that 'Masons care and will always be there!'

RICHARD E. FLETCHER,
PAST GRAND MASTER OF MASONS IN VERMONT,
EXECUTIVE SECRETARY, MSA.

4
INTEGRITY

'YOUR LAWFUL SECRETS WHEN ENTRUSTED TO ME AS SUCH I WILL KEEP AS MY OWN.'

IN common with all responses to deep spiritual experiences, every Freemason has his own personal, inner response to his initiation. These feelings cannot be communicated to another, for there is no language by which they can be fully expressed. Although Freemasonry is not a religion it is concerned with instilling spiritual values in its members, and it does demand that they believe in God.

Thus it is not surprising that the symbolic ritual dramas that are at the heart of the initiation ceremonies should lead the initiate to look within himself and reflect upon the inner meaning of what he is undergoing. Indeed, he is enjoined to do exactly this in the ceremony of almost every Masonic degree. And while the personal, psycho-spiritual experience of each mason must remain, by its nature, utterly private, it is possible to attempt to explain something of the spiritual essence of the Craft to those outside it.

This is not an easy task, for nothing has been more subject to individual, idiosyncratic interpretation than the spiritual meaning of Masonry, and no Masonic jurisdiction has ever issued an 'official' statement about how that meaning should be perceived, other than in the most general terms. Further, as has been emphasized earlier, the overt content of the ceremonies of Craft Masonry is moral rather than religious, although in many of the additional degrees great stress is placed on the spiritual aspects of symbolism contained in their rituals, and it is, of course, open to every candidate to be spiritually enriched by the ceremonies in which he takes part.

There is also a tendency for both masons and non-Masons to invest certain Masonic writings with the authority of Holy Writ, and to base their understanding of the psycho-spiritual content of ceremonies and symbols alike on statements that are no more than personal opinions. Thus the Lectures of the Ancient and Accepted Scottish Rite (Southern Jurisdiction) that are printed in Albert Pike's work *Morals and Dogmas* contain 'teachings' that are in no sense binding on members of the Rite, as their author makes quite clear. Indeed, Pike states categorically that they are 'not dogmatic in the odious sense of that term' and that 'Every one is entirely free to reject and dissent from whatsoever herein may seem to him to be untrue or unsound'. If this wise counsel were more generally followed there would be fewer dogmatic pronouncements made about the Craft, and a great deal of confusion would be avoided.

None the less, certain structural elements are common to almost all Masonic degrees:

1. The candidate undergoes careful preparation; he is symbolically attired and spends a certain time in preparing himself both psychologically and spiritually for the experience that lies before him.

2. He undertakes a symbolic journey, or pilgrimage, towards a spiritual goal that is gradually revealed to him. The journey often involves symbolic trials and dangers as a test of his courage, integrity, and commitment.

3. Some of the journey takes place in literal or figurative darkness, culminating in a dramatic restoration of light, thus emphasizing his change of inner state from the darkness of moral or spiritual ignorance to the light of knowledge and understanding.

4. He is symbolically clothed with robes or regalia – and the symbolism explained to him – to seal this change of state.

5. The essentials of the degree or grade in question are communicated through the senses – usually by sight, touch, and hearing, but often by stimulating also the senses of smell and taste.

There are many other ritual elements that may be incorporated into the ceremony, but those listed above are invariably present. Specific features, of course, will vary from degree to degree; symbolic colours are often important, as are lights of a specific kind and number, and music appropriate to the theme of the degree. In general, the symbolism of any given ceremony is eclectic and its historical or mythic connection with the legend around which the ritual is built is not always obvious, but it is always relevant to the inner state the candidate seeks to attain.

Many of the legends in masonic degrees are biblical in origin and often relate to the building or rebuilding of King Solomon's Temple, as an allegory of the creation of a new, just, and more tolerant society. The moral regeneration of the individual is represented in the Third or Master Mason's, degree by the associated legend of the heroic death and figurative raising of Hiram, the builder of the Temple. It is important to stress that this is not a legend of resurrection from death to new life, for that concept has no place in the workings of the Craft, although it does introduce the idea of Loss and the hope of ultimate Restoration.

In addition to the Craft Degrees, there are many others that set out these themes by way of other legends. When the Master Mason is exalted in the Royal Arch, he completes the work of the Third Degree by engaging in a symbolic rebuilding of the Temple, while many of the other degrees and grades 'beyond the Craft' are specifically designed to reinforce a belief in immortality; to lead the candidate towards true self-understanding; to set him on the path to moral regeneration; or to awaken in him an awareness of the way in which he can restore that which was spiritually lost within him. But all these grades and degrees can ultimately do no more than provide signposts to set the dedicated Freemason on the path of his own spiritual quest. How he proceeds on that journey within is a matter for himself alone, for Freemasonry is not a prescriptive religion, but a way of life.

5
FIDELITY

'I WILL SUPPORT YOUR CHARACTER IN YOUR ABSENCE AS IN YOUR PRESENCE.'

ABOVE all, Freemasonry seeks to instill in its members the virtues of tolerance, honesty, charity, and loyalty. The invisible tie that binds all Freemasons together is their shared experience of the Craft's ethos – not only the work within the Lodge, but also in the wider world. Wherever he goes, and whatever his position in life, the Mason knows that when he meets a brother he is meeting someone who will offer him friendship, moral support, and whatever practical help he may need.

The private aspect of Freemasonry is the visible modes of recognition for each degree and the language of the rituals which are considered as confidential information. They are used within the lodge in the course of its ceremonial working, and nowhere else. The notion that particular signs and handshakes are used to identify fellow Masons in the world outside is simply false. What is important to a Mason is the virtue of fidelity, and he will always respect the confidences of fellow Masons – as he will also respect those of his non-Masonic friends.

A Freemason, above all else is a good citizen as stated in the *Old Charges* and Anderson's *Constitutions:*

'A Mason is a peaceful Subject to the Civil Powers, wherever he resides or works, and is never to be concerned in Plots and Conspiracies against the Peace and Welfare of the Nation.'

In a turbulent world that is undergoing radical and unpredictable political and social change, and when nations, religions and political systems are in a state of constant flux, humanity needs more than ever the fixed point and unchanging values that the Craft can offer. For almost three centuries it has promoted tolerance, justice, and peace, and will continue to do so through changing fortunes.

In its outward structures, the Craft itself is also changing. There are also, undeniably, divisions within the Craft that separate brother from brother. Some of these rifts cannot, by their very nature, be bridged; no true Freemason can ever accept the regularity of Masonic bodies that reject the need for a belief in God. But divisions that arise out of past racial or cultural intolerance can be healed, and in some areas the healing process has already begun. With the consolidation of democracy around the world, the Craft can and will grow, reviving where it withered under hostile dictatorships and taking root in countries where it was previously unknown. But this will take time and will require all the Craft's energy and goodwill.

When a Master Mason's Lodge is opened the Senior Warden announces that they will work with the Centre, 'That being a point from which a Master Mason cannot err'. Just as the Master Mason works with the Centre within the Lodge, so in their daily lives Freemasons everywhere work at the centre of society for the good of all mankind.

Freemasonry is in every sense a society based on trust: a trust that is emphasized at the close of every Masonic meeting when all present unite to express their mutual fidelity.

CHAPTER V

GALLERY OF 275 FAMOUS MASONS

'YOU ARE AS OLD AS YOUR DOUBTS AND AS YOUNG AS YOUR ENTHUSIASM.'

GENERAL DOUGLAS MACARTHUR

IT is an invidious task to have to select a relatively small sample from the many thousands of prominent men who have also been Masons, for how can one make comparisons between achievements in widely differing fields of human endeavour? That is a virtually impossible task, but what can be done is to illustrate the diversity of talents that have been found within the Masonic Fraternity, through outlines of the lives of representative men whose achievements were inspired by the principles and ideals of Freemasonry. The two hundred and seventy-five men whose names appear here – one for each year since the founding of the first Grand Lodge – have been chosen on this basis, and while many of them may not be familiar as Masons, virtually all of them are well known for their work in the world at large.

Among them are kings and presidents; admirals, generals, politicians and diplomats; men of the sciences and of the fine and applied arts; poets and novelists; explorers and adventurers; industrialists and inventors; musicians and actors; showmen and sportsmen; men from every walk of life who have one thing in common– all of them were Masons, and proud to acknowledge their membership of the Craft.

What is most noticeable about the selection, however, is that almost every name is drawn from the past. Where are the famous Masons of the present? Without question, there are many Masons today of similar stature, but, unlike their brethren of the past, few of them are willing to proclaim the fact. There is no single reason why this should be so, but it is in part a reflection of the changed perception of Freemasonry in a modern and politically complex society.

The Craft is no longer seen as a part of the essential social fabric of every community, and this is especially so in larger cities and in academic centres, where the majority of famous brethren live and work. And if society sees Masonry as an institution on its margin, so, alas, will many Masons. This, in turn, may lead them to forget the pride they felt in their membership of the Craft at the time of their initiation. But if they do lose that sense of pride they will be the less able to stand up to the unjustified attacks made upon the Craft by misguided religious zealots.

All men, whether Masons or not, can gain inspiration from the brief lives that follow, and it is to be hoped that when they are reminded of all that their forebears have done, those brethren of today who have achieved success and honour in their chosen fields, will be inspired to have the courage of their convictions and proclaim to all the world that they are members of an ancient and honourable Brotherhood – and proud of it.

ABD-EL-KADER (1808-1883)

The most successful military leader of the resistance to French conquest of Algeria from 1832 to 1847. After five years as a prisoner-of-war in France he settled in the Middle East. In 1860, at great personal risk, he saved many Christians from massacre by rioting Muslims at Damascus. His bravery was widely praised and in France he was awarded the Legion d'Honneur. Subsequently he was invited to join Lodge Henri IV, at Paris, but his initiation into the Craft finally took place in 1864 at Lodge Les Pyramides, at Alexandria in Egypt. After 1877, when the Grand Orient removed the basic landmark of belief in God, Abd-el-Kader gave up his Masonic activities.

ALDRIN, COL. EDWIN 'BUZZ' (BORN 1930)

American astronaut. In 1969 he co-piloted the landing on the moon of the Apollo 11 lunar module, the mission which took the first men to the Moon. The photograph of Aldrin on the Moon has become the classic image of Man's conquest of space. He was initiated in Montclair Lodge No. 144, New Jersey.

ALLENDE, SALVADOR (1908-1973)

A medical doctor who was elected President of Chile in 1970. Three years later he was killed during the military coup that overthrew the democratically elected government. Allende had been a Mason since 1935 when he was initiated in Lodge Progresso No. 4 at Valparaiso.

ANDRADE, EDWARD NEVILLE DA COSTA (1887-1971)

English physicist and Fellow of the Royal Society. In 1923 he published the influential work *The Structure of the Atom.* He was initiated in Savage Club Lodge No. 2190, in 1922.

APPLETON, SIR EDWARD VICTOR (1892-1965)

English physicist, whose experiments on the nature of the upper atmosphere led to the discovery of layers of charged particles now known as the Ionosphere. He was awarded the Nobel Prize for physics in 1947. Appleton was a member of Isaac Newton Lodge, at Cambridge, from the time of his initiation in 1922.

ARMSTRONG, LOUIS (1900-1971)

Black American jazz musician. Equally at home as a trumpet player (from which came his nickname of 'Satchmo') and as a singer, he was acknowledged as the world's leading jazz musician of his day. He was a member of Lodge Montgomery No. 18, Prince Hall Affiliation, New York.

ARNE, THOMAS AUGUSTINE (1710-1778)

English composer. He was most successful as a composer of operas and music for the theatre, but he is best known for the tune *Rule Britannia* and for his setting of the *British National Anthem.*

ASHBEE, CHARLES ROBERT (1863-1942)

English architect and craftsman. He was highly influential in the Arts and Crafts Movement of the 1880s and 90s, buying William Morris's presses and printing fine books at his Essex House Press. In 1888 he set up the Guild of Handicraft in London, which he later moved to Chipping Campden in Gloucestershire. He was initiated in Isaac Newton Lodge No. 859, Cambridge, in 1900.

ASHMOLE, ELIAS (1617-1692)

English antiquarian. His remarkable collection of curiosities was presented to Oxford University in 1677 and has become the Ashmolean Museum. Ashmole's diary records the first known Masonic initiation, when he and Colonel Henry Mainwaring were made Freemasons at Warrington, Lancashire, in 1646.

ASTOR, JOHN JACOB (1763-1848)

German-American financier. He made a huge fortune in the fur trade, which he invested in property in New York. His enormous wealth and the dynasty he founded are equally famous. He was a member of Holland Lodge No. 8, New York City.

ATATURK, MUSTAPHA KEMAL (1881-1938)

Leader of the 'Young Turks' and the father of the modern Turkish state, he was President from 1923 until his death. Ataturk was a member of an Italian Lodge, Macedonia Resorta e Veritas.

AUSTIN, STEPHEN (1793-1836)

American pioneer, known as 'The Father of Texas'. He took over his father's colonizing project and from 1822 was the leader of the first colony of U.S. settlers in Texas. The city of Austin is named after him. He was initiated in Louisiana Lodge No. 109, at Sainte Genevieve, Missouri, in 1815.

AUTRY, GENE (BORN 1907)

Radio, television and screen actor. He was raised in Catoosa Lodge No. 185, Catoosa, Oklahoma.

BAILY, EDWARD HODGES (1788-1867)

English sculptor. His most famous commission was for the Statue of Nelson that stands on Nelson's Column in Trafalgar Square, London, England. He was a member of Jerusalem Lodge No. 233.

BALL, WALTER WILLIAM ROUSE (1850-1925)

English mathematician, known equally for his historical works and his popular books on mathematical puzzles. Initiated in Isaac Newton Lodge No. 859 in 1885.

BANKS, SIR JOSEPH (1743-1820)

English botanist and President of the Royal Society from 1778 until his death. He sailed around the world with Captain Cook in the *Endeavour* from 1768 to 1771, and with the botanical collections and the knowledge that he brought back he turned the Royal Botanic Gardens at Kew into the world-famous institution that it is today.

BARTOLOZZI, FRANCESCO (1727-1815)

Anglo-Italian artist and engraver. He produced exquisite engravings after old masters' drawings and paintings, and engraved the frontispiece to the 1784 edition of *The Book of Constitutions*. He was a member of the Lodge of Nine Muses No. 235, London.

BASIE, WILLIAM 'COUNT' (1904-1984)

Black American jazz pianist and band-leader, who became one of the longest-surviving pioneers of the big-band era. Basie was a member of both a Craft Lodge and Shriner Temple under the Prince Hall Affiliation at New York.

BATEMAN, HENRY MAYO (1887-1970)

English artist and cartoonist, born in New South Wales, Australia. His first exhibition of caricatures was held in 1911, and this led to the long series of cartoons *The man who ...* – for which he is best remembered. He was initiated in The Pen and Brush Lodge, in 1913.

BEARD, DANIEL CARTER (1850-1941)

In 1905, two years before the Boy Scout movement was started in England, he had organized the *Boy Pioneers, Sons of Daniel Boone*. He then organized the Boy Scout movement in America. He was raised in Mariner's Lodge No. 67, New York City.

BELZONI, GIOVANNI BAPTISTA (1778-1823)

Italian traveller, engineer and showman who settled in London in 1803. He carried out excavations in Egypt from 1815, publishing the results in 1820, and was effectively the founder of Egyptology. He was said to be a member of Lodge of Emulation, London.

BENES, EDUARD (1884-1946)

President of Czechoslovakia elected in 1935, he resigned in 1938 on German occupation of Sudeten. President of the Czechoslovakian government in exile with headquarters in London, he was re-elected president in 1946. Initiated in Lodge Ian Amos Komensky, No. 1, at Prague about 1924-1925, passed and raised in Lodge Pravda Vitezi about 1927-1928.

BERLIN, IRVING (1888-1989)

American composer and songwriter whose best-selling songs ranged from 'Alexander's Rag-Time Band' in 1911 to 'White Christmas' in 1942. He is equally well-known for his theatre and film music, which included *Top Hat, Follow the Fleet*, and *Annie Get Your Gun*. The entire royalties on several of his songs he gave to a charity for deprived youth. He was made a Mason in Munn Lodge No.190, New York City, and was active in both the Scottish Rite and as a Shriner.

BLUCHER, GEBHARDT LEBRECHT (1742- 1819)

German soldier. He was Field Marshal General of Prussia and during the Napoleonic Wars he drove the Emperor out of Prussia, crossed the Rhine, and in 1814, entered Paris. In 1815 he aided Wellington in the Battle of Waterloo. He was an active Mason and a member of Lodge Archimedes, at Altenburg.

BOLIVAR, SIMON (1783-1830)

Born in what is now Venezuela, Bolivar led the struggle which lasted for twenty years – to liberate the countries that now make up much of the eastern seaboard of South America from Spanish rule. He is justly known as the 'George Washington' of South America. Bolivar joined the Craft at Cadiz, Spain, and in 1807 entered the Scottish Rite and the Knights Templars at Paris. In 1824 he founded the Lodge Order and Liberty No. 2, in Peru.

BONGO, OMAR [ALBERT BERNARD](BORN 1936)

President of the Republic of Gabon since 1957, he became Grand Master of the Grand Lodge of Gabon in 1983.

BORGLUM, GUTZON (JOHN GUTZON DE LA MOTHE BORGLUM) (1871-1941)

Sculptor and painter, best known for the gigantic Mt. Rushmore national memorial in the Black Hills of South Dakota, officially started in 1927, the fourth head being unveiled in 1939, but the work was completed by his son. An active Mason, he was raised in Howard Lodge No. 35, New York City, on June 10, 1904, and served as its Master in 1910-11. He received his Scottish Rite degrees in 1907. There is a colossal marble head of Lincoln by Borglum in the rotunda of the Capitol of Washington.

His son, **LINCOLN BORGLUM**, was raised in Battle River Lodge No. 92, at Hermosa, South Dakota.

BORGNINE, ERNEST [ERMES BORGNINO] (BORN 1915)

American stage and film actor. Best known for 'tough guy' roles, but he won his Oscar for playing the shy butcher in *Marty* (1955). He is a member of Abingdon Lodge No. 48, Abingdon, Virginia.

BOSWELL, JAMES (1740-1795)

Scottish writer whose biography of Dr. Johnson (1791) is one of the great classics of English literature. He was raised in Canongate Kilwinning Lodge, at Edinburgh in 1759.

BRADLEY, OMAR NELSON (1893-1981)

American General. In World War Two he commanded the 2nd Corps in the Tunisian and Sicilian Campaigns of 1943; the 1st US Army in Normandy; and then, in 1944-45, the 12th Army Group as it drove through to Germany to meet the Russians advancing from the East. From 1949 to 1953 General Bradley was chairman, US Joint Chiefs of Staff. He was raised in West Point Lodge No. 877, Highland Falls, New York State.

BROUGHAM, HENRY PETER, BARON BROUGHAM AND VAUX (1778-1868)

Scottish statesman and reformer. He was a founder of the influential *Edinburgh Review* (1802) but took up the law and entered politics. He encouraged popular education, forming the Society for the Diffusion of Useful Knowledge in 1825 and helped in founding London University in 1828. He worked for the abolition of slavery, and by his famous speech ensured the passage of the Reform Bill in 1831. He was initiated in Fortrose Lodge, Stornoway, Scotland, in 1799.

BRUCE, JAMES (1730-1794)

Scottish explorer. In 1770 he discovered the source of the Blue Nile in Abyssinia. He was a member of Canongate Kilwinning Lodge, at Edinburgh.

BURBANK, LUTHER (1849-1926)

American horticulturist and naturalist. His experiments on plants led to the blight-resistant Burbank potato, and over a fifty-year period his experimental farm at Santa Rosa, California, produced a remarkable range of new fruit and flower varieties. He was raised in Santa Rosa Lodge No. 57, in 1921.

BURKE, EDMUND (1729-1797)

Anglo-Irish statesman and orator. The foremost spokesman for the Whigs, Burke championed John Wilkes; argued for peace with the American colonies; and passionately denounced the use of Indians in the war. He was an advocate for Catholic Emancipation and he wrote a powerful condemnation of the French Revolution. He was a member of Jerusalem Lodge No. 44.

BURNS, ROBERT (1759-1796)

Scottish poet who has been adopted as the national poet of his native land. Burns was an enthusiastic Mason from the day of his initiation into St. David's Lodge No. 174, at Tarbolton, on July 4,1781. He subsequently joined a number of other lodges, including Canongate-Kilwinning No. 2, at Edinburgh, where he was made Poet Laureate of the lodge in 1787. His poems include some which are specifically Masonic, while the words of *Auld Lang Syne* have become an essential part of New Year celebrations around the world.

BYRD, RICHARD E. (1888-1957)

American admiral, pioneer aviator and polar explorer. In 1926 he became the first man to fly over the North Pole, and between 1928 and 1956 he led five expeditions to the South Pole. With his pilot, Bernt Balchen, he dropped Masonic flags at each pole. He was initiated in Federal Lodge No. 1, at Washington, D.C., and in 1935 established First Antarctic Lodge No. 777, under the Grand Lodge of New Zealand.

CAGLIOSTRO, COUNT [BALSAMO, GIUSEPPE] (1743-1795)

Charismatic Italian adventurer and occultist. He came to London in 1776 and received the three Craft degrees in Loge L'Espérance No. 283. During the following year he set up his pseudo-Masonic Egyptian Rite, which had parallel Adoptive Lodges (presided over by his wife, Serafina), and worked a most exotic ritual. They subsequently travelled about Europe peddling the Egyptian Rite and other occult activities to the gullible nobility. Eventually, in 1789, Cagliostro was arrested by the Inquisition at Rome, where he died in prison.

CAMPBELL, SIR MALCOLM (1885-1948)

English motor-racing star. He established many world land speed records at Salt Lake City and at Daytona Beach where he was also a member of various Masonic bodies.

CANTOR, EDDIE (EDWARD ISRAEL ISKOWITZ) (1892-1964)

American singer and entertainer. He starred in many stage and screen musicals, and among the songs he made popular were *If you knew Susie* and *Makin' Whoopee*. He was raised in Munn Lodge No. 190, New York City.

CARSON, CHRISTOPHER 'KIT' (1809-1868)

American frontiersman and Indian scout. Because of his familiary with Indian languages he was largely instrumental in bringing about many of the treaties between the Indian tribes and the US government. He entered the Craft in Montezuma Lodge No. 109, at Taos, New Mexico.

CASANOVA [GIOVANNI JACOPO CASANOVA DE SEINGALT] (1725-1798)

Italian adventurer. His name has become a byword for philandering, but he was an entertaining and witty writer. He was made a Mason at Lyon, in France, probably in 1750.

CAVOUR, COUNT CAMILLO DI (1810-1861)

Italian politician. He founded the journal *Il Resorgimento* and was the political founder of Italian unity. In 1861 he became the first Prime Minister of united Italy. His Masonic activities were largely confined to his native Piedmont.

CHAGALL, MARC (1887-1985)

Russian artist who spent most of his working life in Paris. His art – in a variety of media: painting, gouache, etching, lithography, ceramics, and stained glass – was heavily influenced by Biblical themes. He was made a Mason in 1912, probably in the short-lived lodge at Vitebsk, Belorussia.

CHALMERS, THOMAS (1780-1847)

Scottish theologian and philosopher. He was a prolific author and instrumental in establishing the Free Church of Scotland (1843). He was initiated in Lodge St. Vigean, at Arbroath, Scotland, in 1800.

CHERUBINI, LUIGI (1760-1842)

Italian composer. His principal works were operas, the best known being *Medee* (1797). In French musical circles he exercised considerable influence – notably upon Gluck – after being appointed head of the National School of Music in 1821. He was a member of the lodge Saint Jean de Jerusalem.

CHODERLOS DE LACLOS, PIERRE AMBROISE (1741-1803)

French soldier and writer. He is famous as the author of the epistolary novel *Les Liaisons Dangereuses* (1782). He was Master of the military lodge L'Union, at Amiens.

CHRYSLER, WALTER P. (1875-1940)

American motor car manufacturer. His career in the motor industry began with Buick in 1912, but he went on to set up his own corporation and to become a household name.

CHURCHILL, SIR WINSTON LEONARD SPENCER (1874-1965)

English statesman. He crowned his distinguished career in politics and literature as Prime Minister of Great Britain during World War Two, when his leadership inspired Britain and the free world in the struggle to defeat Nazism. In 1953 he was awarded the Nobel Prize for literature. He was initiated in Studholme Lodge, No. 1591, London, in 1901 and raised in Rosemary's Lodge No 2851, in 1902.

CITROEN, ANDRÉ (1878-1935)

French engineer and motor car manufacturer. In 1919 he built the first mass-produced automobile in Europe. His cars became known worldwide – especially the ubiquitous 2CV – and the name Citroen is now virtually synonymous with French motor cars. He was a member of Lodge La Philosophie Positive, Paris.

CLARK, MARK WAYNE (1896-1984)

General, U.S. Army. Wounded during World War One. In World War Two he was chief of staff of the Ground Forces in 1942, commanded the 15th Army group in Italy 1944-1945. He was also commander in chief of the United Nation Command in Korea in 1952, and commanding general of all U.S. forces to the Far East. He was raised in Mystic Tie Lodge No. 398, Indianapolis.

CLEAVELAND, MOSES (1754-1806)

American lawyer, Revolutionary soldier, and pioneer. He led the exploration and survey party into the North West Territory (later Ohio) for the Connecticut Land Company, and founded the city of Cleveland in 1796. He was initiated in 1779 in a military lodge (American Union) and in 1791 was Worshipful Master of Moriah Lodge, the first to be warranted by the newly founded Grand Lodge of Connecticut.

COBB, TY[RUS] R. (BORN 1886)

American sportsman. He is considered to be one of the greatest baseball players – if not *the* greatest – of all time. He was initiated in Royston Lodge No. 426, Detroit, in 1907.

COBURN, ALVIN LANGDON (1882-1966)

American photographer. He was justly famous for both his portraits and his studies of London and New York. He was a member of The Lodge of Living Stones No. 4957, London.

CODY, WILLIAM F. 'BUFFALO BILL' (1846-1917)

American frontiersman and showman. He achieved early fame as a Pony Express rider and Indian scout. From 1883 he toured America and Europe with his

Wild West Show, a highlight of which was the re-enactment of his hand-to-hand fight with the Cheyenne chief, Yellow Hand. He was raised in Platte Valley Lodge No. 15, Nebraska, and remained an active Mason for all of his life.

COHAN, GEORGE M. (1878-1942)

American singer, songwriter and all-round entertainer. The archetypal 'Yankee Doodle Dandy', Cohan was a Broadway star for forty years. He was raised in Pacific Lodge No. 233, New York City, in 1905, and was also a Shriner.

COLE, NAT[HANIEL] 'KING' (1919-1965)

Black American singer and pianist. One of the most popular of black entertainers, Nat 'King' Cole was initiated in Thomas Waller Lodge No. 49, Los Angeles, Prince Hall Affiliation.

COLLODI, CARLO [CARLO LORENZINI] (1826-1890)

Italian journalist and writer, and author of the children's classic, *Pinocchio* (1883). He was active in the struggle for Italian liberation.

COLT, SAMUEL (1814-1862)

American inventor and manufacturer. His first patent for revolving firearms was taken out in 1835 when he was only 21. The various Colt revolvers that he developed played an important role in the westward expansion of the U.S., and have become a part of the folklore of the 'Wild West'. Colt's Masonic activities were centred on Hartford, Connecticut.

CONDORCET, ANTOINE CARITAT, MARQUIS DE (1743-1794)

French mathematician and philosopher. He was famous for his treatise on political philosophy, *Tableau Historique des Progrès de l'Esprit Humain* (1793-94). He was said to be a member of Lodge Les Neuf Soeurs, at Paris.

COOPER, LEROY GORDON (BORN 1927)

American astronaut. He made record-breaking flights in Mercury 7, 1963 and in Gemini 5, 1965. He is a member of Carbondale Lodge No. 82, Colorado.

DE COSTER, CHARLES (1827-1879)

Belgian novelist. His masterpiece, *Les Aventures de Tyl Ulenspiegel*, is not only hugely entertaining, but also a patriotic denunciation of political oppression. He was initiated in Lodge Les Vrais Amis de l'Union et du Progrès Réunis, at Brussels, in 1857.

CROCKETT, DAVID (1786-1836)

American frontiersman. He was a folk-hero in his native Tennessee, but gained immortality when he fell at the Alamo during the Texan struggle for independence.

DECROLY, OVIDE (1871-1932)

Belgian educationalist. His schools, modelled on the principles laid down by Maria Montessori, have been highly influential in both Belgium and France. He was initiated in 1902, in Lodge Les Amis Philanthropes No. 2, at Brussels.

DE MILLE, CECIL B. (1881-1959)

American film producer-director and a pioneer of Hollywood. His films include *The Squaw Man* (1913), the first major film to be produced in Hollywood, and such spectaculars as *The Ten Commandments* (1923 and 1956), and *Samson and Delilah* (1949). He was a member of Prince of Orange Lodge No. 16, New York City.

DEMPSEY, WILLIAM HARRISON 'JACK' (1895- 1983)

American heavyweight boxing champion of the world in 1919 – retaining the title for seven years. He was a member of Kenwood Lodge No. 800, Chicago, Illinois.

DIEFENBAKER, JOHN GEORGE (1895-1979)

Canadian statesman. He was Prime Minister of Canada from 1957 to 1963. He was an active Mason and a Shriner, in Ontario, where he received the 33º.

DIEHL, CHRISTOPHER (1831-1912)

American librarian. He established the first Masonic public library in America, which became the basis of the present public library at Salt Lake City, where Diehl was raised in Mt. Moriah Lodge No. 70, in 1872.

DOYLE, SIR ARTHUR CONAN (1859-1930)

English novelist and short-story writer. Doyle was a prolific novelist but is best known as the creator of the immortal characters, Sherlock Holmes and Doctor Watson. Doyle introduced Sherlock Holmes to the world in *A Study in Scarlet* (1887), which he followed with three other novels including *The Hound of the Baskervilles* (1902), and 56 short stories featuring the detective. He was raised in Phoenix Lodge No. 257, at Portsmouth, England, in 1893.

DRAKE, EDWIN L. (1819-1880)

American pioneer of the oil industry. He was the first to tap petroleum at its source by drilling (at Titusville, Pennsylvania, on August 27, 1859) for the Pennsylvania Rock Oil Company, the oldest petroleum firm in the world. He was a member of Oil Creek Lodge No. 3, at Titusville, Pennsylvania.

DUNANT, JEAN HENRI (1828-1910)

Swiss humanitarian and founder of the Red Cross (1864) – the voluntary relief body dedicated to the care of those wounded in war. Dunant conceived the idea of the Red Cross when organizing emergency aid for soldiers wounded at the battle of Solferino in 1859. In 1901 he shared with Frederick Passy the first Nobel Peace Prize.

DUNCKERLEY, THOMAS (1724-1795)

English sailor and promoter of Freemasonry. He was a natural son of King George II, but at the age of 10 he ran away to sea and served for 26 years in the Royal Navy. He was an enthusiastic and energetic Mason, doing much to spread the Craft in England. He also consolidated the Royal Arch and was the first Grand Master of the Masonic Knights Templars.

DUVEEN, EDWARD JOSEPH (1869-1939)

English art connoisseur, and the world's foremost art dealer of his time. He was a trustee of major art galleries, including the National Gallery at London and the Museum of Modern Art at New York City. He was initiated in Royal Colonial Institute Lodge No. 3556, in 1912.

EATON, HUBERT (1881-1966)

American chemist. He originated the 'memorial park' plan for cemeteries, with tablets set level with the ground in place of tombstones, thus revolutionizing the whole concept of commemorating the dead. His most famous creation is Forest Lawn Memorial Park at Glendale, California. He was made a Mason in Euclid Lodge, No. 58, Great Falls, Montana.

ÉBOUÉ, FELIX (1884-1944)

French African politician and soldier. The grandson of a slave, he became the first black Governor-General of a French colony (Tchad, 1938). In 1940 he rallied this African colony to the Free French Forces, and by the time of his death had laid the foundations for the de-colonization of French Africa. He was initiated in Lodge France Equinoxiale, at Cayenne, French Guiana, in 1922.

EDWARD VII (1841-1910)

As Prince of Wales he was Grand Master of the United Grand Lodge of England from 1875 to 1901.

EDWARD VIII (1894-1972)

After a reign of less than one year, he abdicated in 1936 in order to marry Mrs. Simpson and was created Duke of Windsor. He was Grand Master of the United Grand Lodge of England in 1936.

ELLINGTON, EDWARD KENNEDY 'DUKE' (1899-1974)

Black American jazz musician. As composer, arranger and pianist, he was a significant figure in American twentieth century music. He was initiated in Social Lodge No. 1, Washington D.C., Prince Hall Affiliation, his impressions of initiation being recorded in the song 'I'm beginning to see the Light' which was sung by Louis Armstrong (q.v.).

FABER, EBERHARD (1859-1946)

American manufacturer. He was head of the famous Eberhard Faber Pencil Co. at Brooklyn, New York State, taking over the post from his father. He was a member of Chancellor Walworth Lodge No. 271, New York City, N.Y.

FAIRBANKS, DOUGLAS, SR. (DOUGLAS ULLMAN) (1883-1939)

American silent screen actor. The most famous swashbuckling actor of all, known especially for *The Three Musketeers* and for his *Zorro* films. He was a member of Beverly Hills Lodge No. 528, California.

FIELDS, WILLIAM CLAUDE (DUKINFIELD) (1880-1946)

American stage, screen and radio comedian. His idiosyncratic style of humour – he appeared as an intolerant, eccentric, hard-drinking misogynist – ensured his lasting fame. He was a member of E. Coppee Mitchell Lodge No. 605, Philadelphia.

FITCH, JOHN (1743-1798)

American engineer and the true inventor of the steamboat. His experimental boats were not taken up and his ideas were utilised by others. He was initiated in Bristol Lodge No. 25, at Bristol, Pennsylvania, in 1785.

FLEMING, SIR ALEXANDER (1881-1955)

Scottish bacteriologist. In 1928 he discovered the antibiotic properties of the penicillium mould. The importance of his discovery cannot be overstated: it led to the saving of countless thousands of lives in World War Two, and in 1945 Fleming was awarded the Nobel Prize for medicine and physiology. He was active in many Craft lodges and in 1942 attained Grand Rank in the United Grand Lodge of England.

FLETCHER, SIR BANISTER FLIGHT (1866-1958)

English architect and architectural historian. His book *A History of Architecture on the Comparative Method* has gone through eighteen editions since it was first published, and is universally acclaimed as the finest work of its kind. He was initiated in Authors' Lodge No. 3456, London, in 1910.

FOLKES, MARTIN (1690-1754)

English antiquarian. He was elected a Fellow of the Royal Society at the age of 23, and was its president from 1741 to 1753. Folkes was responsible for one enduring piece of scientific folklore, being the source

of the story of the falling apple that led to Newton's discovery of the laws of gravitation. In 1724 he was Deputy Grand Master of the Grand Lodge of England.

FORD, HENRY (1863-1947)

American industrialist and philanthropist. Ten years after building his first motor car, he organised the Ford Motor Co. in 1903 and built it into the largest automobile company in the world by developing the 'assembly-line' method of production. In this way the motor car, epitomized by the Model-T Ford, came within the reach of the average man. From 1914 onwards the company operated a revolutionary profit-sharing plan for its workers. He was raised in Palestine Lodge No. 357, Detroit, Michigan, in 1894.

FOURCROY, ANTOINE FRANÇOIS, COMTE DE (1755-1809)

French chemist. He worked with Lavoisier to establish the modern form of chemical nomenclature. He was a member of Lodge Les Neuf Soeurs, at Paris.

FRANKLIN, BENJAMIN (1706-1790)

American statesman, scientist and philosopher. He began his working life as a printer at Philadelphia, where in 1727 he established the future American Philosophical Society. His many inventions and public improvements included street lighting, a heating stove and the lightning rod. He was instrumental in framing the Declaration of Independence, gained French support for the colonists, and negotiated the Peace Treaty with Britain in 1781. He was initiated in 1731 in St. John's Lodge, Philadelphia, Pennsylvania, and was always an enthusiastic Mason.

GABLE, CLARK (1907-1960)

American film actor. For more than thirty years he played leading roles in more than seventy Hollywood films, including *It Happened One Night* (1934), for which he won an Oscar, and the enormously successful *Gone with the Wind* (1939). In 1933 he was initiated in Beverly Hills Lodge No. 528, California.

GARIBALDI, GIUSEPPE (1807-1882)

Italian patriot and hero of the 'Risorgimento', the movement for the liberation and union of Italy. In 1833 he joined Mazzini's revolutionary society, 'Young Italy', and after early reverses took up the struggle for Italian freedom in 1848, bringing it to completion in 1870 when Italian troops freed Rome from Papal control. He was initiated in Lodge L'Ami de la Vertu, at Montevideo, in 1844. At one time he was a member of the French Grand Orient and

became Grand Master of the Grand Orient of Palerma, 33º.

GARRICK, DAVID (1717-1779)

English actor. Garrick is considered to be one of the greatest actors of all time. He was particularly noted for his Shakespearean performances, but he also found success as a playwright and actor-manager. He was a member of St. Paul's Lodge No. 194, London.

GATLING, RICHARD J. (1818-1903)

American inventor. In 1862 he built the 'Gatling Gun', the first practical repeating gun, which was adopted by many armies and which changed the tactics of warfare around the world. He was a member of Center Lodge No. 23, Indianapolis.

GEORGE VI (1895-1952)

He succeeded to the throne when his brother abdicated in 1936. From his initiation in Naval Lodge No. 2612, in 1919, he was an enthusiastic Mason: in 1936 he was installed as Grand Master Mason of Scotland, and in 1938 accepted the rank of Past Grand Master of the United Grand Lodge of England. Between 1939 and 1948 he personally installed three Grand Masters.

GILBERT, SIR WILLIAM S. (1836-1911)

English poet and playwright. He was the librettist for the world famous Savoy Operas *The Pirates of Penzance, The Mikado, Patience*, etc., the music for which was written by Sir Arthur Sullivan (q.v.). He was raised in St. Machar Lodge No. 54, Aberdeen, Scotland, in 1871.

GILLETTE, KING C. (1855-1932)

American manufacturer. He invented the safety razor with which his name has since become virtually synonymous, and perfected the production of the extremely thin blades. For thirty years he was President of the Gillette Safety Razor Company.

GLENN JOHN (BORN 1921)

American astronaut. He was the first American to orbit the earth. On February 20, 1962, he circled the earth three times in less than five hours on the spacecraft Friendship 7. He won election to the US Senate from Ohio in 1974, and was re-elected in 1980 and 1986. Member of Concord Lodge No. 688, at Concord, Ohio.

GOBLET D'ALVIELLA, EUGENE FÉLICIEN, COMTE (1846-1925)

Belgian statesman and historian of religions. He was one of the great pioneers in the study of comparative religion, his book on *The Migration of Symbols* being still in print, and he played an active role in bringing religious tolerance to Belgium.

He was initiated at Brussels in 1870, in the Loge Les Amis Philanthropes, and in 1884 became Grand Master of the Grand Orient of Belgium. In 1909 he was elected to membership of the research lodge Quatuor Coronati, No. 2076, at London.

GODFREY, ARTHUR (BORN 1903)

Radio and television personality, he is a member of Acacia Lodge No. 18, Washington, D.C.

GOETHE, JOHANN WOLFGANG VON (1749- 1832)

German poet. Goethe not only instituted the Romantic School, but is without question the greatest figure in all German literature – both *Faust* and *Wilhelm Meister* are classics of world literature. His restless mind also sought the truth in various scientific fields. His last words were 'Mehr Licht' ('More Light'), and while his ideas have since been discarded they acted as a powerful stimulus in his day. He was initiated in Amalia Lodge at Weimar on 23 June 1780, and remained an active Mason for many years.

GOMPERS, SAMUEL (1850-1924)

Founder and first president of the American Federation of Labor. He was a member of Dawson Lodge No. 16, Washington, D.C.

DE GREY, GEORGE FREDERICK SAMUEL ROBINSON, EARL (later first Marquis of Ripon) (1827-1909)

English statesman, and from 1870-1874 Grand Master of the United Grand Lodge of England. He held many Cabinet appointments in successive Liberal governments, and from 1880 to 1884 was Governor-General of India. His name has been immortalized in Earl Grey tea.

GRIFFITH, DAVID W. (1880-1948)

American film pioneer, and the industry's first major producer-director. He is, perhaps, best remembered for his classics *The Birth of a Nation* (1915) and *Intolerance* (1916). He was a member of St. Cecile Lodge No. 568, New York City.

GRIS, JUAN [JOSE GONZALES] (1887-1927)

Spanish painter. Gris came to Paris in 1906 and worked at first with Picasso and other artists. In 1922 he created an important series of stage sets for the Diaghilev Ballet, but his lasting place in art is as one of the greatest and most original artists of the Cubist movement. He was initiated in Lodge Voltaire, at Paris, in 1923.

GRISSOM, VIRGIL 'GUS' (1926-1967)

American astronaut. In 1965, as pilot of Gemini 3, he undertook the first manned manoeuvre in space.

He was tragically killed in the fire that destroyed Apollo I in 1967. He was a member of Mitchell Lodge No. 228, in Indiana.

GROCK [KARL ADRIAN WETTACH] (1880-1959)

Swiss circus clown, famous throughout Europe not only as a clown but also as an acrobat and circus musician. He was a member of the Swiss Grand Lodge Alpina.

GUILLOTIN, JOSEPH IGNACE (1738-1814)

French physician. As a deputy of the French States-General in 1789, he argued for a device that would enable capital punishment to be both speedy and painless; the machine has ever since borne his name. Guillotin was one of the founders of the Grand Orient of France.

HAHNEMANN, SAMUEL (1755-1843)

German physician and founder of Homoeopathy, the system of medical treatment based on the idea that 'like is cured by like'. Hahnemann set out the principles of his system in 1810, in his book *Organon der Rationellen Heilkunde*. Despite some opposition, Homoeopathy is widely practised today. Hahnemann was initiated in lodge Zu den Drei Seebatten, at Hermanstadt, Germany, in 1777.

HAIG, DOUGLAS, FIRST EARL (1861-1928)

English soldier and field-marshal. In World War One, Haig was Commander-in chief of the British Expeditionary Force to France. In 1916 he was the architect of the 'Battle of the Somme'. He was initiated in Elgin Lodge No. 91, at Leven, Scotland, in 1881.

HALL, MANLY PALMER (1901-1990)

American metaphysical writer. He founded the Philosophical Research Society in 1919 and devoted his life and prolific writings to the promotion of a healthy approach to esoteric subjects. He was raised in Jewel Lodge No. 374, at San Francisco, in 1954.

HALL, PRINCE (1748-1807)

The first black American Freemason. Prince Hall was a free man and a Methodist minister at Cambridge, Massachusets, when he was made a Mason in 1775 in an Irish military lodge. In 1784 the charter for African Lodge No. 459 – which still survives – was issued by the Grand Lodge of England, but the lodge was not set up until 1787, the charter having taken three years to arrive. On June24, 1791 the African Grand Lodge was founded with Prince Hall as Grand Master. Much controversy and uncertainty surrounds the early years of the Grand Lodge, but Prince Hall Masonry is now firmly established across the U.S. and in many other parts of the world.

HARDY, OLIVER (1892-1957)

American comedian and film actor. He gained world-wide recognition for his partnership with the English comedian Stan Laurel. He was a member of Solomon Lodge No. 20, Jacksonville, Florida.

HAYDN, FRANZ JOSEF (1732-1809)

Austrian composer. He was the first great symphonic composer, but is equally famous for his masses, chamber music, and the two oratorios, *The Creation*, and *The Seasons*. Encouraged to become a Mason by Mozart, he was initiated at Vienna in 1785, in the lodge Zur Wahren Eintracht.

HEDGES, CORNELIUS (1831-1907)

He was the 'Father' of Yellowstone National Park, America's first national park. He was initiated in Independence Lodge No. 87, Independence, Iowa.

HEINE, HEINRICH (1799-1856)

German poet. His poems combine a romantic lyricism with a fierce irony and often reflect their author's passionate beliefs in political freedom and social justice. He was initiated at Paris in 1844, in lodge Les Trinosophes.

HELVETIUS, CLAUDE-ADRIEN (1715-1771)

French philosopher, and one of the 'encyclopédistes'. His most important work was on ethics, *De l'Esprit* (1758), in which he sets out a form of Utilitarianism (the desirability of working towards the greatest good for the greatest number). He was a member of Lodge Les Neuf Soeurs, at Paris.

HENSON, JOSIAH (1789-1883)

American black slave, Methodist minister. His escape from slavery in Kentucky and his journey into Canada inspired Harriet Beecher Stowe's novel *Uncle Tom's Cabin*. He was a member of Mount Moriah Lodge No. 4, Dresden, Ontario.

HERDER, JOHANN GOTTFRIED VON (1744-1803)

German writer and philosopher. A friend of Kant and later of Goethe, Herder was the effective father of Romanticism and the initiator of the 'Sturm und Drang' (Storm and Stress) movement. He was initiated at Riga, in 1766, in Lodge Zur Schwert.

HILTON, CHARLES C. (1843-1905)

American hotelier. After managing hotels in Chicago he set up the Hotel Hilton, thus laying the foundations for the world's best-known chain of hotels. He was initiated at Chicago in 1866, in William B. Warren Lodge No. 309.

HOBAN, JAMES (1762-1831)

American architect who designed and built both the original White House (1792-1800) and its replacement after the War of 1812. He was a founder of Federal Lodge No. 1, at Washington, D.C.

HOE, RICHARD M. (1812-1886)

American engineer. He invented the rotary press, web press (both in 1847), and other improvements in printing machinery that led to modern newspaper printing methods. He was initiated in Columbia Lodge No. 91, Philadelphia, Pennsylvania.

HOGARTH, WILLIAM (1697-1764)

English painter and engraver. Famous for his many caricatures and satirical engravings, which strip bare the social hypocrisies of his day. Several of his engravings, notably *Night* and *The Mystery of Masonry brought to Light by the Gormogons*, have Masonic themes. He was an active Freemason, serving as Grand Steward of the Grand Lodge of England in 1735.

HOGG, JAMES (1770-1835)

Scottish poet, known as the 'Ettrick Shepherd', from his original occupation. He was a friend of many of the Romantic poets. He was made a Mason in 1831, in Lodge Canongate Kilwinning, Edinburgh.

HOOVER, J. EDGAR (1895-1972)

American law officer. From 1924 until his death he was the highly successful – if sometimes controversial – Director of the Federal Bureau of Investigation. He was a member of Federal Lodge No. 1, Washington, D.C.

HOPKINS, SIR FREDERICK GOWLAND (1861-1947)

English biochemist. His work on proteins in 1900 led to the concept of the 'essential amino acid' and in 1929 his later pioneering work in vitamin research brought him the Nobel Prize for medicine and physiology. He was initiated in Aesculapius Lodge No. 2410 in 1904.

HORLICK, ALEXANDER J. (1873-1950)

American industrialist. He became President of the Horlick's Malted Milk Corporation, having worked in the family company from 1893 and helped it to grow to its present international status. He was a member of Belle City Lodge No. 92, Racine, Wisconsin.

HORNSBY, ROGERS (1896-1963)

An original member of the Baseball Hall of Fame and an outstanding baseball player. He was a member of Beacon Lodge No. 3, St. Louis, Missouri.

HOUDINI, HARRY [ERICH WEISS] (1874-1926)

American conjurer and escape artist. His stage performances were legendary, and his books on conjuring were widely acclaimed. He was made a Mason in 1923, in St. Cecile Lodge No. 568, New York City.

HOUSTON, SAM (1793-1863)

American pioneer. After an eventful early life he went to Texas in 1832, taking command of the armed forces when independence was declared in 1836. He defeated Santa Anna at the battle of San Jacinto, and later in the same year was elected first President of the Republic of Texas. The admission of Texas to the Union in 1845 was largely due to his efforts. He was initiated in Cumberland Lodge No. 8, Nashville, Tennessee, in 1817.

IRWIN, JAMES BENSON (BORN 1930)

American astronaut who piloted the lunar module 'Falcon' on the Apollo 15 mission. In July 1971, the mission made the fourth landing on the moon where Irwin and astronaut David R. Scott spent nearly 67 hours. Their explorations featured the first of a vehicle called the 'lunar rover'. He is a member of Lodge Tejon No 104, Colorado Springs, Colorado.

ISMAIL PASHA (1830-1895)

Khedive (Viceroy) of Egypt 1863-1879. He encouraged the building of the Suez Canal, and in 1879 presented an obelisk to the U.S. which was erected in New York. He was Grand Master of the Grand Lodge of Egypt.

JENNER, EDWARD (1749-1823)

English physician whose discovery of the principle of vaccination – obtaining human immunity to smallpox by inoculation with cow-pox – led ultimately to the complete eradication of smallpox, which had been one of the greatest scourges of humanity. Jenner was a member of Faith and Friendship Lodge No. 270, at Berkeley, England.

JERROLD, DOUGLAS WILLIAM (1803-1857)

English playwright. He was a prolific and popular author of humorous works, publisher of popular journals and a major contributor to *Punch* in its early years. He was initiated in Bank of England Lodge No. 329, in 1831.

JOFFRE, JOSEPH JACQUES CESAIRE (1852-1931)

French Field-Marshal who commanded the Allied armies in France during World War One. In 1914 he halted the German advance on Paris at the crucial Battle of the Marne – during which he had fresh troops driven to the battle-front from Paris by taxi!

He was initiated in 1875 in Loge Alsace-Lorraine, at Paris.

JOHNSON, JOHN A. 'JACK' (1878-1946)

American black boxer. In 1908 he gained the heavyweight boxing championship of the world, and did not lose it until 1915. He was initiated in Lodge Forfar and Kincardine No. 225, Dundee, Scotland, in 1911.

JOLSON, AL [ASA YOELSON] (1886-1950)

American singer and screen actor. He was noted for his blackface minstrel songs, and achieved fame as the star of the first talking picture, *The Jazz Singer* (1927). He was a member of St. Cecile Lodge, No. 568, New York City.

JONES, MELVIN (BORN 1880)

American businessman. In 1917 he was one of the founders of Lions International, a worldwide philanthropic association of businessmen, and for many years after was both Secretary General and Treasurer. He was a member of Garden City Lodge No. 141, Chicago, Illinois.

KANE, ELISHA KENT (1820-1857)

American physician, and arctic explorer. In 1850 he took part in the first Grinnell expedition to search for Sir John Franklin, and in 1853 commanded the second expedition, undergoing severe hardships, but returning as a hero. He was initiated in Franklin Lodge No. 134, at Philadelphia, in 1853.

KEAN, EDMUND (1787-1833)

English actor. He was the greatest tragedian of his day, excelling in Shakespearean roles. He was a member of St. Mark's Lodge, No. 102, Glasgow, Scotland.

KING, CHARLES GLEN (BORN 1896)

American biochemist. He was noted for his work in the field of nutrition, especially on enzymes and synthetic fats, but his greatest achievement came in 1932 when he isolated Vitamin C (which he synthesized in the following year). He was initiated in Whitman Lodge No. 49, Pulman, Washington, in 1919.

KIPLING, RUDYARD (1865-1936)

English writer who was awarded the Nobel Prize for literature in 1907. Most of his writing, both prose and verse, concerns India, where he was born and spent his adult life until 1889. Among his most popular works are his stories for children: *The Jungle Books*, *Just So Stories*, and *Stalky & Co*. Much of his writing contains Masonic allusions (notably *Kim*, and *The Man who would be King*) while *The Mother Lodge* is probably the most frequently quoted of all Masonic poems. He was

initiated in Hope and Esperance Lodge No. 782, Lahore, India, in 1887. On settling in England he became a founder of two lodges – Builders of the Silent City (in 1927), and Authors' Lodge – and was appointed Poet Laureate of Canongate Kilwinning Lodge, at Edinburgh.

KIRBY, WILLIAM FORSELL (1844-1912)

English entomologist. He published many important works on butterflies and moths, including almost all of the British Museum handbooks on the subject. He was also a folklorist and produced a standard translation of the Finnish epic, *Kalevala*. His interest in the esoteric aspect of Masonry led to his bringing the author A. E. Waite into the Craft. Both men were members of Runymede Lodge No. 2430, Wraysbury, Buckinghamshire.

KITCHENER, HORATIO HERBERT (1850-1916)

English soldier, and lst Earl Kitchener of Khartoum and Broome (1914). He was honoured and decorated for his part in the campaigns in the Sudan between 1884 and 1898, and subsequently played a prominent role in British military affairs. At the outbreak of war in 1914 he was Secretary of State for War and organized the British Expeditionary Force – gaining immortality through the recruiting poster showing his pointing finger with the words 'Your Country Needs You'. He was lost at sea in 1916 when he went down with the cruiser, H.M.S. *Hampshire*. He entered the Craft while on service in Egypt.

KNOX, HENRY (1750-1806)

American soldier and lst Secretary of War under Washington. In 1779 he took the first steps in creating the U.S. Military Academy, and in 1782 was commander of West Point. He is believed to have joined the Craft in St. John's Regimental Lodge, at Morristown, New Jersey

KOSSUTH, LAJOS (1802-1894)

Hungarian patriot. In 1848 he was appointed Governor of Hungary during the short-lived independence from Austria. After a decade of wandering he joined Garibaldi in Italy, where he remained for the rest of his life. He was initiated in 1852, in Cincinnati Lodge No. 133, at Cincinnati, Ohio.

LAGUARDIA, FIORELLO H. (1882-1947)

American politician. He served with distinction as a diplomat, and was three times Mayor of New York City – whose domestic airport is named after him. He was initiated in Garibaldi Lodge No. 542, New York City, in 1913.

LALANDE, JOSEPH JEROME DE (1732-1807)

French astronomer. In 1801 he published the first significant catalogue of stars listing nearly 50,000 – and from 1768 he directed the Paris Observatory. He was a founder of Lodge Les Neuf Soeurs.

LANCASTER, SIR OSBERT (1908-1986)

English artist, cartoonist and writer, whose sardonic commentary on English social life delighted the British public for fifty years. He was initiated in Apollo Lodge No. 357, at Oxford, in 1928.

LAPLACE, PIERRE SIMON, MARQUIS DE (1749-1827)

French mathematician and astronomer. His planetary theory, which rounded off Newton's work, is expounded in his massive work on celestial mechanics (1799-1825), but he is equally famous for postulating the nebular theory of the origin of the solar system. He held Grand Rank in the Grand Orient of France.

LATROBE, BENJAMIN H. (1764-1820)

Anglo-American architect. Latrobe came to the U.S.A. in 1796, and subsequently designed and constructed many famous buildings, from the Roman Catholic cathedral at Baltimore, to the rebuilt Capitol at Washington (1815-17). He also made alterations in the White House, and designed and installed the first water system in the U.S., at Philadelphia. He was initiated in 1788 in the oldest of all Masonic Lodges in England: Antiquity No. 2, at London.

LEMON, MARK (1809-1870)

English author and playwright. In 1841 he was a founder of the humorous journal, *Punch*, and its editor from the beginning until his death in 1870. He was initiated in Globe Lodge No. 23, at London, in 1854.

LESSING, GOTTHOLD E. (1729-1781)

German dramatist and critic. Among his many writings were two Masonic pieces, the poem *Nathan the Wise*, and the dialogue *Ernst und Falk*. He was initiated in the lodge Zu den Drei Goldenen Rosen, at Hamburg, in 1771.

LEVER, WILLIAM HESKETH, 1ST VISCOUNT LEVERHULME (1851-1925)

He was created viscount in 1922. He was the first initiate of William Hesketh Lever Lodge No 2916, at Port Sunlight, England, which was founded in his honour and consecrated on June 4, 1902. He was initiated the following July 8th. In 1929 he was appointed Senior Grand Warden of the Grand Mark Lodge of England.

LINCOLN, ELMO [OTTO ELMO LINKENHELTER] (1889-1952)

American screen actor. He became famous as the first actor to portray *Tarzan of the Apes* (1918). He was a member of Elysian Lodge No. 418, Los Angeles, California.

LINDBERGH, CHARLES (1902-1974)

American aviator. In May 1927 he made the first non-stop solo flight from America (Roosevelt Field, N.Y.) to Europe (Paris). He was initiated in Keystone Lodge No. 243, Saint Louis, Missouri, in 1926.

LIPTON, SIR THOMAS JOHNSTONE (1850-1931)

Scottish merchant and yachtsman. He was equally famous as a distributor of tea (from his plantations in Ceylon), and as a challenger for the America Cup in his yacht, *Shamrock*. He was initiated in Scotia Lodge No. 178, Glasgow, Scotland, in 1870.

LISZT, FRANZ VON (1811-1886)

Hungarian composer and virtuoso pianist. His music remains among the most popular composed for the piano, while the rapturous reception given to his concert performances led to the coining of the word 'Lisztomania'. He was initiated in 1841, in Lodge Zur Einigkeit at Frankfurt.

LIVINGSTON, EDWARD (1764-1836)

American lawyer, described by Sir Henry Maine as 'the first legal genius of modern times'. He drafted the Civil and Criminal Codes of Louisiana, drawing them ultimately from Roman as opposed to English law, as had been the custom in other States. He was active as a Mason first in New York and later in New Orleans.

LLOYD, HAROLD C. (1893-1971)

American screen actor. One of the best-known comedians of the silent screen, he was famous for his dangerous stunts. He was initiated in Alexander Hamilton Lodge No. 535, Hollywood, California, in 1925.

LOCKE, RICHARD A. (1800-1871)

American journalist. He was the author of the famous 'Moon Hoax' of 1835 which created a sensation by claiming that Sir John Herschel had observed the inhabitants of the Moon and recorded their doings. He was a member of Benevolent Lodge No. 28, New York City.

LOUTHERBOURG, PHILIP JAMES (1740-1812)

German artist. Most of his working life was spent in Britain. Although best-known as a landscape artist, he produced a series of water colour designs for Cagliostro's Egyptian Rite of Freemasonry.

MACADAM, JOHN LOUDON (1756-1836)

Scottish engineer. His road-making experiments began at Ayr, Scotland, and were continued at Falmouth, in Cornwall. His process for rendering roads waterproof, or macadamizing, was taken up in all parts of the world. He was probably made a Mason in America, but was Masonically active in Scotland.

MACARTHUR, DOUGLAS (1880-1964)

General of Army (5-star) in 1944. In World War One he was Chief of Staff of 42nd Division. He retired in 1937 but returned to active service as commander of the US armed forces in the Far-East in 1941-51. In August 1945 as Allied Supreme Commander he accepted the surrender of Japan, and commanded the occupational forces there until 1951.

He was made a Mason 'at sight' by Samuel Hawthorne, Grand Master of Philippines on January 17, 1936, and he affiliated with Manila Lodge No 1, Manila. He received 32° of the Scottish Rite at Manila the same year, and was a life member of the Nile Shrine Temple, Seattle, Washington.

MACDONALD, SIR JOHN ALEXANDER (1815-1891)

Canadian statesman. In 1867 he was responsible for uniting the Canadian provinces into the Dominion of Canada, of which he became the first Prime Minister until 1873. He held the office again from 1878 until his death. He was initiated in St. John's Lodge No. 758, at Kingston, Ontario, in 1844.

MACKENZIE, HENRY (1745-1831)

Scottish novelist, best-known for *The Man of Feeling* (1771). He was a member of Lodge Canongate Kilwinning, Edinburgh.

McMANUS, GEORGE (1884-1954)

American cartoonist. He became famous with his comic-strip 'Bringing up Father' which ran for a period of 41 years and inspired both touring stage shows and a series of films. He was initiated in 1908, in Dirigo Lodge No. 30, New York City.

MARSHALL, GEORGE C. (1880-1959)

American soldier and statesman. In World War One he was with the American Expeditionary Forces, then aide-de-camp to General Pershing. He was Chief of Staff with the rank of General 1939-1945, and General of the Army (5-star) in 1944. In 1945, he became ambassador to China. Secretary of State 1947-1949, he was the author of the Marshall Plan for European economic recovery for which he was awarded the Nobel Peace Prize in 1953. Made a Mason 'at sight' on December 16, 1941, by Ara M. Daniels, Grand Master of the Grand Lodge of the District of Columbia, in the Scottish Rite Cathedral of the District.

MARSHALL, JOHN (1775-1835)

As Chief Justice of the U.S. Supreme Court, 1801-1835, he shaped the court to become the final authority on questions of constitutionality. Member of Richmond Lodge No. 13, Richmond, Virgiana.

MASARYK, JAN (1886-1948)

Czechoslovak statesman. The son of Tomas Masaryk, the first president of his country. As a true patriot he fought for the liberation of his country while exiled in England during the Nazi occupation, and from 1945, as Foreign Minister, he strove for freedom against the Communists who eventually drove him to suicide in 1948. He was initiated in Jan Amos Komensky Lodge No.1, at Prague.

MAYER, LOUIS B. (1885-1957)

American film producer. In 1924 his corporation merged with that of Sam Goldwyn to form Metro-Goldwyn-Mayer, one of the most enduring of Hollywood production companies. He was a member of St. Cecile Lodge No. 568, New York City.

MAYO, DR. CHARLES H. (1865-1939)

American physician. With his brother William he founded the Mayo Clinic and the Mayo Foundation for Medical Education and Research at Rochester, Minnesota. The Mayo Clinic – which began in the Masonic Temple building at Rochester – is a completely voluntary association of physicians – the largest of its kind in the world. The Research Foundation is now a branch of the University of Minnesota. Dr. Mayo was initiated in Rochester Lodge No. 21, in 1890, as were his father before him and his son Charles, after him.

MAZZINI, GIUSEPPE (1805-1872)

Italian patriot. After banishment in 1832 he organized the secret revolutionary society 'Young Italy', and for the rest of his life worked tirelessly for the liberation and unification of Italy. He became Grand Master of the Grand Orient of Italy.

MELLON, ANDREW W. (1855-1937)

American industrialist. He was president of the Mellon National Bank and from 1921 to 1932 Secretary of the Treasury. The A. W. Mellon Educational and Charitable Trust was founded in 1930, and in 1937 he donated his highly important private art collection to the nation. He was made a Mason 'at sight' by the Grand Master of Pennsylvania, at Pittsburgh, in 1928.

MENNINGER, KARL A. (BORN 1893)

Psychiatrist who received international recognition in the treatment of mental illness. His many writings widely influenced public attitudes toward mental illness. He was a member of Topeka Lodge No. 17, Topeka, Kansas.

MESMER, FRANZ ANTON (1734-1815)

Austrian physician. He conducted experiments during the 1770s on the supposed curative powers of magnets, concluding that some kind of healing power lay within himself. In 1778 he went to Paris and put his therapy, Animal Magnetism, into practise. Although it was condemned by contemporary scientists, the real processes at work behind Mesmerism (as it came to be called) led to the understanding and use of Hypnotism in the nineteenth century. He was affiliated with the French Lodge Les Philadelphes.

MEYERBEER, GIACOMO (1791-1864)

German composer. He was among the most influential of opera composers in the early nineteenth century and is best known for such grand operas as *Robert le Diable* and *Les Huguenots*. He was a member of the French Lodge Les Frères Unis Inséparables.

MICHELSON, ALBERT ABRAHAM (1852-1931)

American physicist. In 1882 he successfully measured the speed of light, following this with his experiments of 1887, with Edward Morley, that proved the constant nature of the velocity of light. In 1907 Michelson received the Nobel Prize for physics, the first American to receive a Nobel prize in the sciences. He was initiated in Washington Lodge No. 21, New York City, in 1874.

MIX, TOM [THOMAS EDWIN] (1880-1940)

American screen actor. He began his film career in 1910 and made over four hundred Western movies. He was initiated in Utopia Lodge No. 537, Los Angeles, California, in 1925.

MONTGOLFIER, JACQUES ETIENNE (1745-1799)

French inventor. With his brother, Joseph Michel, he developed the first practical hot-air balloon. Their first flight was made in 1783, followed by another at Paris which was watched by a crowd of 300,000 that included Benjamin Franklin. Montgolfier was initiated in Lodge Les Neuf Soeurs, at Paris, in 1784.

MOZART, WOLFGANG AMADEUS (1756-1791)

Austrian composer. Mozart's musical genius shines through all his work, and his Masonic enthusiasm is reflected in a number of his compositions – most dramatically in the opera *The Magic Flute* which was first performed shortly before his death. He was initiated in 1784 in Lodge Zur Wohltatigkeit, in Vienna.

MUCHA, ALPHONSE MARIE (1860-1939)

Czech painter and designer. Mucha was responsible for many of the most attractive posters and other designs in the Art Nouveau style, which his work helped to popularize. He was an enthusiastic Mason and in 1923 was elected Sovereign Grand Commander of the Czechoslovakian Supreme Council of the Scottish Rite.

MURPHY, AUDIE (1924-1971)

American film actor and the most decorated American soldier of World War Two. His most important role was in *The Red Badge of Courage* (1951). He was a member of the Scottish Rite at Dallas, Texas.

NASMYTH, ALEXANDER (1758-1840)

Scottish painter. Although best known as a portrait painter (notably of his friend, Robert Burns) he is also considered to be 'the father of Scottish landscape art', and he was the inventor of the bowstring bridge used at Charing Cross and Birmingham railway stations. He was a member of Canongate Kilwinning Lodge, at Edinburgh.

NYS, ERNEST (1851-1920)

Belgian jurist. As a member of the Hague Tribunal, Nys was responsible for the Convention covering the treatment of prisoners-of-war. He wrote on both legal topics and Freemasonry.

O'CONNELL, DANIEL (1775-1847)

Irish patriot. The 'Liberator' advanced the causes of both Irish freedom and Catholic Emancipation more than any other man of his day – and this by relying solely on constitutional means. He was raised in Lodge No. 189, Dublin, in 1797, but later left the Craft because of Catholic opposition to Freemasonry.

OGLETHORPE, JAMES E. (1696-1785)

English soldier and politician. In 1729 he began his work to improve the lot of debtors in the London prisons, and in 1732 he obtained a royal charter for the colony of Georgia which he settled in the following year, founding the city of Savannah and becoming the first Governor. He was the first Worshipful Master of King Solomon's Lodge No. 1, at Savannah, Georgia.

OLDS, RANSOM E. (1864-1950)

American automobile pioneer. In 1886 he built the first three-wheeled 'horseless carriage', and in 1893 produced his first four-wheeled motor car. He was for many years president (later chairman) of the Reo Motor Car Co., and the Oldsmobile was named after him. He was a member of Capitol Lodge, No. 66, Lansing, Michigan.

OPIE, PETER MASON (1918-1982)

English author. He was, with his wife, the world's greatest authority on the folklore of the child. Among his many books is the classic *Oxford Dictionary of Nursery Rhymes* (1951). He was a member of Prince of Wales's Lodge No. 259.

OSTWALD, WILHELM (1853-1932)

German chemist. He was a founder of modern physical chemistry, and in 1909 he was awarded the Nobel Prize in chemistry for his work on catalysis. His other principal research was in the field of colour mixing and colour harmony. He was Grand Master of the Grand Lodge Zur Aufgehenden Sonne, Bayreuth.

OTIS, JAMES (1725-1783)

American Revolutionary statesman famous for the phrase: 'taxation without representation is tyranny'. He was made a Mason in St. John's Lodge, Boston, Massachusetts, in 1752.

PABST, CHARLES F. (BORN 1887)

American dermatologist, who coined the term 'athlete's foot' for fungal infection of the feet. He was raised at Brooklyn, New York, in Aurora Grata Day Star Lodge No. 756, in 1921.

PARKER, SIR [HORATIO] GILBERT (1862-1932)

Canadian author. His many novels and short stories were largely concerned with Canadian history; the most famous, *The Seats of the Mighty* (1896), deals with the fall of Quebec in 1759. He was a member of Authors' Lodge No. 3456, London, England.

PEALE, NORMAN VINCENT (BORN 1898)

One of the best known Protestant clergymen in America. Author of several best-selling books. Member of Milwood Lodge No. 1062, Brooklyn, N.Y.

PEARY, ROBERT E. (1856-1920)

American explorer. He began his Arctic explorations in Greenland in 1886, and after a series of unsuccessful expeditions, he finally, in 1909, became the first man to reach the North Pole. He was a member of Kane Lodge No. 454, New York City.

PEDRO I, DOM ANTONIO PEDRO DE ALCANTARA BOURBON (1798-1834)

In 1822 he declared Brazil independent of Portugal and was crowned emperor. He abdicated in 1831, and returned to Portugal where he was proclaimed king (Pedro IV). He was elected Grand Master of the Grand Orient of Brazil in 1821.

PENNEY, JAMES C. (1875-1971)

He was the founder of J. C. Penney Co, a major department store chain in the United States. He was initiated in Wasatch Lodge No 1, Salt Lake City, Utah.

PERSHING, JOHN JOSEPH (1860-1948)

American soldier. Already a distinguished officer, 'Black Jack' Pershing led the American forces in Europe in World War One. When they entered Paris he visited Lafayette's grave and said, 'Lafayette, here we are !' He was initiated in Lincoln Lodge No. 19, Lincoln, Nebraska, in 1888.

PIKE, ALBERT (1809-1891)

American lawyer, author and soldier. After service as a Confederate General in the Civil War, he devoted his life to advancing the cause of the Scottish Rite. From 1859 until his death he was Sovereign Grand Commander of the Scottish Rite, Southern Jurisdiction, and not only rewrote all the rituals but established the theoretical basis and determined the whole ethos of the Rite.

POPE, ALEXANDER (1688-1744)

English poet and satirist. A friend of Swift – and apparently a member of the same Lodge, No. 16, in London – he is remembered for his *Rape of the Lock*, with its Rosicrucian theme, and for his translations of the *Iliad* and the *Odyssey*.

PRESIDENTS OF U.S.A.

WASHINGTON, GEORGE (1732-1799)

First President, 1789-1796. The hero of American Independence was initiated on November 4, 1752, in the lodge at Frederickburg, Virginia, and raised in 1753.

MONROE, JAMES (1758-1831)

Fifth President, 1817-1825. He was initiated in Williamsburg Lodge No. 6 at Williamsburg, Virginia, when he was hardly 18 years of age. He stopped studying and left for the battle front. He became Fellowcraft and Master in a military Lodge during the war.

JACKSON, ANDREW (1767-1845)

Seventh President, 1829-1837. He received the three Craft degrees in Harmony Lodge No. 1, at Nashville, Tennessee. He was Grand Master of the Grand Lodge of Tennessee, October, 1822-October 1824. Honorary member of Federal Lodge No. 1, at Washington, D.C., he was also a Royal Arch Mason.

POLK, JAMES KNOX (1795-1849)

Eleventh President, 1845-1849. Initiated, passed and raised in 1820 in Columbia Lodge No. 21, Columbia, Tennessee. He was Junior Deacon in 1820 then Junior Warden of that same lodge. He was also a member of Mark and Royal Arch.

BUCHANAN, JAMES (1791-1868)

Fifteenth President, 1857-1861. Initiated on December 11, 1816 in Lancaster Lodge No. 43, at Lancaster, Pennsylvania, passed and raised in 1817. Junior Warden in 1821 and 1822, then Worshipful Master in 1825. Became life member in 1858; he was also Deputy Grand Master of the Grand Lodge of Pennsylvania.

JOHNSON, ANDREW (1808-1875)

Seventeenth President, 1865-1869, who succeeded Lincoln. He was initiated, passed and raised in Greenville Lodge No. 19, at Greenville, Tennessee, in 1851. A Knight Templar, he was also the first President who took up the degrees of the Scottish Rite in which he received the 32° in June 1867.

GARFIELD, JAMES ABRAM (1831-1881)

Twentieth President in 1881. He was initiated on November 19, 1864 in Colombus Lodge No. 246, at Garrettsville, Ohio, passed the same year and raised in 1864. He was Chaplain in 1868 and 1869. He was also a member of Pentalpha Lodge No. 23, at Washington, D.C., of the Mark and Royal Arch, and of the Scottish Rite, and he was a Knight Templar.

McKINLEY, WILLIAM (1843 1901)

Twenty-fifth President, 1897-1901. Initiated in Hiram Lodge No. 21, at Winchester, Virginia, on May 1, passed on May 2, raised on May 5, 1865. He was affiliated with Canton Lodge No. 60 at Canton, Ohio. He was a member of Mark and Royal Arch, and a Knight Templar.

ROOSEVELT, THEODORE (1858-1919)

Twenty-sixth President, 1901-1909. He was initiated on January 2, 1801, passed on March 27 and raised on April 24 same year in Matinecock Lodge No. 806, at Oyster Bay, New York State. Made honorary member of Pentalpha Lodge No. 23, at Washington, D.C., he took an active part in numerous Masonic ceremonies.

TAFT, WILLIAM H. (1857-1930)

Twenty-seventh President, 1909-1913. He was also President of the Supreme Court of Justice in 1921. He was made a Mason 'at sight' on June 18, 1909, by Grand Master Charles S. Hoskinson. He was affiliated with Kilwinning Lodge No. 356, on April 14, at Cincinnati, Ohio, then made Honorary member of Crescent lodge No. 25, at Cedar Rapids, Iowa.

HARDING, WARREN G. (1865-1923)

Twenty-ninth president, 1921-1923. He was initiated on June 18, passed on August 13 and raised on August 23, 1920. He became Honorary member of Albert Pike Lodge No. 36, at Washington, D.C., in 1921. He was also a member of the Mark and Royal Arch, a Knight Templar and 33° of the Scottish Rite, the first President who ever became a Shriner.

GALLERY OF 275
FAMOUS MASONS

ROOSEVELT, FRANKLIN DELANO (1882-1945)
Thirty-second President, 1933-1945. He was initiated on October 11, passed on November 14, and raised on November 28, 1911, in Holland Lodge No. 8, New York City. Elected Honorary Member of Stansburg Lodge No. 24, at Washington, D.C.. He was present when his three sons were raised: Elliott on February 17, 1933, James and Franklin D. Jr. in November 1935, all of them in Architect Lodge No. 519, New York City. He was also a member of the Scottish Rite.

TRUMAN, HARRY S. (1884-1972)
Thirty-third President, 1945-1953. He was initiated on February 9, and raised on March 18, 1909 in Belton Lodge No. 450, at Belton, Missouri. He served as Junior Warden of that Lodge, 1940-41. He was Grand Master of the Grand Lodge of Missouri, also a Knight Templar and a 33º in the Scottish Rite.

JOHNSON, LYNDON B.(BORN 1908)
Thirty-sixth President, 1963-1969. He was initiated on October 30, 1937, in Johnson City Lodge No. 561, at Johnson City, Texas.

FORD, GERALD R. (BORN 1913)
Thirty-eighth President, 1974-1977. He was initiated on September 30, 1949, in Malta Lodge, at Grand Rapids, Michigan. He was raised on May 18, 1951, in Colombia Lodge No. 3, at Washington, D.C., by proxy of Malta Lodge. He was awarded the Distinguished Achievements Medal in 1974.

PRESTON, WILLIAM (1742-1818)
English Masonic author. His book *Illustrations of Masonry* (1772) was the most popular Masonic book in England for some seventy-five years. He was Master of the prestigious Lodge of Antiquity No. 2, and exercised a crucial influence on the development of both Masonic ritual and the philosophy that underlies it.

PULLMAN, GEORGE M. (1831-1897)
American engineer. In 1858 he remodelled two railway coaches into sleeping cars, and in 1863 built the prototype, named 'The Pioneer', of the present Pullman car. The manufacturing company, Pullman Palace Car Co., was set up in 1867 and in the following year the first dining cars were built. Pullman was a member of Renovation Lodge No. 97, Albion, New York.

PUSHKIN, ALEKSANDER (1799-1837)
Russian poet. His greatest works, *Evgene Onegin* (1823-1830), and *Boris Godunov* (1825), have been widely translated and also presented as both opera and ballet. He was initiated in 1821 in Lodge Ovid, at Kischinev.

RAFFLES, SIR THOMAS STAMFORD (1781-1826)
English colonial governor. He spent much of his life in the East Indies where he was for five years Lieutenant-Governor of Java. In 1819 he founded the city of Singapore as 'a free port and the trade thereof open to ships and vessels of every nation'. On his return to England he founded the Zoological Society, of which he was first president. He was initiated in Lodge Virtute et Artis Amici, in Java, was Master of Lodge Friendship, Soerabaya, in 1813. Member of Rose-Croix Chapter La Vertueuse, Batavia, Djarkata.

REVERE, PAUL (1735-1818)
American silversmith and Revolutionary War patriot. In addition to his silver work, he was the first to roll sheet copper in America, he designed the first official seal for the colonies, and produced the first banknotes. His ride in 1775 from Boston to Lexington to warn of the approach of British troops was immortalized in Longfellow's poem *The Midnight Ride of Paul Revere*. From 1794 to 1797 he was Grand Master of the Grand Lodge of Massachusetts.

RICHET, CHARLES ROBERT (1850-1935)
French physiologist. Between 1887 and 1902 he worked on the production of an immune serum and discovered the phenomenon of anaphylaxis (now called allergy). For his research, in 1913 he was awarded the Nobel Prize for medicine and physiology. In later years Richet devoted himself to psychical research. He was a member of Lodge Cosmos under the Grand Lodge of France.

RICHTER, JOHANN PAUL FRIEDRICH (1763-1825)
German novelist. A prolific author, influenced by Goethe, he was, in his day, probably the most widely-read novelist in Germany. He was a member of Lodge Pforte zum Tempel des Lichts, at Hof.

RICKENBACKER, EDWARD V. (1890-1973)
American aviator. During World War One he commanded the 94th Hero Pursuit Squadron and became the leading American 'Ace'. After the war he worked in civil aviation, but returned to military work in World War Two, and was awarded the Distinguished Service Cross with nine clusters, and the Congressional Medal of Honour for his bravery on special missions. He was a member of Kilwinning Lodge No. 297, Detroit, Michigan.

RICKEY, BRANCH (1881-1965)
Major league baseball player and manager. As manager, he won four world championships. Initiated in Tuscan Lodge No. 360, St. Louis, Missouri.

THE RINGLING BROTHERS (ALBERT, ALFRED, AUGUST, CHARLES, HENRY, JOHN, AND WILLIAM)

American showmen. Founded in 1884 by their father, August Ringling, the world famous Ringling Brothers' Circus became known as the 'Greatest Show on Earth'. All seven brothers – and their father – were members of Baraboo Lodge No. 34, Baraboo, Wisconsin.

ROBINSON, 'SUGAR RAY' (BORN 1921)

American black boxer. Light heavyweight boxing champion of the world in 1951 and five times World Middleweight champion (1951/52 to 1958). He was a member of Joppa Lodge No. 55, Prince Hall Affiliation, New York City.

ROGERS, ROY (BORN 1912)

American cowboy, screen star. Member of Hollywood Lodge No. 355, Hollywood, California.

ROTHSCHILD, NATHAN MEYER (1777-1836)

Anglo-German financier. He established the London branch – the most important one – of the famous Merchant Bank founded by his father. His brother James, who was also a Mason, founded the Paris branch of the bank. He was a member of Emulation Lodge No. 21.

ROUGET DE LISLE, CLAUDE JOSEPH (1760-1836)

French composer. In 1792 he wrote the stirring patriotic song, *Chant de guerre pour l'armée du Rhin*, which was renamed *La Marseillaise* and became the French National Anthem. He was a member of Loge Les Frères Discrets, at Charleville.

ROUX, ANDRÉ (1928-1992)

French lawyer and Grand Master of the French National Grand Lodge. His work as Grand Master ensured continuing international support for his Grand Lodge as the only recognised Masonic body in France.

SABATINI, RAPHAEL (1875-1950)

English romantic novelist. Among his most popular works – many of which were made into cinema films – were *Scaramouche, Captain Blood,* and *The Sea Hawk*. He was initiated in 1919 in Jerusalem Lodge, No. 197, London.

SAINT-MARTIN, LOUIS CLAUDE DE (1743-1803)

French speculative philosopher. He developed a unique system of Christian mystical thought which he published under the name of *The Unknown Philosopher*. To some extent it derives from his mentor, Martines de Pasqually, and the work of both men has been incorporated in the quasi-Masonic system of Martinism. He was a member of many of the more exotic Masonic Orders of his day.

SALTEN, FELIX [FELIX SALZMANN] (1869- 1945)

Austro-Hungarian writer of children's stories. His most famous creation was *Bambi*, the story of an orphaned deer immortalized in the Walt Disney cartoon film version. He was a member of Lodge Zur Wahreit in Vienna.

SARNOFF, DAVID (1891-1971)

American radio and television executive. All of his life was spent in the radio industry, first with the Marconi Company and then with the Radio Corporation of America, of which he became President at the age of 39. He was known as the 'father of American television'. He entered the Craft in Strict Observance Lodge No. 94, New York City, in 1921.

SAVAGE, RICHARD (1697-1743)

English poet and playwright. A close friend of Dr. Johnson, his early death prevented full recognition of his abilities. In 1737 he was Master of Richmond Lodge, No. 55, London.

SAX, ANTOINE JOSEPH (ADOLPH) (1814-1894)

Belgian instrument maker. He invented the Saxhorn (1845) and Saxophone (1846), and ushered in a new range of musical expression. He was initiated in Lodge Les Vrais Amis de l'Union in 1842.

SCHOELCHER, VICTOR (1804-1893)

French politician. In 1848 he was instrumental in bringing about the abolition of slavery in the French colonies. He was initiated in Loge Les Amis de la Vérité, at Paris.

SCOTT, ROBERT FALCON (1868-1912)

English polar explorer. On his second Antarctic expedition, 1911-1912, Scott reached the Pole just five weeks after the Norwegian, Amundsen, but on the return journey he perished with his entire party. From diaries recovered later it is clear that members of the part displayed outstanding heroism. He was a member of Drury Lane Lodge No. 2127, London.

SCOTT, SIR WALTER (1771-1832)

Scottish novelist and poet. The vast literary output of 'The Wizard of the North' included poems such as *The Lady of the Lake* and *The Lay of the Last Minstrel*; and such historical novels as *Ivanhoe, Quentin Durward,* and *The Talisman*. He was initiated, passed and raised at an emergency meeting of Saint David Lodge No. 36, Edinburgh, on March 2, 1801.

SELLERS, PETER (1925-1980)

English stage, screen and radio actor. He was best known for his comic roles in such films as *The Millionairess* (1961), *The Pink Panther*, and *Dr. Strangelove* (1963), and in the BBC radio *Goon Show*. He was initiated in Chelsea Lodge No 3098, London.

SHACKLETON, SIR ERNEST H. (1874-1922)

English explorer. The greatest of all Antarctic explorers, he died on his third major expedition and is buried in South Georgia.

SHILLIBEER, GEORGE (1797-1866)

English inventor. He pioneered the omnibus, first in Paris and then, in 1829, in London. He was initiated in Etonian Lodge, Windsor, in 1827.

SIBELIUS, JAN (1865-1957)

Finnish composer. The most powerful Scandinavian composer and the greatest Masonic musician after Mozart. He was one of the founding members of Finnish Masonry, being initiated in Suomi Lodge No. 1, Helsinki, within hours of the creation of the Grand Lodge of Finland in 1922. Sibelius composed a considerable body of music for Masonic occasions.

SIMPSON, WILLIAM (1823-1899)

English artist. He achieved fame as a war artist in the Crimea, being known afterwards as 'Crimean Simpson'. From 1860 he was the 'special artist' of the illustrated London News and followed major and minor campaigns around the world. He was a member of Quatuor Coronati Lodge No. 2076.

SKELTON, RICHARD B. 'RED' (BORN 1913)

Comedian and television star. He was raised in Vincennes Lodge No. 1, Vincennes, Indiana, in 1939.

SMIRKE, SIR ROBERT (1781-1867)

English architect. He designed many prominent buildings in London in the classical style, including Covent Garden Theatre, the Royal Mint and the British Museum. He also carried out the restoration of York Minster in 1829. Smirke was a member of Antiquity Lodge No. 2, London.

SMITH, JOSEPH (1805-1844)

American founder of the Church of Jesus Christ of Latter-day Saints – the Mormons. His Church grew out of the teachings of the strange Book of Mormon that he claimed had been revealed to him by an angel. He was initiated in Nauvoo Lodge, Nauvoo, Illinois, but was expelled for his misuse of the ceremonies which later became the basis of the Temple Ceremonies of his Church.

SOANE, SIR JOHN (1753-1837)

English architect whose most famous work was the Bank of England which he rebuilt in 1788. He collected a remarkable museum of paintings and other works of art which he presented to the nation in 1833. He was a member of Grand Mare Lodge No. 1.

SOUSA, JOHN PHILIP (1854-1932)

American composer and bandmaster. From 1880 to 1892 he led the band of the U.S. Marine Corps, and later his own band. His marching tunes – among them *Washington Post* and *Stars and Stripes for Ever* – became world famous, and 'The March King', as he was called, exerted an enormous influence on martial music. He was a member of Hiram Lodge No. 10, at Washington, D.C.

STENDHAL [HENRI BEYLE] (1783-1842)

French novelist and critic. His most famous novels are *Le Rouge et le Noir* (Red and Black) (1830) and *La Chartreuse de Parme* (1839). He was a member of the French Lodge Sainte Caroline.

STILL, ANDREW T. (1828-1917)

American physician. After losing three children during an epidemic of spinal meningitis in 1864, he devised the treatment of osteopathy (manipulation of the skeletal structure), and began to practice it in 1874. In 1892 he founded the American School of Osteopathy. He was a member of Palmyra Lodge No. 23, Baldwin, Kansas.

STRATTON, CHARLES S. (1838-1883)

American midget. He was made famous by P. T. Barnum, who exhibited him as 'General Tom Thumb'. He later married another midget, Lavinia Warren, and they were exhibited around the world. He was a member of St. John's Lodge No. 3, Bridgeport, Connecticut.

STRESEMAN, GUSTAV (1878-1929)

German statesman. He negotiated the return of the Ruhr to Germany in 1925, and signed the *Treaty of Locarno* with Briand in 1926 – for which he was awarded the Nobel Peace Prize.
He was a member of Lodge Friedrich der Grosse.

STUKELEY, WILLIAM (1687-1765)

English antiquarian and Fellow of the Royal Society. His best known work was an account of Stonehenge (1740), and he was responsible for the romantic image of Druidism that persisted for more than a century after his death.
He was made a Mason at the Salutation Tavern, London, in 1721.

SULLIVAN, SIR ARTHUR SEYMOUR (1842-1900)

English composer. He is remembered for his collaboration with Sir W. S. Gilbert (q.v.) in the Savoy Operas, but he also composed overtures, oratorios, a *Te Deum*, and the music for such songs and hymns as *The Lost Chord*, and *Onward Christian Soldiers*. He was Grand Organist of the United Grand Lodge of England in the Jubilee year, 1887.

SWIFT, JONATHAN (1667-1745)

Irish poet, satirist, and Dean of St. Patrick's, Dublin. Of his many importantt works – *A Tale of a Tub*, the *Journal to Stella*, the *Drapier's Letters* – the greatest is, beyond question, *Gulliver's Travels* (1726). He is believed to have been a member of Lodge No. 16, which met at the 'Goat at the foot of the Haymarket'.

THOMAS, LOWELL (BORN 1892)

American explorer and author. He was the first writer to bring *Lawrence of Arabia* to public notice. His books on his travels in India, South East, and Central Asia were extremely popular. He was raised in St. John's Lodge, Boston, Massachusetts, in 1927.

THOMSON, JAMES (1700-1748)

Scottish poet. Although *The Castle of Ignorance* (1748) is accepted as his masterpiece, he is best-known for *The Seasons* (1726-1730). He was initiated in 1737 in the lodge that met at the Old Man's Coffee House, London.

THORWALDSEN, BERTEL (1768-1844)

Danish sculptor. His most famous work is the colossal statue of a lion, at Lucerne, Switzerland. He was a member of Zorubabel Lodge, Copenhagen.

TIRPITZ, ALFRED VON (1849-1930)

German naval officer. He was responsible for the creation of a modern navy for the German Empire, and it was his policy of unrestricted submarine warfare that brought America into World War One. He was a member of Lodge Zur Aufrichtigen Herzen, at Frankfurt.

TRAVIS, WILLIAM B. (1811-1836)

American Commander of the Alamo. His heroism, and that of the men he led, inspired the Texans in their struggle for freedom. He was initiated in Alabama Lodge No. 3, Claiborne, Alabama, in 1829.

TROLLOPE, ANTHONY (1815-1882)

English novelist. He is best known for his *Barsetshire* novels of English clerical life, and for his series of political novels concerning the Palliser family. He was initiated in Banagher Lodge No. 306, Banagher, Ireland, in 1841.

TSCHIRSKY, OSCAR (1866-1950)

Swiss-American chef. In 1893 he became chef at the Waldorf Astoria, and as 'Oscar of the Waldorf' brought fame to the hotel. He was a member of Metropolitan Lodge No. 273, New York City.

VIVEKANANDA, SWAMI NERENDRAMAH DATTA (1863-1902)

Indian ascetic who became the leading exponent of both Hinduism and Yoga in the west. In 1893 he attended the Parliament of Religions at the World's Fair in Chicago. He was initiated in Hope and Anchor Lodge No. 1, Calcutta, in 1884.

VOLTAIRE [FRANÇOIS MARIE AROUET] (1694- 1778)

French writer and philosopher. He was a brilliant satirist and a defender of victims of religious intolerance. The Church condemned him as an atheist (although he was really a Deist) and he left France on more than one occasion, for England, Prussia, and Switzerland. On 7 April 1778, two months before his death, Voltaire was escorted by Benjamin Franklin into Lodge Les Neuf Soeurs, at Paris, and was initiated into the Craft.

WADLOW, ROBERT PERSHING (1918-1940)

He was the tallest human being on record, being almost nine feet in height. He was made a Mason in Franklin Lodge No. 25, Alton, Illinois, in 1939.

WAITE, ARTHUR EDWARD (1857-1942)

English writer and Masonic historian. He was this century's most prolific exponent of esoteric ideas, and especially of the spiritual aspects of Masonry. He was initiated in Runymede Lodge No. 2430, Wraysbury, Buckinghamshire, in 1901.

WALLACE, LEW(IS) (1827-1905)

American soldier and novelist. After distinguished service in the Civil War he resumed his legal practice and entered politics. His writing career began in 1873 with *The Fair God*, and his most famous work, the classic *Ben Hur*, appeared in 1880. He was initiated in 1850 in Fountain Lodge No. 60, Covington, Indiana.

WARNER, JACK L. (1892-1978)

American film producer. He was the last member of the four Warner brothers who started their company in 1923 and pioneered sound pictures in 1927 with *The Jazz Singer*, whose star, A1 Jolson, was also a Mason. Warner was initiated in Mount Olive Lodge No. 506, Los Angeles, California, in 1938.

WASHINGTON, BOOKER T[ALIAFERRO] (1859- 1915)

American black educator and author. He was highly influential both through his works on the American black and as a promoter of racial harmony. He was made a Mason 'at sight' by the Grand Master of the Prince Hall Grand Lodge of Massachusetts.

WAYNE, JOHN [MARION MICHAEL MORRISON] (1907-1979)

American film star. He was the archetypal Western hero and starred in more films than any other actor, but he did not receive an Oscar until 1969 for *True Grit*. He was a DeMolay.

WEBB, MATTHEW (1848-1883)

English swimmer. He was the first man to swim the English Channel (1875), and he performed other feats of endurance until he was drowned in 1883 while attempting to swim through the rapids and whirlpool at the foot of the Niagara Falls. He was initiated in Neptune Lodge No. 22, in 1877.

WELLINGTON, ARTHUR, DUKE OF (1769- 1852)

He defeated Napoleon at the Battle of Waterloo in 1815, aided by Blucher (q.v.). His father was Grand Master of the Grand Lodge of Ireland in 1776. The 'Iron Duke' was initiated in the family lodge No. 494, at Trim, on December 7, 1790.

WHITEMAN, PAUL (1891-1967)

American jazz musician, known as the 'King of Jazz'. Many of the most famous jazz musicians of the pre-war period played in his orchestra. He was a member of St. Cecile Lodge No 568, New York City.

WILDE, OSCAR O'FLAHERTIE WILLS (1854-1900)

Anglo-Irish wit and dramatist. His plays, which remain deservedly popular, include *Lady Windermere's Fan*, and *The Importance of being Earnest*. At the end of his life he wrote the famous poem, *The Ballad of Reading Gaol*. He was initiated in Apollo Lodge No. 357, Oxford, in 1875.

WOOD, REV. JOHN GEORGE (1827-1889)

English naturalist and author. He was the most prolific author on natural history of his day, and the greatest populariser of the subject among the general public. His principal publisher was his fellow Mason, George Routledge. He was a member of St. Paul's Lodge No. 194, London.

ZANUCK, DARRYL F. (1902-1979)

American film producer. He was a co-founder of 20th-Century Productions in 1933 (which became 20th-Century-Fox in 1935). He was a member of Mount Olive Lodge No. 506, Los Angeles.

ZIEGFELD, FLORENZ (1869-1932)

American theatrical producer. His spectacular *Ziegfeld's Follies* were produced on the New York stage from 1907 onwards. He was initiated in Accordia Lodge No. 277, Chicago, Illinois, in 1866.

ZOFFANY, JOHN (1733-1810)

English portrait painter, born in Germany. His portraits were highly acclaimed, and in 1768 he was a founder member of the Royal Academy. He was a member of the Lodge of Nine Muses, London.

GLOSSARY

Accepted Mason – Originally a non-operative accepted into an operative masons' lodge. Now a Freemason, as in Free and Accepted Mason.

Additional Degrees – In England, *basic* Freemasonry consists of the three Craft degrees and the Royal Arch, with the highest being the third degree of Master Mason. In other countries, particularly America, the other degrees and Orders are additional to the three degrees and are referred to as higher degrees.

Adoptive Masonry – Freemasonry for women, which originated in France in 18th century. There are today a number of feminine Grand Lodges in Britain and Europe but they are not recognised as being Masonic by regular Grand Lodges.

Allied Masonic Degrees – In 1880 a Grand Council of the Allied Masonic Degrees was formed in England to superintend a number of unconnected degrees which had no governing bodies. Today it governs the degrees of St. Lawrence the Martyr, Grand Tylers of Solomon, Red Cross of Babylon, Knight of Constantinople and Grand High Priest. A similar Grand Council, covering these and other degrees, exists in the USA.

Ancient and Accepted (Scottish) Rite – A system of thirty-three degrees developed out of the 18th century French Rite of Perfection of twenty-five degrees. Outside the British Isles it is referred to as the Scottish Rite, many of the original French degrees having *Ecossais* in their titles. In Britain it is a Christian Order but in most other countries it is as universalist as the Craft.

Androgynous degrees – Degrees open to men and women, e.g. the Eastern Star (q.v.).

Anno Lucis – Literally the year of light. The system of dating documents in Craft Freemasonry was derived from Archbishop Usher's chronology. Usher, by studying the Old Testament computed that the world was formed 4004 years before the birth of Christ, therefore in Masonic terminology AD 1992 becomes Anno Lucis 5996. In most Masonic constitutions the system was simplified by adding only 4000, making AD 1992 into AL 5992.

Apron – The principal item of a Craft Freemasons' regalia. Derived from the lambskin apron worn by the operative stone masons to protect their clothing. In Freemasonry the wearing of the apron points out that regardless of their stations in life, in Freemasonry all men are equal.

Ars Quatuor Coronatorum – The *Transactions* of Quatuor Coronati Lodge No. 2076, London, the premier Lodge of Masonic Research. The 103 volumes so far published are a treasure house of Masonic knowledge.

Ashlar – Literally stones for building. The rough ashlar represents the candidate coming into Freemasonry unpolished, and the perfect ashlar represents the state he hopes to reach by practising the principles and tenets of Freemasonry.

Blue Masonry – An American term for Craft Freemasonry, derived from the celestial blue of heaven which is said, in the ritual, to be the covering of a Masons' lodge.

Broken Column – A symbol of those in need. In many lodges the alms box is in the form of a broken column.

Capitular Masonry – An American term for Royal Arch Masonry (q.v.).

Cardinal Virtues – The four cardinal virtues which a Freemason is exhorted to practice are Prudence, Temperance, Fortitude and Justice.

Chapter – Masonic short-hand for the Royal Arch (q.v.), derived from the basic unit in that Order being called a Chapter.

Charges – The duties a Freemason owes to his God, the law, his family and society in general. They are explained in set pieces of ritual delivered in the three Craft ceremonies.

Charter – In many Grand Lodges and Grand Chapters the formal document which is the lodge's or chapter's authority to meet and practise regular Freemasonry.

Clandestine – A clandestine lodge etc. is one which meets without any regular authority from an established Masonic body. Its members would not be acceptible in regular Freemasonry.

Co-Masonry – A system for men and women formed in France in 1894 and exported from there to England in 1902. Regarded as irregular by regular Freemasonry.

Companion – The name given to members of Royal Arch Masonry to distinguish them from Craft Masons.

Constitution – Lodges working under the United Grand Lodge of England are described as being of the English Constitution; those under the Grand Lodges of Ireland etc. are described as being of the Irish, Scottish, French etc. Constitutions.

Constitution, Book of – The basis upon which a Grand Lodge practises Freemasonry and the basic rules and regulations by which it conducts its affairs and governs the relationships between it and its lodges and its individual members.

Craft – A distinctive term used to define and separate lodge Freemasonry from the other Masonic degrees and Orders. The Craft refers specifically to Freemasonry as practised in lodges under a Grand Lodge.

Deacons – The officers in a Craft lodge who assist the Master in carrying out the ceremonies by conducting the candidates and acting as messengers.

Degrees – In Freemasonry, degree is used in its sense of a progressive step, hence a candidate in the Craft progresses by three degrees or steps to become a Master Mason.

District Grand Lodge – In the English and Scottish Constitutions lodges abroad in a specific area are grouped together in District Grand Lodges headed by a District Grand Master with a team of District Grand Officers, e.g. the District Grand Lodges of Jamaica, East Africa, New Zealand etc.

Eastern Star – An androgynous Order formed in the USA in the 1850s by Robert Morris. Although requiring the presence of Freemasons at its meetings the Order is not Masonic per se.

Entered Apprentice – The first degree of Craft Masonry. The ceremony by which a candidate becomes a Freemason. Derived from the apprenticeship system in the operative crafts.

Exposures – From the 1720s there has been popular curiosity as to the rituals and secrets of Freemasonry, which has been satisfied from time to time by the publication of so-called exposures purporting to reveal the secrets.

Fellowcraft – The second degree in Craft Masonry; the ceremony of passing an Entered Apprentice (q.v.) to the status of a Fellowcraft.

Festive Board – The refreshment and fellowship enjoyed after a Masonic meeting, often including the honouring of loyal and Masonic toasts.

Free – Originally in Freemasonry to be free was to be freeborn and not in servitude.

Freemason – A member of Freemasonry. One who is a Free and Accepted rather than an operative stone mason.

Freemasonry – A generic term covering the whole of the Masonic system. Freemasons as a body rather than as individuals.

General Grand Chapter – An umbrella body in the USA to which many of the State Royal Arch Grand Chapters subscribe. A discussion body with no executive power, any recommendations it makes having to be voted on by the individual Grand Chapters before they can be adopted.

Grand Chapter – The governing body of, and supreme authority over, a group of Royal Arch Chapters. Grand Chapters are usually organised on a national or State basis.

Grand Lodge – The governing body, and sovereign authority over, a group of lodges, usually organised on a national or State basis. The Grand Lodge is the final authority and law making body, its membership is by right of office or Masonic status and not elective.

Grand Master – The senior member of a Grand Lodge. The Grand Master's powers are defined by the Book of Constitutions, making him a constitutional ruler and not an autocrat.

Grand Orient – Literally Grand East. Title adopted by some European and South American bodies as an alternative to Grand Lodge.

Great Architect of the Universe – Masonic vocative for God enabling men of different religions to refer and pray to God without offending their religious susceptibilities. To a Christian the Great Architect is the Trinitarian God of his faith, to a Muslim it is Allah, etc. The Great Architect is neither an attempt to combine God as He is seen in different religions nor a separate Masonic god.

Higher Degrees – In the Ancient and Accepted (Scottish) Rite the degrees from the 30th to the 33rd. Used erroneously as a description for degrees beyond the Craft (see Additional Degrees).

Immediate Past Master – Having completed his period as Master of a Lodge a brother becomes the Immediate Past Master of the Lodge and by virtue of that office assumes the chair of the lodge in the absence of the Master.

Inner Guard – A junior officer of the lodge who guards the door from inside the lodge room.

Installation – The formal ceremony of placing the presiding officer in the chair and investing him with his authority to preside. In some Craft constitutions and in a number of the additional degrees the installation includes the conferring of additional signs and words restricted to those who have occupied the Chair.

Irregular Masonry – A number of groups exist calling themselves Masonic which are not recognised as such and are said to be irregular. Recognition as a regular Masonic body is only granted to those which subscribe to certain agreed principles, in particular that a belief in a Supreme Being is essential in every candidate; that the Volume of the Sacred Law is present at all meetings; that the discussion of politics and religion are banned at all meetings; and that only men are admitted into membership.

Jewels – Freemasons refer to badges of rank and office and other Masonic medals as jewels. Many of them are indeed jewels of the goldsmith's, silversmith's and enameller's arts.

Knights of Malta – A Christian Masonic degree based upon the medieval Knights Hospitallers and emphasizing the Christian virtues.

Knights Templar – A Christian Masonic Order based upon the medieval Knights Templar and emphasizing the Christian virtues.

Landmarks – In Freemasonry a landmark is some aspect of the system which has been present 'from time immemorial' and whose removal would alter the essential nature of Freemasonry. Many have attempted to provide definitive lists of landmarks but many of the items included in those lists are simply time honoured customs and basic rules for conducting Masonic meetings. Examples of landmarks would be the insistence on all candidates having a belief in a Supreme Being; the ban on political and religious discussions together with Freemasons *as a body* giving political or religious opinions; the use of ritual.

Lewis – In operative Masonry a lewis is a metal clamp inserted in a large stone to enable it to be lifted or lowered. In Freemasonry a Lewis is the son of a Freemason.

Lodge – The basic unit in Craft Freemasonry. A lodge is a group of Freemasons given authority by the Grand Master and/or Grand Lodge to meet and practice Freemasonry.

Mark Masonry – An additional degree which in England has its own Grand Lodge and subordinate Lodges but which in other constitutions forms part of the Royal Arch system.

Master – The presiding officer of a lodge elected by the members to rule the lodge and carry out the ceremonial. In most constitutions the Master serves for one year and a successor is then elected to replace him. In a few European systems the Master continues in office for life, or until he decides to retire.

Master Mason – The third degree of Craft Masonry, the final step by which a candidate becomes a Freemason and is then able to take office in his lodge and progress towards the Mastership of it.

Mother Lodge –
(a) The lodge in which a candidate was introduced into Freemasonry, and which will have special place in his affections throughout his Masonic career.
(b) In the 18th century an independent lodge which gave authority to others to meet as lodges. The best known example is Mother Kilwinning in Scotland which,

although one of the founders, broke away from the Grand Lodge of Scotland and for nearly sixty years exercised its immemorial authority to constitute new lodges until it, and its daughter lodges, rejoined the Grand Lodge of Scotland in 1802.

Obligations – The serious promises taken by Freemasons to uphold the principles and tenets of Freemasonry and to preserve the secrets (signs and words) of the particular degree. Despite popular belief the obligations do not bind Freemasons to support each other regardless of the circumstances. A Freemason would be breaking his obligations if he gave protection to anyone guilty of '...murder, treason, felony or any other offences contrary to the laws of God or the ordinances of the realm'.

Old Charges – A series of 124 known documents (of which 112 survive) dating from c.1390 to the mid-18th century often referred to as the Gothic Constitutions or title deeds of the Craft. In two parts, they consist of a largely legendary history of the Mason craft followed by a series of Charges in which the Mason's duties to God, the law and society in general are laid down.

Operative Mason – A stone mason who cut and prepared stone for building.

Passing – The ceremony of the second degree in which the Entered Apprentice is passed to the degree of a Fellowcraft.

Past Master – A Mason who has served as Master of his lodge.

Provincial Grand Lodge – In England lodges outside London are grouped in Provinces, based on the old Counties with the larger Provinces divided into two. The Provincial Grand Lodge is presided over by the Provincial Grand Master who is appointed by the Grand Master to act as his Deputy within the Province. The Provincial Grand Master annually appoints a team of Provincial Grand Officers to assist him in administering his Province. The same system is used in Ireland and Scotland.

Quarterly Communications – The quarterly meetings of a Grand Lodge at which administrative business is carried out.

Raising – The ceremony of the third degree in which a Fellowcraft is raised to the status of a Master Mason.

Red Cross of Constantine – A Christian Masonic degree based upon the story of Helena, Constantine and the finding of the true cross.

Royal and Select Masters – Alternately known as the Cryptic Degrees. In England the Royal and Select Masters is a separate series of degrees filling in gaps between the Craft and the Royal Arch legends. Their equivalent in other constitutions form part of the Royal Arch series.

Royal Arch – In England the Royal Arch is regarded as the completion of the Master Mason degree. In other constitutions it is a separate degree independent of the Craft and usually the climax of a series of degrees linking it to the Craft. In both the intent is the same. Having learned in the Craft paractical lessons in how to live a life pleasing in the eyes of God and of service to mankind, the candidate in the Royal Arch is, without transgressing the bounds of religion, led to contemplate the nature of and his relationship with his God. Members of the Royal arch are called Companions, and meet in Chapters under the authority of a Grand Chapter.

Royal Ark Mariner – An additional degree based upon the story of Noah and his ark. In England it is a separate degree attached to the Mark (q.v.). In other constitutions, where it exists, it either forms part of the Royal Arch series or is part of the Allied Masonic Degrees (q.v.).

Royal Order of Scotland – Dating back to at least the 1740s the Royal Order of Scotland is governed by a Grand Lodge in Edinburgh with Provincial Grand Lodges throughout the world. It has two degrees the rituals for which, mostly in blank verse, draw together strands found in many of the additional degrees.

Scottish Rite – *see* Ancient and Accepted (Scottish) Rite.

Secret Monitor – An Order of three degrees based upon the biblical story of David and Jonathan and the virtues of friendship and service.

Shriners – The Ancient Arabic Order of Nobles of the Mystic Shrine, formed in New York in the early 1870s. Entry is restricted to those having the 32nd degree in the Scottish Rite or being Knight Templars. Principally a means of raising enormous sums of money for charity. The Shriners are well known in America for their parades with marching bands and members in fancy dress costumes.

Societas Rosicruciana in Anglia – The SRIA, and its sisters the Societas Rosicruciana in Scotia and the Societas Rosicruciana in Civitatis Feodoratis, whilst not Masonic Orders *per se* require their members to be Master Masons. Their aim is the study and understanding of Western and Eastern religions and esoteric subjects.

Speculative – Literally non-operative Masons. Used in the original sense of to meditate upon a theme or subject. Thus an operative mason is involved in the practicalities of his trade, but a speculative mason uses the idea of building and the tools involved to remind him of the principles and tenets he has sworn to uphold.

Supreme Council 33° – The governing body in the Ancient and Accepted (Scottish) Rite. Each Supreme Council is sovereign over the Rite in its particular geographical area. It usually consists of nine active members led by a Sovereign Grand Commander. The Supreme Council governs the 4th to the 33rd degrees, ceding authority over the first three to the Grand Lodge(s) from which it draws its membership.

Swedish Rite – In Scandinavia a rite of ten connected degrees is worked corresponding to the Craft, Royal Arch, Knights Templar and Ancient and Accepted (Scottish) Rite in other Constitutions. The preliminary degrees are universalist but the higher degrees are intensely Christian.

Tracing Boards – In operative terms a board on which the architect or builder traced out the ground plan of the new structure. In Freemasonry a pictorial and symbolic representation of the principles of a particular degree.

Tyler – The officer of the Lodge who guards the door from the outside. The derivation of the title is obscure.

Universalism – A term applied in two senses to Freemasonry.
(a) Freemasonry is universal in that it exists throughout the world, and
(b) it is universal in that, barring the requirement for a belief in a Supreme Being, it embraces men of all races, creeds and opinions.

Volume of the Sacred Law – To the vast majority of members the VSL is the Bible 'that great light which is from above'. To Muslims, Hindus, Parsees, etc. the VSL is the book which is held sacred within their particular religion.

Wardens – The Senior and Junior Wardens, with the Master, are the principle officers of a lodge. Their offices are derived from the guild system.

Warrant – The formal document by which a lodge is authorised by its Grand Lodge to practice Freemasonry. In some constitutions it is referred to as a Charter.

Working Tools – The working tools of an operative mason (the square, level, plumb etc.) are used as symbols to remind Freemasons of the principles and tenets of the Craft.

York Rite – The system in the United States of America which encompasses the Mark, Cryptic, Royal Arch and Knight Templar Orders. Derived from the English Ancients Grand Lodge which worked all of these Orders within its lodges and claimed descent from a supposed Assembly of Masons held by Prince Edwin at York in 926 AD.

BIBLIOGRAPHY

The following list is in not a comprehensive bibliography of Freemasonry – which would run into many thousands of titles – but is designed as a general guide to further reading for both Masons and non-Masons. Many of the books listed contain their own, often substantial, bibliographies which will help the reader who seeks further and more specialised information.

ANDERSON, James. *The Constitutions of the Freemasons*, 1723 [and] *The New Book of Constitutions ...*, 1738. Facsimile reprint. Foreword by Eric Ward. London, 1976. The earliest administrative documents of the modern Craft. With introductions. by L. Vibert and W.J. Hughan.

ARS QUATUOR CORONATORUM. *Transactions of Quatuor Coronati Lodge* No. 2076, London, 1888 onwards (the latest issue is Volume 103). The annual volumes of *Transactions* of the premier lodge of Masonic research. The contents cover almost every aspect of Masonic knowledge. A concise index to Vols. 1 to 80 was published in 1971.

BAYNARD, S.H. *History of the Supreme Council 33° Ancient & Accepted Scottish Rite of Freemasonry, Northern Jurisdiction of the USA.* Boston, 1938, 2 volumes. The standard history.

BUISINE, Andrée. *La femme et la Franc-Maçonnerie dans les pays de langue anglo-saxonne.* Dijon, France,1990. A documented thesis for a State Doctorate.

CARR, Harry (ed.). *The Early French Exposures.* London, 1971. Translations, with extensive comment, of the unauthorised texts that are the earliest printed European Masonic rituals.
——, *The Freemason at Work.* Revised edition. London, 1981. A collection of over 200 of the questions and answers that have been printed in the lodge summonses and *Transactions of Quatuor Coronati Lodge.*

COIL, Henry Wilson. *Coil's Masonic Cyclopaedia.* Revised by W.M. Brown, W.L. Cummings and H.V.B. Voorhis. New York, 1961. The best single volume Masonic reference work. A new edition is currently in preparation.

COLLECTED PRESTONIAN LECTURES. Three volumes. London, 1984-1988. Volume 1: 1925-1960 ed. Harry Carr; Volume 2: 1961-1974 ed. Cyril Batham; Volume 3: 1975-1987 ed. Rev. N. B. Cryer. These prestigious lectures, on a wide variety of Masonic topics and each delivered by a recognised authority, are given each year under the aegis of the United Grand Lodge of England.

DENSLOW, William R. *10,000 Famous Freemasons.* Trenton, Mo., 1957-1961. 4 volumes. An important source of biographical information for American Masons, but relatively weak for Britain and Europe.

DYER, Colin. *Symbolism in Craft Freemasonry.* London, 1976. An excellent guide to an understanding of the symbols utilised in the three Craft degrees.
——, *Preston and his work.* Shepperton, 1987. An excellent study of Preston and his work. It includes the complete texts of Preston's highly important 'Lectures'.

GOULD, Robert Freke. *History and Antiquities of Freemasonry.* Third edition revised by H. Poole. London, 1951. 4 vols. The best edition of the most comprehensive general history of the Craft, but it omits much of the material on European Freemasonry that appears in the original edition of 1882-1887, while American Masonic history is given in greater detail in the long 'addenda' to the editions printed in the United States.

HAFFNER, Christopher. *Workman Unashamed.* Shepperton, 1989. A careful study of Freemasonry in relation to religion. It shows clearly that there is no conflict between being a Mason and being a practising Christian.

HAMILL, John. *The Craft. A History of English Freemasonry.* Wellingborough, 1986. A concise, reliable and comprehensive history.

HAMILL, John & GILBERT, Robert A. *World Freemasonry. An illustrated History.* London, 1991. An informative illustrated guide.

HENDERSON, Kent. *Masonic World Guide.* Shepperton, 1984. An invaluable reference work, giving details of every recognised Grand Lodge throughout the world.

HORNE, Alex. *King Solomon's Temple in the Masonic Tradition.* Wellingborough, 1972. A study of the history, significance and symbolism of the Temple.

HUGHAN, W.J. *The Origin of the English Rite of Freemasonry.* Third edition, revised by J.T. Thorp. Leicester, 1925. A classic study that is still of great value, more than a century after its original publication in 1884.

JACKSON, A.C.F. *Rose-Croix: A History of the Ancient and Accepted Rite for England and Wales.* Second edition. Shepperton, 1987. The standard history of the Rite in England.

JONES, Bernard E. *Freemasons' Guide and Compendium.* Revised edition. London, 1957. A thorough and accurate account of the history, nature and working of the Craft.

JONES, Bernard E. *Freemasons' Book of the Royal Arch.* Revised by Harry Carr and A.R. Hewitt. London, 1970. A detailed study of the history, structure and symbolism of the Royal Arch.

KNOOP, Douglas & JONES, G.P. *The Genesis of Freemasonry.* 1947 (Reprinted, London, 1978). The classic presentation of the 'Three Stage' theory of Masonic history.
——, *The Medieval Mason.* Third, revised edition. Manchester, 1967. The history and development of Operative Masonry.

KNOOP, D., JONES, G.P. & HAMER, D. *The Early Masonic Catechisms.* Second edition, edited by Harry Carr. London, 1963. The texts of the earliest manuscript and printed Masonic rituals of the British Isles.
——, *Early Masonic Pamphlets.* 1945 (Reprinted, London, 1978). A selection of the earliest printed texts relating to Freemasonry–each with comment.

LANE, John. *Masonic Records 1717-1894.* Second edition. London, 1895. Detailed, analytical lists of all the Lodges under all the English jurisdictions to that date. Similar lists have been compiled of both Scottish (by George Draffen, 1950) and Irish (by Philip Crossle, 1973) lodges.

LANTOINE, Albert. *Histoire de la Franc-Maçonnerie Française.* Paris, 1925. 2 volumes. The best work to date on French Masonic history.

LE FORESTIER, René *La Franc-Maçonnerie Templière et Occultiste aux XVIIIe et XIXe siècles.* Deuxième édition. Préface d'Antoine Faivre. Paris, 1987. 2 volumes. A most important study of the esoteric offshoots of the Craft in Europe.

LENNHOFF, Eugen. *The Freemasons.* Translated from the German. 1936 (Reprinted, Shepperton, 1978). A reliable history, important for its account of Freemasonry in Europe.

LENNHOFF, Eugen & POSNER, Oskar. *Internationales Freimaurerlexikon.* Zurich, 1932. A thoroughly objective and truly comprehensive work of reference.

MACKEY, Albert G. *Encyclopaedia of Freemasonry and kindred sciences.* Revised and enlarged by R.I. Clegg. Chicago, 1929. 2 volumes. A sound and deservedly popular reference work. Clegg's edition retains all the earlier revisions of W.J. Hughan and E.L. Hawkins.

MACNULTY, W. Kirk. *Freemasonry. A journey through Ritual and Symbol.* London, 1991. A pictorial survey of Masonic symbolism.

MASONIC BOOK CLUB. Bloomington, Ill., 1970 onwards. For more than twenty years the annual publications of the Masonic Book Club have provided members with both reprints of historically significant Masonic texts (e.g. by Conder, Coustos, Dassigny, Johnson, Dermott, Oliver, Preston, Prichard) and works of reference (e.g. Hunt's *Masonic Concordance to the Bible*), and such important modern works as Transou's *Masonic Almanacs*, and Macleod's *The Old Gothic Constitutions.*

PARTNER, Peter. *The Murdered Magicians. The Templars and their Myth.* Oxford, 1982. A study of the historical Knights Templar and of the Romantic myths that have grown up around them.

PICK, Fred L. & KNIGHT, G. Norman. *The Pocket History of Freemasonry.* Revised by Frederick Smyth. London, 1991. A fully updated edition of a popular and valuable work.

PIKE, Albert. *Morals and Dogma of the Ancient and Accepted Scottish Rite of Freemasonry.* Charleston, 1871 (Frequently reprinted, and after 1925, with the 'Digest Index' of T.W. Hugo).

PRESTON, William. *Illustrations of Masonry.* 11th edition. 1801. Reprinted, with an Introduction by Colin Dyer. Wellingborough,1985. One of the great classics of Masonic literature.

ROBERTS, Allen. *House Undivided. The Story of Freemasonry and the Civil War.* Missouri Lodge of Research, 1961. A detailed study of the role of the Craft in the conflict between North and South.

SADLER, Henry. *Masonic Facts and Fictions.* 1887. Reprinted with an Introduction by John Hamill. Wellingborough, 1985. A valuable account of the early years of the premier Grand Lodge and of the development of the Antients Grand Lodge.
——, *Masonic Reprints and Revelations, including original Notes and additions.* 1898. An important contribution to our knowledge of early English and Irish Masonry.

SMYTH, Frederick. *Brethen in Chivalry.* Shepperton, 1991. A history of the Masonic Orders of Knights Templar and Knights of Malta.

STEVENSON, David. *The Origins of Freemasonry.* Cambridge, 1988. An attempt to argue for a Scottish origin of the Craft.

WAITE, Arthur Edward. *A New Encyclopaedia of Freemasonry.* London, 1921. 2 volumes (Frequently reprinted). Useful for the history of the many additional degrees and obscure offshoots of the Craft.
——, *The Brotherhood of the Rosy Cross.* London, 1924 (Reprinted, New York, 1961). A history of the Rosicrucian movement and of all the Masonic Rites, degrees and grades based upon it.

WOLFSTIEG, August. *Bibliographie der Freimaurerischen Literatur.* 1911. 3 volumes. (Reprinted, with Bernhard Beyer's supplementary volume of 1926, Hildesheim, 1964. 4 vols.). Apart from a small number of specialised works, very few Masonic bibliographies have been published in this century. Wolfstieg's is by far the best and most extensive.

INDEX

ACKNOWLEDGEMENTS

The publishers and editors would like to express their gratitude to the following organizations, photographers, and individuals who have assisted them with information and visual material:

Academyof Motion Pictures, Arts & Sciences, USA 187 top. APA Photo Agency, Singapore 110-111. Art Directors Photo Library, London 102-103, 109. Austrian National Bibliotheque 12. Bettmann Archives, New York. Bibliotheque National de Paris 108. Bridgeman Art Library, London 42, 60, 67, 120, 205, 122-123, 154, 167, 170, Cahiers du Cinema, Paris 179, Christie's, London 156-157. Commonwealth War Graves 132-133. Edimedia, Paris 182 below, 201 right, Explorer, Paris 73, 106 below, 149, 158, 172. F.P.G. International, New York 104-105, 114, 138 left, 144, 159, 164 below, 165, 176, 181, 182 left, 184, 188 below, 191, 197. Freemasons Hall, London 14-15, 23, 26, 28, 32, 35, 37, 38, 56, 135, 150, 162, Ghislaine Leber Iconographie, Paris 19, 21, 29, 30-31, 40, 53, 82-83, 85, 96 below, 97, 136, 148, 152, 166, 169, 178, 190, 193, 199, 201, above right. Giraudon, Paris 16, Grand Lodge of New York 117, 161. Hulton Picture Company, London 62, 70, 72, 78, 88, 89, 106 right, 126, 147, 174 right, 175, 180 right, 197 inset. Inglefield, Eric 146. Jean-Loup Charmet, Paris 17, 64, 65, 84, 87, 112, 113, 115, 116, 125, 128, 129, 130, 155, 185, 200, Kharbine-Tapabor, Paris 141, 157 below, 173, Kobal Collection, London 63, 127, 180 left, 183, 186, 187 above, 188-189, Lewis, Frederick 138 below. Life Picture Service, New York 48-49. Maxwell Mackenzie *66, 92-93, 160. Münchner Stadtbibliothek am Gasteig 94, 95 left, NASA 52, 139. Nathan-Murat, Roger 209. National Park Service, USA 145. Peter Roberts, Collection, UK 142 above left, 143 top. Petit, Pierre 224. Philadelphia Masonic Hall 98-99. Pictor International 137. Redfern, David, London 174 left, 177. Robert Harding Picture Library, London; 101 right, 119. Royal Botanical Gardens London 194-195. Royal Institute of British Architects London 101 below. Royal National Lifeboat Institution, UK 213. Spanberg, Eleanor 163 Supreme Council Northern Jurisdiction, USA 44, 47 above, 58, 196, 202, 211, Supreme Council Southern Jurisdiction, USA 10, 24, 45, 46, 47 below, 90. Texas Scottish Rite Hospital for Children 218-219. Topham Picture Source, London Tre Trykare AB Sweden 143 above.

*A print of 'George Washington laying the Cornerstone of the United States Capitol, September 18, 1793' (page 66) is available for purchase by writing to The Supreme Council, 33°, SJ, USA, 1733 Sixteenth Street, NW Washington, DC 20009-3199

This book was produced entirely on the Apple Macintosh, using QuarkXpress.